CW00471853

The New Antiquarians:

50 years of archaeological innovation in Wessex

The New Antiquarians: 50 years of archaeological innovation in Wessex

edited by Rowan Whimster

CBA Research Report 166
Council for British Archaeology
2011

Published in 2011 by the Council for British Archaeology
St Mary's House, 66 Bootham, York, YO30 7BZ
Copyright © 2011 Authors and Council for British Archaeology
British Library cataloguing in Publication Data
A catalogue record for this book is available from the British Library
ISBN 978 1 902771 85 4

Designed and typeset by Carnegie Publishing Ltd
Printed by Information Press, Oxford

The publisher acknowledges with gratitude a grant from English Heritage
towards the cost of publication

Front cover: Flint arrowheads from the grave of the Amesbury Archer
(© Wessex Archaeology); gold pendant from Saxon cemetery at St Mary's Stadium,
Southampton (© Wessex Archaeology)

Back cover: Excavations at Stonehenge in the 1950s (© English Heritage); students on a
Practical Archaeology course, 2008 (© Wessex Archaeology)

Contents

List of figures

List of tables

Contributors

Michael Allen

Michael Allen has worked as an environmental archaeologist for 24 years, 18 of them with Wessex Archaeology. The projects with which he has been involved range from Stonehenge to the publication of the *Mary Rose* excavation. He now offers freelance snail analysis, environmental and geoarchaeological services.

Martin Biddle

Trained in the field by Mortimer Wheeler, Sheppard Frere and Kathleen Kenyon, Martin Biddle and Birthe Kjølbye-Biddle excavated and published together for 45 years, at Winchester, Repton and St Albans, at Qasr Ibrim in Nubia and in the Church of the Holy Sepulchre in Jerusalem.

John Chandler

John Chandler is author and publisher of books about Wiltshire, was formerly the county's local studies librarian and until recently general editor of the Wiltshire Record Society. He is a visiting research fellow at the Regional History Centre, University of the West of England.

Clare Conybeare

Clare Conybeare was Chair of CBA Wessex from 2004 to 2009. She lives in Wiltshire where, for many years, she has worked in museums as an archaeological curator and in collections management for the National Trust.

Mike Corfield

Mike Corfield has been a conservator in Wiltshire, Wales and at English Heritage from where he retired as Chief Scientist in 2002. Mike has a long standing interest in canals, especially their history, he has been a member of the Kennet and Avon Canal Trust for 40 years and is a currently a Vice President.

Barry Cunliffe

Sir Barry Cunliffe taught at Bristol and Southampton Universities before holding the Chair of European Archaeology at Oxford from 1972 to 2007. In Wessex, he has directed excavations at Danebury, Portchester, Chalton, Hengistbury and most recently Brading in the Isle of Wight. A former President of the CBA, he has also served as President of the Society of Antiquaries and Interim Chairman of English Heritage.

Timothy Darvill

Timothy Darvill is Professor of Archaeology in the School of Conservation, Bournemouth University, specialising in the Neolithic of north-west Europe, prehistoric pottery studies, and Archaeological Resource Management. In 2008 he excavated with Geoff Wainwright inside Stonehenge, and currently has fieldwork projects in the Isle of Man, the Cotswolds, and Pembrokeshire.

Sue Davies

Sue Davies is Chief Executive of Wessex Archaeology, one of the leading heritage practices in the UK. She is also Chair of the UK National Commission for UNESCO Culture Committee and a former Chair of the Institute for Archaeologists. Sue was awarded an OBE for services to heritage in 2008.

Antony Firth

Antony Firth is Head of Coastal and Marine at Wessex Archaeology where he has worked since 1996. He started as a volunteer diver on the Isle of Wight Maritime Heritage Project and carried out some of the first diving investigations of the Hampshire and Wight Trust for Maritime Archaeology whilst researching his PhD in the Management of Archaeology Underwater at the University of Southampton.

Andrew Fitzpatrick

Andrew Fitzpatrick is Head of Communications at the leading heritage practice Wessex Archaeology. An expert in the later prehistory of western Europe, he has led a series of major excavations including those at Boscombe Down where the burials of the Amesbury Archer and the Boscombe Bowmen were discovered.

Peter Fowler

Peter Fowler is a field archaeologist and World Heritage consultant. He was Secretary to the Royal Commission on Historical Monuments (England), then Professor of Archaeology at Newcastle University. His books include *Landscape Plotted and Pieced ... in Fyfield and Overton, Wiltshire* (Soc Antiqs 2000), *Farming in the First Millennium* (CUP 2002), and *Landscapes for the World* (Windgather Press 2004).

Charles French

Charles French is Reader in Geoarchaeology and academic director of the McBurney Geoarchaeology Laboratory in the University of Cambridge. He specialises in the analysis and interpretation of buried landscapes using geomorphological and micromorphological techniques, and is involved in landscape archaeology projects in the East Anglian fenlands, the chalk downlands of Wessex, Herm in the Channel Islands, Patagonia, India, Ethiopia, Bosnia and Serbia.

Michael Fulford

Michael Fulford is Professor of Archaeology at the University of Reading where he was appointed lecturer in 1974. His involvement with the archaeology of Wessex began with his PhD on New Forest pottery and has continued ever since, particularly through his excavations of Iron Age and Roman Silchester, which have been focused on insula ix since 1997.

Martin Green

Martin Green is a farmer and conservationist who began his own independent archaeological fieldwork in 1966. He subsequently collaborated in major surveys of the region with Reading and Glasgow Universities (1977–84) and Cambridge University (1998–2006). He is a Fellow of the Society of Antiquaries and received an Honorary Doctorate from Reading University in 2006.

Alison Hamer

Alison Hamer is a maritime archaeologist at English Heritage with specific responsibility for the management of the sites designated under the Protection of Wrecks Act 1973. Prior to this she was Education Officer at the Hampshire and Wight Trust for Maritime Archaeology.

Phil Harding

On leaving school, Phil became a circuit digger. He eventually 'came home to roost' in Wiltshire in 1975 and has been here ever since, now working for Wessex Archaeology. A flint knapper, lover of stone tools, especially handaxes, blues music and real ale, he is probably most familiar to people as a member of Channel 4's *Time Team*.

Mike Heyworth

Mike Heyworth is Director of the Council for British Archaeology, based in York. He first became involved in archaeology whilst a schoolboy in Romsey (Hants) in 1975, working with the Test Valley Archaeological Committee. His first experience of excavation was working on the site of Old Down Farm in Andover.

David Hinton

David A Hinton began his career at the Ashmolean Museum, Oxford, before moving to the University of Southampton, from which he retired as an Emeritus Professor of Archaeology in 2008. His publications include *Gold and Gilt, Pots and Pins* (2005), and he has worked on various field projects, in Hampshire, on Purbeck, in Wareham, and at the Anglo-Saxon chapel at Bradford-on-Avon.

Robert Hosfield

Robert Hosfield is a lecturer at the University of Reading, where he teaches and researches British and European Palaeolithic archaeology. He is particularly interested in handaxe variability and has excavated at the Wessex Lower Palaeolithic sites of Broom and (currently, with Dr John McNabb) Corfe Mullen.

Roger Mercer

Roger Mercer was an Inspector of Ancient Monuments before moving to the Department of Archaeology at University of Edinburgh. In 1990 he became Secretary of the Royal Commission on the Ancient and Historical Monuments of Scotland whence he retired in 2004. He has excavated and surveyed numerous prehistoric sites and landscapes in Scotland and south-west England.

Garry Momber

Garry Momber is the Director of the Hampshire and Wight Trust for Maritime Archaeology. Along with running the Trust, he has a particular interest in submerged landscapes. In addition to work in the Western Solent, Garry has led diving projects to investigate and interpret occupation of drowned lands from the Atlantic to the Middle East.

Alan Morton

Born in Jersey 60 years ago, Alan Morton followed ancient trade routes northwards to Southampton. At the time of writing he ensures that archaeological work is carried out in the city. If this is being read after 21 September 2009, he's retired and someone else now does that job.

Richard Osgood

Richard Osgood works for the Ministry of Defence as one of its archaeologists, ensuring the protection of such archaeological landscapes as the Salisbury Plain training area. He has also recorded the excavation of the remains of Second World War aircraft and is the co-director of an archaeological excavation of Great War deposits in Belgium.

Mike Parker Pearson

Mike Parker Pearson is a professor of archaeology at Sheffield University, having previously worked as an Inspector of Ancient Monuments for English Heritage. He has excavated in many parts of the world, most recently at Stonehenge. His interests in British prehistory include burial practices, domestic life and ceremonial monuments.

Mike Pitts

Mike Pitts began his career as a professional archaeologist, directing excavations at Stonehenge and elsewhere. In 1984 he left that to write, photograph and travel, start a small publishing business and open a restaurant in Avebury (*Stones*). Since 2000 he has been a freelance journalist (editing *British Archaeology* since 2003), while continuing to conduct original research.

Joshua Pollard

Joshua Pollard is Reader in Archaeology at Bristol University. He has worked in various locations in the UK (Cambridge, Newcastle, Belfast and Newport), but finds himself continually drawn to the Wessex chalk. Over the last decade he has acted as co-director of fieldwork projects investigating the Avebury and Stonehenge monument complexes.

Katharine Scott

Katharine Scott studied archaeology and palaeontology, firstly in Cape Town and then at Cambridge. Since 1989 she has directed excavations at various Upper Thames quaternary sites, most notably the 200,000-year-old site at Stanton Harcourt, now one of the largest excavated fossil assemblages of its age in Britain.

Roland Smith

Roland Smith has been a professional archaeologist for over 25 years, working mostly for Wessex Archaeology in Salisbury. Having lived and worked in Wessex for nearly all of his 50 years, Roland has a close association with and love of the archaeology of the region.

Peter Stanier

Peter Stanier graduated from Southampton University in 1973 and is a freelance industrial archaeologist, lecturer and writer based in Dorset. An authority on West Country quarrying and mining, he also edits the Association for Industrial Archaeology's quarterly *Industrial Archaeology News*. He is the Industrial Archaeology Representative for the CBA Wessex Region.

Geoffrey Wainwright

Geoff Wainwright was Chief Archaeologist of English Heritage for 20 years and has been President of the Society of Antiquaries, the Prehistoric Society and the Cambrian Archaeological Association. He is currently Chairman of Wessex Archaeology and with Timothy Darvill is researching the connections between Preseli and Stonehenge.

Rowan Whimster

Rowan Whimster began his archaeological career studying Iron Age burial practices, but was soon distracted by the fascination of aerial archaeology, firstly at Cambridge University and later with the Royal Commission on Historical Monuments. Based in north Wiltshire, he works as a freelance editorial consultant and is currently a Vice President of the CBA.

Foreword

Of all the regions of England, few can claim to have made so many contributions to archaeological knowledge and practice as Wessex. It was on its chalk hills that John Aubrey first discerned the depth of England's prehistoric past, and it was those same downlands that served as an outdoor laboratory for so many of the pioneers of modern archaeology – Sir Richard Colt Hoare and William Cunnington in the 18th century; Lieutenant-General Pitt-Rivers in the 19th; O G S Crawford, Mortimer Wheeler and Stuart Piggott in the first half of the 20th century.

It is, however, the most recent half-century that has seen the greatest explosion in activity and knowledge – the same decades in which the Wessex group of the Council for British Archaeology has worked tirelessly to co-ordinate an ever-growing army of professional and voluntary organisations and individuals with a shared commitment to exploring, understanding, protecting and celebrating the region's quarter-million years of human settlement.

One constant during this eventful time is the way new archaeological research depends on the systematic evaluation of hundreds and thousands of previous excavations and field surveys. In our own era of commercially funded rescue archaeology and a daunting mountain of published reports and unpublished grey literature, this kind of expert synthesis has become more important than ever before. It is only by taking stock of what we already know – and more importantly do not know – that we can agree among ourselves the research priorities of the future: the questions to ask; the places to look; the methods to deploy.

The authoritative period-based and thematic overviews that form the backbone of this present book fulfil just that purpose. They not only remind us of the extraordinary archaeological achievements of the last fifty years, but also set out the challenging lists of questions that need to be addressed by the next generation of Wessex antiquarians. On the one hand they are the keys to unlocking yet more of our fascinating shared history. On the other they will help us safeguard, whether nationally, regionally or locally, its most fragile and irreplaceable elements for the enjoyment of generations yet to come.

The New Antiquarians also reminds us that no amount of centralised planning will ever replace the contribution of the inspired individual or dedicated group of enthusiasts. As this book repeatedly shows, it is the excitement of discovery and thirst for understanding that has made archaeology the immensely popular yet rigorously professional discipline that it is today. Happily, we can never accurately predict what has still to emerge from the earth or the bed of the sea, but there are two things of which we can be certain. The first is that the process of discovery and enlightenment will continue unabated. The second is that it will depend, as it does now, on the willingness of professionals and amateurs to pool their resources and expertise in a shared cause – the elucidation of our common but extraordinary past.

Edward Impey
Director of Heritage Protection and Planning, English Heritage

Introduction

Wessex is a country without borders, a cultural region whose identity has shifted through time. Once the home of the West Saxons, it was reinvented as the fictional setting for Thomas Hardy's vision of 19th-century rural England. Later still, Stuart Piggott adopted it to describe the homeland of the early Bronze Age cultures of central southern England, and O G S Crawford and Alexander Keiller made it the subject of their pioneering work in aerial survey. While each of these incarnations had the chalk uplands of Wiltshire and Dorset at its heart, they all tended to leave the outer boundaries of Wessex vaguely defined. It was only with the formation in 1958 of the Wessex group of the Council for British Archaeology that the region gained a more formal historical identity.

For the CBA's purposes, Wessex would be taken to mean the counties of Berkshire, Hampshire, Wiltshire and Dorset, including the offshore territories of the Isle of Wight and the Channel Islands. Not only did they encompass the chalk uplands that had played such a powerful role in the development of prehistoric society in southern England, but they were also the stamping ground of some of the most seminal figures in the history of British archaeology – the innovative men and women who built modern scientific archaeology on the antiquarian foundations laid by John Aubrey and William Stukeley.

In 2008 CBA Wessex celebrated its 50th birthday – half a century that had witnessed extraordinary changes in archaeological methods and understanding. Commercial archaeology, large-scale landscape studies and new scientific dating techniques have revolutionised our understanding of the region's past. At the same time, increasing public interest and involvement has changed archaeology from a minority activity to a subject that today enjoys huge public interest and support.

To mark this anniversary CBA Wessex organised a two-day conference in November 2008 to review the achievements of the past half-century and to look forward to the challenges of the next. Although based on the presentations made at the conference, the volume you hold in your hand was never intended to be a conventional set of conference proceedings. Instead, it was our intention to publish a colourful and provocative book that would interleave specialist papers with personal recollections (green pages), accounts of some of the region's most influential sites (purple pages) and creative discussion about the future direction of academic, professional and public archaeology in Wessex – cradle of the first antiquarians and an ever-vital test-bed for their pioneering successors.

Within CBA Wessex it was the vision and unrelenting energy of Clare Conybeare, Andy Manning, Francis Taylor and John Winterburn that brought the conference into being. Since then, the editing and production of the *New Antiquarians* has depended on the expert support of Julie Gardiner of Wessex

Archaeology and Catrina Appleby, Frances Mee and Rose Gordon at the CBA, and we are similarly indebted to the Marc Fitch Fund and English Heritage for their very generous grants towards the design and printing of the book.

A special vote of thanks is also due to the Ordnance Survey who generously hosted the conference at their headquarters in Southampton. From our present-day perspective, with its plethora of commercial archaeological units, university departments, local authority historic environment services and voluntary societies, it is easy to forget the pivotal role the OS played in archaeological life at the time of the CBA Wessex's formation in 1958. Long before the invention of county sites and monuments records and at a time when the number of professional archaeological posts could be counted on two hands, it was the annotated maps and card indexes of the Ordnance Survey Archaeology Division that served as the starting point for any serious archaeological research within the region. As time went on, more pressing demands caused the OS to transfer its archaeological recording responsibilities to local authorities and the National Monuments Record, but to this day there is still one vital function that it retains: the authoritative depiction of historic sites on the nation's leisure and touring maps. In this age of GPS, twitter and social-networking it remains the single most powerful means of communicating the historical depth and wealth of the British landscape – the very same cause to which CBA Wessex, this book and all of its contributors are so passionately devoted.

Rowan Whimster

The Wessex Story

CBA Wessex: 50 remarkable years

Clare Conybeare

The New Antiquarians: 50 years of archaeological innovation in Wessex was a conference arranged to mark the anniversary of the foundation of the Wessex regional group of the Council for British Archaeology – CBA Wessex as it has come to be known. The period that it spanned, 1958–2008, has witnessed a remarkable maturing in the discipline of archaeology in Britain. This is well demonstrated in Wessex, a region the iconic status of which has attracted antiquarians and scholars for centuries.

The event gathered together many of those who had been involved to review our understanding of the past and consider what new techniques may herald the future. The papers presented summarise the animated debate that took place, the theories propounded, the ideas that were floated and the memories that were stirred. In celebrating the archaeology we honour the people who, over many millennia, have lived in the area and whose lives have helped to shape it. Their endeavour forms the foundation of our studies today.

From the beginning, CBA Wessex was a successful group. The bedrock of its membership, drawn from a wealth of backgrounds, has always been the volunteer, the enthusiast and the amateur. The CBA *Annual Report* for 1958 records that Group 12 (as it was then known) 'is at last in operation'. It was far from the first regional group, as these had been coming into being since the formation of the CBA itself in 1944. It began with nine members, augmented by representatives of museums and local societies, at a meeting held at Salisbury Museum in May. In October, Sir Ian Richmond addressed the first open meeting and an audience of 170.

By 1964, the newsletter had been launched with the aim of 'encouraging co-ordination of regional activities in research and preservation'. In 1965, 270 people attended the open meeting in Devizes. Launch of the *Archaeological Review* followed a couple of years later. The common theme in these early years was the relentless pace of destruction of archaeological evidence without record.

During the 1970s, attendance at open meetings was routinely 200–300 and the newsletter of 1974 lists 74 archaeological and related bodies active in Wessex. Berkshire joined the region in 1975 and, in 1976, news of the Channel Islands was included for the first time. During the 1980s and 1990s the newsletter reflected the growth of professional units and archaeological consultancy. Today, membership is a little under 600 and the Group is one of the CBA's largest and most active.

Over this half-century, some notable individuals have dedicated years to voluntary fieldwork and research, making their particular mark in the archaeological record. A few must stand to represent the many who have worked in the field and enriched our understanding. John Bernard Calkin, a teacher by training, studied the archaeology of Purbeck and the Bournemouth area throughout the middle of the 20th century. He focused on early flint working and the Kimmeridge shale industry and helped to catalogue the Druitt collection as part of his close involvement with the Red House Museum, Christchurch.

Norman Field, a modern languages teacher, used the young members of Poole Grammar School's archaeological society to help him investigate local sites. He excavated at Bucknowle Roman villa and was passionate about the need to protect surviving ancient landscapes. Max Dacre, for many years chair of the Andover Archaeological Society, worked on the Kimpton late Bronze Age urnfield and on the Portway near Andover.

John Musty began his career as a scientist at what is now known as the Defence Science and Technology Laboratory, Porton Down, near Salisbury. Encouraged by another significant archaeological figure and fellow scientist, J F S Stone, he excavated the medieval pottery kilns at Laverstock, the Anglo-Saxon cemetery at Winterbourne Gunner, Clarendon Palace, Ford Saxon barrow, and Gomeldon deserted medieval village. In 1966, he was appointed head of the Ancient Monuments Laboratory, a position he filled with distinction.

A long-standing secretary of the Berkshire Archaeological Society, Maitland Underhill was tireless in his drive to record the architectural details of churches and buildings under threat in the county, as well as excavating at East Camp, Bracknell and the Romano-British site at Canhurst Farm.

Archaeological research has benefited in other ways from the endeavours of the enthusiastic volunteer. Dennis Sloper used his engineering skills to undertake meticulous experimental work on Kimmeridge shale. Using archaeological evidence, he produced authentic tools to illustrate the methods, techniques, and time required to replicate Roman shale artefacts and the fine Bronze Age shale cups from the Amesbury area now in the collection at Salisbury Museum.

Most of the major excavations used volunteers as diggers. When undergraduate labour was not readily available, the local archaeological society usually was. The county societies, too, played an important role. Their journals provided, and continue to provide, an avenue for publication and the societies act as a focus in each county, advocating preservation when industrial and residential development proposals, road schemes, and changes to agricultural or forestry practices threaten. Membership of county societies is holding up well today, most in Wessex having almost doubled in size since the 1950s.

The role of the volunteer to make a visible difference in practical conservation management is both significant and important. Currently, CBA Wessex has two Friends of Ancient Monuments (FOAM) groups active in clearing scrub and undergrowth from field monuments in the Lake Barrow group near Stonehenge and at Odiham Castle. This work supports the preservation of monuments and their presentation, and is about the practical linking of people and historic places.

Never has the public been better informed about archaeology and this awareness is regularly refreshed by the media. Our challenge is to ensure that the opportunities for training for the interested amateur are sustained in day schools, evening classes, and other extramural teaching. In this environment, professional and amateur archaeologists meet to disseminate knowledge and share enthusiasm. Evidence suggests that where there is provision for active participation in research, fieldwork, and practical conservation, there is no shortage of volunteers. Working alongside the professional archaeologist, the amateur has a crucially important role, one that CBA Wessex will continue to champion.

Wessex: landscape, people and revolution

Barry Cunliffe

To offer a succinct overview of the achievements of archaeologists working in Wessex over the last 50 years is no easy task. So rich is the archaeology and so active have been the practitioners attracted to the region that the accessible record is truly massive. The only option open to a reviewer is to be unashamedly selective in the hope of hitting some of the highlights of what has been a remarkable contribution to the development of the discipline in its formative period.

Wessex is undoubtedly a favoured region – a congenial landscape with a variety of productive soils held in a network of routeways running across the chalk and limestone uplands and along the river valleys. It is also blessed with a long littoral zone providing an interface with the near Continent and a safe passage for those engaged in cabotage. Taking a broader view, Wessex lies between westward-facing Britain looking outwards towards the Atlantic and eastward-facing Britain looking across the North Sea to continental Europe. Thus it is a natural node articulating the flow of people, ideas, and commodities. Those who could command the flow had the power to benefit themselves and their communities. It is little wonder, therefore, that Wessex enjoyed such a vibrant and varied culture throughout prehistory and into historical times.

The richness of the archaeological record in this comparatively restricted region of central southern Britain has attracted antiquarian attention since the time of Aubrey and Stukeley. Later, the excavations of Cunnington and Colt Hoare in the early 19th century offered ample demonstration of the range of prehistoric material culture that was to be had for the digging, even if it was not immediately apparent how to interpret it. With the foundation of the county societies – Wiltshire in 1853, Dorset in 1875, Hampshire in 1885, and Berkshire in 1892 – the nascent discipline of archaeology was given new focus and opened up to a broader spectrum of the increasingly educated populace. Meanwhile public museums proliferated – encouraged by the *Libraries, Museums and Gymnasiums Act* of 1845 – making the results of archaeological endeavour available to all. General Pitt-Rivers saw the importance of all this to maintaining the stability of

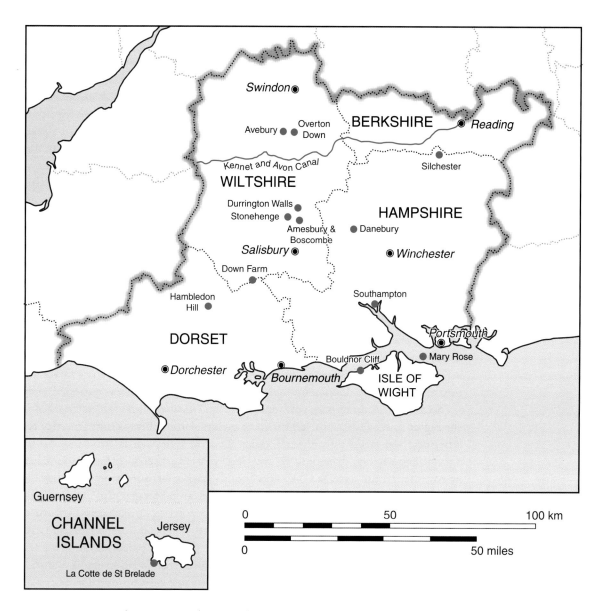

Fig 1.1 Location map
showing the area of
Wessex

society against revolutionary tendencies when he said, on opening the Dorchester
Museum in 1884: 'The knowledge of the facts of evolution and the process of
gradual development is the one great knowledge that we have to inculcate, and
this knowledge can be taught by Museums – provided they are arranged in such
a manner that those who run may read – the working classes have but little time.'
At the time he was deeply involved in developing the ground rules of modern
excavation on his Cranborne Chase estates.

Wessex archaeology, then, has an impressive pedigree. By the end of the 19th
century it was established and vigorous. The first half of the 20th century saw
it take the lead in so many branches of the discipline. Field survey was advanced
dramatically by men like J P Williams-Freeman – a Hampshire doctor who

NEW ANTIQUARIANS

produced a seminal book, *Field Archaeology as Illustrated by Hampshire* in 1915 – Heywood Sumner, whose beautiful surveys of earthworks still inform and delight, and Leslie Grinsell who single-handedly recorded every barrow in Wessex and beyond. Air photography was first brought to prominence by O G S Crawford in a stunning and innovative publication, *Air Survey and Archaeology* (1924) and, later, in his collaborative work with Alexander Keiller, *Wessex from the Air* (1928). And in excavations Wessex excelled itself. One thinks of the campaign to study Iron Age hillforts conducted by the Cunningtons in Wiltshire, Christopher Hawkes in Hampshire, and by Mortimer Wheeler in Dorset, culminating in his magisterial report on Maiden Castle (Wheeler 1943). In parallel with this, Alexander Keiller was exploring the Neolithic monuments of Windmill Hill and Avebury (Smith 1965), where the young Stuart Piggott was learning his trade.

In the post-war period major set-piece excavations continued. Richard Atkinson began his programme of excavations at Stonehenge in 1950, publishing a popular account six years later (Atkinson 1956), though we have had to wait 40 years for the definitive report (Cleal *et al* 1995). Stuart Piggott's work at the West Kennet long barrow in 1955–56 was published more promptly (Piggott 1962), while the major campaign on the Iron Age hillfort and Roman fort at Hod Hill, directed by Ian Richmond between 1951 and 1958, was published within the decade (Richmond 1968).

So it was that in 1958, when the Wessex group of the CBA was set up, its members could look back with some pride on the achievements of their predecessors. Many of the great innovators of British archaeology had worked in the region and Wessex excavations featured large on any list of classic site reports. The stage was well set for the next act.

The last 50 years has seen a revolution in British archaeology and Wessex has, as so often in the past, led the way: the discipline has been professionalised in a way that none of us could have anticipated, our understanding of the past has become far more nuanced than in those early pioneering days, and the volume of archaeological data grows exponentially. The story of the coming of age of British archaeology deserves a thorough treatment: here all we can do is to select a few highlights that reflect the part that Wessex has played in that saga. To provide some order to the great mass of available material we will consider three themes, survey and documentation, excavation, and synthesis and dissemination.

Survey and documentation

One could fairly argue that it was in Wessex – in Hampshire – that field archaeology really began with the publication of Williams-Freeman's volume dealing with the earthworks of Hampshire (Williams-Freeman 1915). Yet even before that a young Oxford undergraduate, studying for a diploma in geography, was preparing a thesis on the landscape of the Andover district, offering the first step in an approach we now call 'landscape archaeology'. The thesis was presented in 1910 but its author, O G S Crawford, did not publish it until he was in post as the Ordnance Survey's Archaeological Officer (Crawford

1921). By this time he was busy compiling the map-based archaeological record for the Survey while publishing his highly original work on aerial survey and archaeology (Crawford 1924). Later came the first (and only) 6 inch sheet of the map of Celtic earthworks of Salisbury Plain (Ordnance Survey 1933) and the period map of Neolithic Wessex (Ordnance Survey 1934) – all of them pioneering publications.

Crawford's systematic work in preparing the Ordnance Survey's index of archaeological sites was continued by Charles Philips, Leo Rivet, and, when the Survey eventually moved back to Southampton, by Dick Feachem – the last in a succession of dedicated Archaeological Officers – all good academic archaeologists in their own right. The transfer of the record to the National Monuments Record in 1983 following the recommendations of the Serpell Report and the subsequent incorporation of that body into English Heritage in April 1999 have ensured the maintenance and accessibility of a resource of outstanding value. Since the 1970s county authorities have begun to develop records of their own, usually under the authority of County Archaeological Officers. These Sites and Monuments Records (SMRs), now Heritage Environment Records (HERs), maintained largely to inform planning decisions, are now a primary database for all archaeological research and feed into the national record. Crawford's legacy is something of which we can be justifiably proud.

The advent of metal-detecting as a popular pastime created what was undoubtedly a threat to the wellbeing of the archaeological record but a programme of education, the reform of the *Treasure* Acts, and the setting up of the Portable Antiquities Scheme (PAS) in 1997 have transformed the situation by providing a mechanism by which responsible detectorists can report their finds. The result has been spectacular. Since its inception the Scheme now holds records of 365,000 finds made throughout the country, details of all of which are accessible online. Together, the HERs and the PAS offer a record that is unparalleled anywhere in the world.

Whilst these major new developments have been taking place country-wide, two, more traditional, institutions of record have continued to serve the region. The *Victoria County History*, established in 1900, published its survey of the archaeology of Wiltshire in two volumes (Pugh and Crittall 1957; Crittall 1973) and the Royal Commission on Historical Monuments (England) completed its five-volume (eight-part) survey of Dorset (RCHM(E) 1952; 1970a; 1970b; 1972; 1975). Though both were publications of considerable and lasting value, such was the amount of new archaeological material being produced almost daily that county-wide surveys of this kind were long out of date even before they were published. More to the point, the county SMRs (HERs) had made published county listings redundant: what were needed were regional or thematic surveys unrestricted by county boundaries.

Thus it was that already in 1979 the Royal Commission on Historical Monuments (later to become part of English Heritage) began to change its mode of production with the publication of two volumes, a survey of the long barrows of Hampshire and the Isle of Wight (RCHM(E) 1979a) and an assessment of Stonehenge and its environs (RCHM(E) 1979b). Then followed surveys of the Danebury Environs region (Palmer 1984), Bokerley Dyke (Bowen 1990), the Salisbury Plain Training Area (McOmish et al 2002), and Wessex Hillforts (Payne et al 2006). Meanwhile, county societies were making their contribution with surveys of the South Dorset Ridgeway (Woodward 1991), the Marlborough Downs (Gingell 1992), and the Berkshire Downs (Richards 1978). These primary surveys are of outstanding value and have made a major contribution to the sub-discipline of field archaeology as well as to our overall understanding of the Wessex landscape.

I have, of necessity, been selective in choosing these publications for specific mention. There has been much more besides published in monographs and in the county proceedings; nor should one forget the plethora of small town surveys that appeared in the 1970s usually under the auspices of County Archaeological Officers. If they were all put together one suspects that hardly a corner of Wessex has escaped the avid attention of an archaeological surveyor.

A more recent, and overarching, development has been the creation of the National Mapping Programme (NMP), set up by English Heritage in 1990s with the intention of providing an air photographic survey of the entire country using the totality of the photographs available. The particular value of this scheme is that, given the resources, it can be continuously updated and made available online. With some 30% of the country already covered, it is fast becoming an immensely valuable resource quite unparalleled in the rest of the world. The coverage of the Wessex region is at present somewhat patchy but ongoing projects are beginning to fill the gaps.

The last 50 years have seen a massive change in the availability of mapped data. When CBA Wessex was set up in 1958 those of us working in the region had to visit the offices of the Ordnance Survey at Chessington to make copies of the 6 inch maps and their accompanying index cards or brave the austerity of the Royal Commission offices in Salisbury to view the earthwork surveys (all before the advent of the photocopier!). Now with the SMRs (HERs), the PAS records, and the NMP data available, or soon to be available, online research into the Wessex landscape has been totally transformed.

Excavation

It is tempting to say that the word 'excavation' covers a multitude of sins in that it is a term conditioned by a variety of motives, practices, and competencies. Broadly speaking we may divide excavation into three categories: *rescue excavations* designed to evaluate the potential of sites and to mitigate the effects of development; *research excavations* the prime purpose of which is to forward knowledge by addressing carefully specified research questions; and *recreational excavation* intended to provide public enjoyment or content for television programmes. While, of course, all three often overlap, the categories provide a helpful way of structuring the discussion.

Although rescue excavations had been carried out at various times in the first half of the 20th century the scale of the potential problem was not fully realised until the publication of *A Matter of Time* (RCHM(E) 1960), illustrating the highly destructive effects of commercial gravel digging. The book had a massive impact which mobilised the archaeological community, leading to the formation of *Rescue*. Thereafter the speed of change was dramatic. To cope with the escalating threat commercial excavation units emerged, while to offer some assurance of professional standards the *Institute of Field Archaeologists* was set up (since renamed the *Institute for Archaeologists*). In parallel with all this, pressure was put on Government which resulted in the publication of two *Planning Policy Guidance* notes, 15 and 16, directing local planning authorities to ensure that the archaeological and built heritage were properly considered in the face of development programmes. The result has been a huge increase in the number and size of rescue excavations and, with it, the creation of a commercial sector which is now by far the biggest employer of archaeologists in the country.

The Wessex region has benefited from rescue activity in many ways. In the late 1960s and '70s there were a number of linear threats to the landscape – motorways such as the M3, M27, and M4 and pipelines, most notably the Southern Gas-Feeder pipeline (Catherall *et al* 1984). All were dealt with mainly by local committees or small units created for the purpose and resulted in series of publications. Most of the excavations were partial and of limited extent, adding only details to our knowledge, but a few, like the M3 work on the Iron Age settlements at Micheldever Wood (Fasham 1987) and Winnall Down (Fasham 1985; Fasham *et al* 1989), were more extensive and produced reports significantly more useful to research.

Another kind of development threat to the countryside has been the rapid expansion of small market towns like Basingstoke and Andover to provide accommodation for London overspill. In both cases local part-time archaeologists have risen to the challenge, most notably Mary Oliver and her colleagues in Basingstoke and the late Max Dacre in Andover. Constant on-the-spot observation over the years has ensured that little has been lost and the aggregate of the work has led to the two areas being among the best-studied landscapes of our region.

In the field of urban rescue archaeology Wessex has led the way with major campaigns of excavation in Winchester, Southampton, and Dorchester. Martin Biddle's great programme of work within the ancient centre of Winchester in the 1960s set entirely new standards across Europe and, as a result, completely revolutionised our understanding of medieval urban archaeology. Such was the complexity of the work, however, that the publication programme has not yet been completed. This is, to a large extent, a reflection of the fact that in those pioneering days post-excavation programmes were usually severely under-resourced, the imperative being to get on with the excavation before it was too late. In Southampton, Colin Platt and his colleagues embarked upon a rather more limited campaign of excavations in 1966–69 but, in addition, took on the task of bringing together the final publication of three earlier campaigns of rescue excavations spanning the period 1953–61. The result is a major publication of lasting value (Platt and Coleman-Smith 1975). At Dorchester in the late 1960s and early 1970s work was arranged under the overall auspices of the Dorchester Excavation Committee which employed a series of directors to deal with sites as they became threatened. The excavations were individually published in separate monographs and in the Dorset society's proceedings.

The urban redevelopment boom of the period 1960–75 had led to the formation of a number of local excavation committees which facilitated the work of site directors, but with the instigation of *PPG* 15 and 16 all this was to change. Since the 1980s most rescue excavation, whether rural or urban, has been undertaken by commercial units employed directly by developers. This has benefits and disbenefits too many to explore here. Suffice it to say that competitive tendering for work, and the understandable desire by the developer to accept the lowest price, have inevitably led to a lowering of standards – a tendency to do the minimum required by the contract rather than to respond fully and creatively to the opportunities offered by the site. The situation could be much improved if the local planning authority, which approves the design brief for the excavation, was prepared to recognise that the prescribed procedures should incorporate a high degree of flexibility and that to meet the needs of the individual site there should be continuous dialogue and modification as the work develops. These are not easy matters to contend with in the face of development pressures but the problem is significant and needs to be confronted.

In the field of research excavations the Wessex region has done spectacularly well. There are a number of cases where the need for rescue has been creatively combined with a well-planned research agenda. Geoff Wainwright's Neolithic henge programme, which saw the excavation of Durrington Walls, Marden, and Mount Pleasant (Wainwright and Longworth 1971; Wainwright 1971; 1979a), is a case in point. By carefully focusing the appropriate level of resource on a group of related sites major advances were made in our understanding of these hitherto ill-characterised monuments. Another example of this same creative approach was the excavation of the Iron Age settlement at Gussage All Saints (Wainwright 1979b). Here, Wainwright argued that properly to understand the fragments of Iron Age settlements being exposed in rescue work we needed to excavate totally one settlement and to publish it thoroughly. Gussage All Saints was chosen because it was typical of its class and the site was plough-threatened. The 20-year programme of excavation at the hillfort of Danebury (Cunliffe 1995) also began in the context of research-led rescue. Here the research aim was to attempt to understand a Wessex hillfort through extensive excavation, made necessary by the threat of woodland felling and replanting.

An outstanding characteristic of Wessex research excavation has been the realisation that to make significant advances in knowledge, over and above the level of simply accreting data, requires a major commitment to excavation over an extended period and an equal commitment to rapid post-excavation analysis and publication. The 20 years of work at Danebury (1969–88) have already been mentioned. Other long-term projects have included Roger Mercer's excavations on the Neolithic causewayed enclosure on Hambledon Hill (1974–86), Mike Fulford's work at Silchester (1974 and ongoing), my excavations at Portchester Castle (1961–72), and the *Mary Rose* project which began with the rediscovery of the wreck in 1971 and is still continuing. In addition to these site-based research projects, Wessex has been host to a number of innovative landscape and excavation programmes. Among the more ambitious we should include Julian Richards' Stonehenge Environs project (Richards 1990), Alasdair Whittle's work in the Avebury/Silbury region (Whittle 1997), Mike Parker Pearson's Stonehenge Riverside project (ongoing), Richard Bradley's Cranborne Chase project (Barrett *et al* 1991), Chris Gingell's Marlborough Downs project (Gingell 1992), and my Danebury Environs programmes (Cunliffe 2000; 2008).

We can fairly say that Wessex has, over the last 50 years, been the scene of an astonishing number of research programmes of very high quality, all of which can claim their rightful places in international debates.

Turning finally to recreational excavation, the 'amateur' tradition has served the region well and there are many instances of weekend excavations, run by and for volunteers, focusing attention on major research issues and producing publications of outstanding value. Particularly impressive were the Roman villa excavations at Hallstock, 1967–85 (Lucas 1993), and Tarrant Hinton, 1963–84 (Graham 2006). Both represent considerable achievements. Wessex has also had its fair share of television-led excavations but, apart from the BBC-sponsored excavation at Silbury Hill directed by Richard Atkinson, they have added little of note.

Synthesis and dissemination

We are fortunate in that all four of our Wessex counties and the Channel Islands have active county-based societies with first-rate annual publications supported by monograph series, and our principal commercial unit, Wessex Archaeology, is also a significant publisher. The region is rather unusual in that two of the county societies also run major museums – at Dorchester and Devizes. Taken together this firmly founded infrastructure provides a valuable interface between research and the public.

There has also been a real effort over the years to communicate the region's archaeology, through works of synthesis, to a wide audience. There are no fewer than four books dealing specifically with Wessex archaeology in general (Stone 1958; Grinsell 1958; Fowler 1967; Cunliffe 1993). Others treating more specific themes include Bill Putnam's *Roman Dorset* (2007), Joshua Pollard and Adrian Reynolds' *Avebury. The Biography of a Landscape* (2002), David Hinton's *Alfred's Kingdom* (1977), Richard Atkinson's *Stonehenge* (1956), to mention only a selection, and, of course, the constant flow (or flood?) of varied offerings which Stonehenge inspires. No one can doubt that our region is well catered for.

Looking to the future

This rather breathless sprint through the highlights of the last 50 years of Wessex archaeology shows, I believe, what an exceptional contribution our region has made to the discipline at large and there is no reason to doubt that it will continue to lead in the decades to come. The essential record base – the HERs, the Portable Antiquities Scheme and the National Mapping Programme – is second to none in the world. The question is how, over and above maintenance and enhancement, can it be improved still further? The answer must be in increased accessibility. There are no technical reasons why the totality of the record should not be made available online, perhaps in a format based on the ever-popular *Google Earth*. If this were done it would be quite feasible to include the large number of geophysical surveys now available and even excavation plans with links to publications and databases. While it might be argued that the costs involved could hardly be justified by the size of the academic user-base, such a facility would have a wide appeal among a growing public becoming increasingly interested in their heritage and the landscape in which they live. There are real possibilities here which deserve to be actively explored.

It is a reasonable assumption that the need for rescue excavation will continue even though the intensity of that need will vary with the economic health of the country at large. There are, however, problems that need to be addressed. The old idea of 'preservation by record' has led to a rather mechanistic approach to recording and the presentation of results. Discussions now in progress, to refocus the purpose of these excavations on providing an intelligible narrative about human activity, should do much to improve the situation. It will require a less box-ticking and more mind-engaged attitude to the process of excavation. Value could then be judged in terms of useful and usable information retrieved and communicated. For some commercial units this may require a major programme of staff retraining.

An associated problem with commercial excavation is that only a small percentage is published in an accessible medium, much remaining in the 'grey literature' reports produced for the developer client. Strenuous efforts should be made to persuade all commercial contractors to follow the lead of Wessex Archaeology who are currently planning to put all their reports on their website. Were all units to do this, the situation would be dramatically transformed.

A further concern is one of standards. It is a regrettable fact that some, probably a minority, of commercial units are not always working to acceptable standards. Firm action by the curators (the County Archaeologists) would do much to improve things but in the end responsibility lies with the IfA – a policy of unannounced field inspections would do much to provide the necessary corrective!

The future of research excavation and fieldwork is less certain, not through lack of enthusiasm or ideas but simply because the increase in standards of recording and analysis is making projects very expensive to run at a time when funds are in short supply. Added to this, universities now require staff undertaking excavations to pay full economic costs to the institution, which makes excavations employing staff exorbitantly expensive. Planning long-term projects is also a hazardous process because few funding bodies will commit themselves to more than three or four years of funding.

The answer, I believe, is to be more adventurous in managing projects. By organising work through a trust set up for the purpose the problem of full economic costs can to some extent be mitigated. Closer relationships between universities and commercial units involving exchange of staff would bring many benefits to both, while the involvement of local volunteers cuts costs and helps to build local loyalties as well as an experienced amateur force who may develop projects of their own. There are several examples within Wessex where projects are already working successfully in this way. If funding problems encourage more to follow this model it will be to the benefit of the entire archaeological community.

The last 50 years have been a time of massive change when archaeology has come of age. Wessex has, throughout, been in the forefront of the advance and can be rightly proud of its record. We now have a sound and varied infrastructure: aware local authorities, strong and active county societies, well-established university departments, and commercial units with excellent track records. There is every reason why the next 50 years should be even more glorious.

2

Earlier Prehistory

Prologue

Timothy Darvill

Riding high in the 'Hit Parade' 50 years ago was a song by the Everly Brothers entitled *All I have to do is dream*; a fitting soundtrack perhaps for the state of knowledge about early prehistory when CBA Wessex was formed back in 1958. But things have changed a great deal over the decades, and the Wessex area in particular has contributed much to expanding knowledge and changing the way we think about these early times.

For the Palaeolithic perhaps the greatest achievement has been John Wymer's work, over many years, which culminated in his contribution to the Southern Rivers Project. This not only gave a secure context for numerous early finds of flint and stone tools through the integration of geomorphology and quaternary geology, but also gathered together a record of material languishing in museums and collections across the region. It served to emphasise the great volume, diversity, and wealth of evidence that exists for these early periods. The discovery of preserved *in situ* flaking floors and the remains of Britain's oldest inhabitant at Boxgrove, West Sussex, only a stone's throw outside our region, reminds us what there is still to find. Red Barns in Hampshire further illustrates the potential, and we might also remember the Middle Palaeolithic site at La Cotte on Jersey (see below pp 16–17) with its Neanderthal remains, excavated by Charles McBurney in the 1960s and later by Paul Callow in the early 1980s to reveal what appears to be a kill site more resembling the Head Smashed In buffalo jump on the great plains of Alberta in Canada than a hunting camp in the low hills overlooking the Solent River as it meandered across the floor of what is now the English Channel.

Much has also changed in what was conventionally referred to as the Mesolithic, following Miles Burkitt's systematic application of the term in Britain in the 1920s. In some quarters the term itself has been abandoned in favour of a more strictly chronological framework of millennia and centuries for the early postglacial re-colonisation of north-west Europe by *Homo sapiens sapiens*. Everywhere, a more nuanced approach can be seen that recognises cultural diversity, technical and social adaptations to fast-changing environments, and shifting relationships between people living in what is now Britain and those living away to the south and east on what would have been the periphery of the great North European Plain.

The work at Portland, and Hengistbury Head, Dorset, and the recognition of peat-covered submerged land surfaces in the Solent and in Poole Harbour have collectively contributed much to the understanding of early post-glacial times.

For the Neolithic, now understood as the 4th and early 3rd millennia BC, much of the work through the 1960s and '70s focused on the long barrows and enclosures that featured so strongly in Stuart Piggott's masterful review of *Neolithic Cultures in the British Isles* published in 1954. Fussell's Lodge, Wiltshire, and Nutbane, Hampshire, were two long barrows excavated in the year CBA Wessex was formed, while Wayland's Smithy was the focus of attention in 1962–63. All these sites are still at the forefront of debates about the use and meaning of long barrows which are now widely recognised as the earliest architectural tradition in the British Isles. The strange triangular-shaped stone-built barrow excavated by Ian Kinnes in the early 1980s at Les Fouaillages, Guernsey, both serves to connect the British megalithic tombs with their continental antecedents and provides the only instance of linearbandkeramik pottery in the British Isles, albeit from what is clearly the French side of La Manche.

The publication in 1965 by Isobel Smith of Alexander Keiller's earlier excavations at Windmill Hill and Avebury set a benchmark not just for the interpretation of a causewayed enclosure and great henge, but also for the way that excavations at prehistoric sites in general are researched and reported. Extensive excavations by Roger Mercer at Hambledon Hill, Dorset, in 1974–82 (see pp 44–45 below), followed by smaller-scale re-examinations of Maiden Castle, Dorset, in 1985–86 to coincide with the first World Archaeological Congress in Southampton, and Windmill Hill in 1988 provided much new information on the chronology and use of these sites. But through the last two decades or so much effort has been directed towards previously little-studied kinds of site such as flint scatters, pit clusters, and, most recently, the recognition that early farming communities in southern Britain did, in fact, as long suspected by some, live in rectangular timber dwellings like their continental cousins.

Two themes stand out strongly from the results of 50 years' study of early prehistory in Wessex. First is the increasingly blurred boundaries between the cultural and the natural; the way that people, plants, animals, the physical landscape, and, in later times at least, built monuments form part of a seamless socially constructed world which cross-referenced all these different dimensions. Second is the impact of climate change, sea-level change, and natural catastrophes on people's lives. That we now live within an interglacial period is widely accepted and, while humankind has undoubtedly impacted on the environment in all sorts of destructive ways, these are far outweighed by natural oscillations in the planet's warming and cooling systems that are still very poorly understood. In our own region these changes have contributed greatly to relative sea-level changes in the English Channel amounting to a rise of more than 10m over the last 10,000 years. If the results of our archaeological researches can be condensed to a sound-bite for today's environmentally conscious communities then, as far as global warming goes, we might do well to follow former US President Bill Clinton in echoing a line from 1970s' soft-rockers Bachman-Turner Overdrive in declaring: You ain't seen nothin' yet!

New sites, new techniques, new understandings: 50 Years of Palaeolithic–Mesolithic research in Wessex

Robert Hosfield

The last 50 years have seen a series of important developments in our approaches to, and understanding of, the Palaeolithic and Mesolithic periods in Wessex. Approaches have become increasingly multi-disciplinary, drawing particularly upon the geosciences (eg Allen and Gibbard 1993; Westaway *et al* 2006), while also benefiting from a greatly expanded range of excavation methods (eg Momber 2000) and absolute dating techniques (eg Briant *et al* 2006).

Understanding of the earliest prehistoric periods in Wessex has expanded through new discoveries and excavations at key sites (Fig 2.4), both old and new, including La Cotte de St Brelade (Callow and Cornford 1986; Scott, this volume pp 16–17), Red Barns (Wenban-Smith *et al* 2000), Broom (Hosfield and Chambers in press), Harnham (Whittaker *et al* 2004), Hengistbury Head (Barton 1992), La Sagesse Priory (Conneller and Ellis 2007), Avington, Wawcott, and Crown Acres (Froom 2005), and Thatcham (Wymer 1962), amongst many others. These discoveries and fieldwork have also been set against the enhanced understanding of the regional archaeological picture which has emerged since 1958, through a series of key regional and national syntheses (Roe 1968; Jacobi 1981; Wymer 1977; 1999; Wessex Archaeology 1993), new landscape projects (eg Allen and Gardiner 2000; Bates *et al* 2004) and palaeoenvironmental investigations (eg French *et al* 2003; Chisham 2004).

This paper provides an overview of selected key developments in both methodologies and knowledge, with reference to examples of Palaeolithic and Mesolithic research in Wessex since 1958. The reader is also referred to the relevant sections in the recent Research Frameworks for both the south-west (Wiltshire and Dorset: Webster 2008) and the Solent-Thames (Hampshire; Berkshire; Isle of Wight).

The state of knowledge in 1958

Understanding of the Palaeolithic and Mesolithic periods in Wessex in 1958 was in many respects well-developed, reflecting a long history of site-specific investigations in the region (eg Dale 1896; 1912; Burkitt *et al* 1939; Calkin and Green 1949) and the continued discovery of new material. Examination of the four regional Wessex journals (for Berkshire, Dorset, Hampshire, and Wiltshire

continued on p 18

La Cotte de St Brelade, Jersey

Katharine Scott

Picture sheer cliffs rising out of a vast expanse of grassland and you may imagine how the island of Jersey, just 20 miles off the coast of France, would have appeared to an ice-age hunter. Having traversed the plain that is now the sea, imagine also how pleased the hunter would have been to find a shelter that not only offered protection from the elements but a view across the grassland with its herds of large mammals and other potential prey.

One such shelter is La Cotte de St Brelade. Not strictly speaking a cave but rather a massive partly roofed fissure in the granite cliffs, it nevertheless became a site of repeated occupation from prehistoric times until almost the present day. It is unique in Western Europe, with archaeological deposits that extend back some 200,000 years, including almost a quarter of a million stone tools and spectacular heaps of mammoth and woolly rhinoceros remains.

Flint tools were first discovered at the site in 1881, but it was not until more extensive excavations were undertaken during the 1950s by Father Christian Burdo that it became apparent that La Cotte was, in reality, a vast cavern with deposits some 30m in depth (Burdo 1960). By the time Professor Charles McBurney of Cambridge University embarked on research at the site in 1961, it was clear that La Cotte de St Brelade was a highly significant Palaeolithic site. Between 1961 and 1978 McBurney not only added massively to the collection of excavated material, but was able to bring to the site his extensive knowledge of other Palaeolithic sites in Europe and North Africa (McBurney and Callow 1971; Callow and Cornford 1986).

Crucial to understanding the sequence of prehistoric events at La Cotte was the emerging scientific evidence for the effect that fluctuations in climate would have had on sea levels over the past 2 million years. During each of a succession of ice ages, the massive build up of ice in the northern hemisphere (although not extending anywhere near as far south as Jersey) resulted in a fall in sea level which, in turn, connected islands such as Jersey to the continental mainland. Thus, before the advent of the boat, the island could only be reached during an ice age.

Fig 2.1 La Cotte de St Brelade: the headland at low tide showing the cave
(© Paul Callow)

Fig 2.2 Charles McBurney at La Cotte de St Brelade, showing the main section in the background
(© Paul Callow)

Fig 2.3 Jersey stamp issued in 2007 illustrating possible scenarios at La Cotte de St Brelade: mammoths being driven off the cliffs by fire and hunters dragging a carcass into the cave (© Jersey Post Ltd; www.jerseypost.com)

Although people were present at La Cotte during the last ice age, the bulk of the excavated deposits date to the penultimate ice age 190,000–130,000 years ago. Initially the environment was temperate and partly wooded but the uppermost deposits indicate open and extremely cold conditions. At this time, the island would have appeared as a large plateau surrounded by grassy plains and the climate would have ranged from cool to very cold. Herds of mammoth, woolly rhinoceros, horse, reindeer and bison grazed the valley between what is now the continental mainland and the plateau.

In the uppermost of the Palaeolithic levels the McBurney team uncovered two extraordinary piles of mammoth and woolly rhinoceros bones, including a number of complete skulls and tusks. The difficulty of dragging such cumbersome objects to the cave from the valley below led me, who helped excavate these heaps, to propose that the mammoths and rhinos had in fact come in through the fissured 'roof' of the cave. The role of the human hunters in driving these animals off the headland is speculative but the way some of the bones were stacked against the cave wall and other damage certainly indicates their presence around this very large meat supply (Scott 1980 and 1989).

The artefacts, studied by Paul Callow and Jean Cornford, exhibit a number of changes in style and raw material through time. For example, side scrapers predominate in the lower levels and typical Acheulian handaxes appear relatively late in the sequence, perhaps reflecting tasks associated with woodland versus open habitats. There is certainly a marked change in the raw materials being used, most probably indicating the unavailability of certain rocks during periods of marine incursion. Fascinating is the evidence that the tool makers had the same proportion of right- to left-handedness as is found among modern humans.

The large unexcavated section of the cave was walled up in 1978 to allow future excavators to benefit from improved techniques. It is nevertheless a very dramatic site to visit. One can imagine the early hunters gazing out from the huge cavern as they made their tools and butchered carcasses. The sea now crashes on the rocks below the cave entrance but, at low tide, one can almost picture the grassy plains extending into the distance. This extinct dwelling and hunting ground is a unique archaeological microcosm of the drama that was playing itself out in greater Europe.

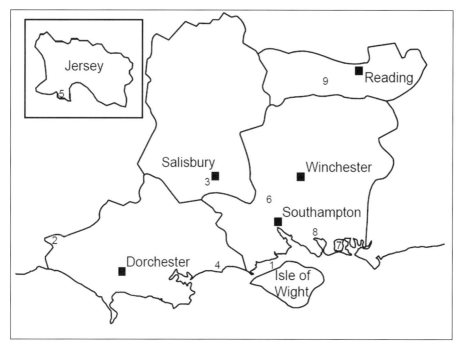

Fig 2.4 Selected Palaeolithic and Mesolithic sites in Wessex, as discussed in the text.
1: Bouldnor Cliff;
2: Broom;
3: Harnham;
4: Hengistbury Head;
5: La Cotte de St Brelade (inset box);
6: La Sagesse Priory;
7: Langstone Harbour;
8: Red Barns;
9: Thatcham
(© Dr Rob Hosfield)

for 1958 reveals the reporting of artefacts from Dorset (Fagan 1958), Berkshire (Wymer 1958), and Wiltshire (Annable 1958). However the last major attempt at synthesising this material had been Evans (1897), over 60 years previously (although occasional county-level investigations, eg Crawford *et al* 1922, had also been undertaken), while the potential for absolute dating (initially restricted to the Upper Palaeolithic and Mesolithic periods) had only very recently emerged.

Regional and strategic perspectives since 1958

The key syntheses of Roe (1968), Wymer (1977; 1999), Jacobi (1981), and Wessex Archaeology (1993) during the last 50 years have provided a much improved understanding of the regional picture of Palaeolithic and Mesolithic settlement in Wessex: the first comprehensive and large-scale perspectives since Evans (1897). In recent years these syntheses (eg Wessex Archaeology 1993) have also incorporated advances in digital mapping to permit the integrated presentation of archaeological, geological, and historical data-sets.

Such advances are important, since the region's Lower and Middle Palaeolithic archaeology in particular (predominantly occurring in riverine settings and handaxe-dominated) is characterised by a complicated combination of hominin behaviours, the locations of sediment traps, and modern archaeological sampling (Hosfield 1999). Such complications require explicit assessment in order for the regional, as opposed to the site-based, archaeological record to be meaningfully interpreted (eg Ashton and Lewis 2002 for the Middle Thames valley).

The last decade has also seen the emergence, and updating, of national and regional Research Frameworks for both the Palaeolithic and Mesolithic periods (eg Prehistoric

Society 1999; Pettitt *et al* 2008; Hosfield *et al* 2008) and the lithic archaeology which dominates them (eg English Heritage 1998; 2000; Lithic Studies Society 2004). These documents have guided and influenced on-going research, highlighting key questions and gaps in knowledge.

Understanding landscapes and climates

Alongside the enhanced documentation of regional archaeological distributions, the last 50 years have seen extensive developments in the understanding of the early prehistoric landscapes of Wessex, both their principal landforms (eg river systems) and the climatic and habitat (fauna/flora) changes.

Landforms

One of the key Pleistocene landforms of Wessex is the now-extinct Solent River (Fig 2.5a). From the earliest studies (eg Darwin-Fox 1862; Bury 1923; 1933) the river was described as having its headwaters in west Dorset (the Frome and the Piddle), flowing through Poole and Christchurch Bay and the West and East Solent, and then turning south and, during low sea-level stands, joining the Channel River. This interpretation has remained generally accepted until recent years. The archaeological importance of the Solent River concerns the rich assemblages of Lower and Middle Palaeolithic artefacts collected from its deposits over the last 150 years (for a fuller recent summary of the Lower and Middle Palaeolithic archaeology of the Solent River landscape, see Hosfield *et al* 2009, while Bridgland 1994 summarises both the river terraces and the early Palaeolithic archaeology of the Middle Thames in north-east Berkshire).

Research over the last 50 years, particularly since 1980, has re-mapped the key Solent River terraces (eg Bristow *et al* 1991;

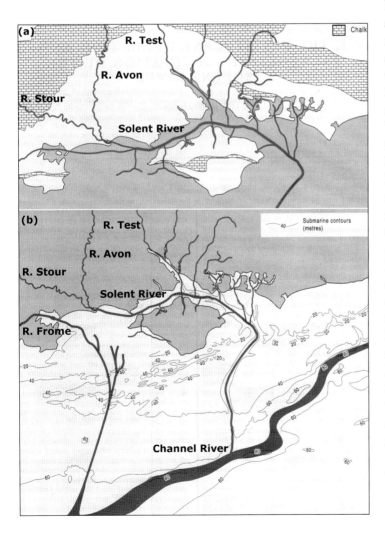

Fig 2.5 The Solent River (after Bridgland 2001, figs 1 & 6)

Allen and Gibbard 1993), reconstructed off-shore palaeo-channels (Dyer 1975; Velegrakis *et al* 1999), and developed relative and absolute geochronological models (Allen and Gibbard 1993; Bridgland 1996; 2001; Westaway *et al* 2006). This work has led to certain modifications in the understanding of the river's palaeography: for example Velegrakis *et al* (1999) and Bridgland (2001) have argued for a beheading of the Solent River in a low sea-level stage of the late Pleistocene, with the newly formed 'Upper Solent' (an extension of the River Frome) turning south in Poole Bay and flowing out through the breached Isle of Purbeck–Needles chalk ridge and joining the Channel River to the south-west of the Isle of Wight (Fig 2.5b). The ages of the river's terraces remain much debated, although continued applications of optically stimulated luminescence (OSL) dating to the Solent terrace deposits (eg Briant *et al* 2006; 2009b; 2009c; Briant and Schwenninger 2009) should help to resolve the problem. In the interim, detailed, and sometimes controversial, models have been suggested by Allen and Gibbard (1993), Bridgland (1996; 2001), and Westaway *et al* (2006).

Climate and habitat

The last 50 years have seen major advances in understanding of Pleistocene and early Holocene chronologies and climatic cycles. While much of this research has been undertaken at national and global levels (eg the oxygen isotope and ice core frameworks), a short summary is provided below (Tables 2.1 and 2.2), as reference for the following discussions. The key issue from a Pleistocene perspective is the evidence for long-term glacial/interglacial cycles and shorter-term climatic oscillations.

Although the geology of much of Wessex frequently does not support pollen preservation there are exceptions, while molluscan preservation is very good. Understanding of late Pleistocene and early Holocene landscapes has therefore been developed in Wessex through the investigation of floodplain peats, palaeochannels, and other features. The Cranborne Chase project (French *et al* 2003) is a key example, where investigation of the pollen (Scaife in French *et al* 2003) has identified open herb communities in the late Pleistocene, with scattered juniper and possibly birch scrub. A second profile has documented the early Mesolithic expansion of juniper followed by birch, and the subsequent arrival of pine, oak, elm, and hazel (typical of the early woodland succession in central southern England; see also Hosfield *et al* 2008). Interestingly, herb and scrub communities also persist into the early Mesolithic (unlike in other parts of southern Britain at this time, where woodland is dominant) and Scaife (in French *et al* 2003) relates this to the survival of refugia of the late Devensian chalk flora.

In areas of Wessex where pollen is poorly preserved or absent, land snails from features such as periglacial involutions and tree-throw pits have provided further insights into environmental conditions in the late Devensian and early Postglacial period (eg Evans *et al* 1993). For example, evidence from South Street and Cherhill in Wiltshire indicates the distinctively cold and open conditions

Table 2.1: Pleistocene climatic and chronological (MIS) framework
(after Hosfield *et al* 2008, table 2.1)

OIS	Years BP	British Quaternary Stages	Climate	Archaeological Period (approximate)
2	24,000–13,000	Devensian	Predominantly Cold	Upper Palaeolithic
3	59,000–24,000			
				Middle Palaeolithic
4	71,000–59,000			
5a–d	117,000–71,000			
5e	128,000–117,000	Ipswichian	Warm	
6	186,000–128,000	Wolstonian	Cold	
7	245,000–186,000		Warm	
8	303,000–245,000		Cold	Lower Palaeolithic
9	339,000–303,000		Warm	
10	362,000–339,000		Cold	
11	423,000–362,000	Hoxnian	Warm	
12	478,000–423,000	Anglian	Cold	
13	524,000–478,000	Cromerian	Warm	

Table 2.2: Late glacial and Holocene environmental and chronological framework
(after Hosfield *et al* 2008, table 2.2)

Radiocarbon Years BP	British Sub-Stage	Chronozone	Pollen Zone	Archaeological Period
6,900–6,000	Holocene (Early Temperate)	Atlantic	VIIa	Late Mesolithic
9,200–6,900	Holocene (Early Temperate)	Boreal	V–VI	Early and Late Mesolithic
10,000–9,200	Holocene (Pre-Temperate)	Pre-Boreal	IV	Early Mesolithic
11,300–10,000	Late-Glacial	Loch Lomond stadial	III	Late Upper Palaeolithic
13,000–11,300	Late-Glacial	Windermere inter-stadial	II	

of the late Glacial (Ashbee *et al* 1979; Evans and Smith 1983), while Allen's reconsideration (in French *et al* 2003) of molluscs from the Dorset Cursus suggested a rare example of a Mesolithic chalkland environment of deciduous woodland with clearings. The chalk and limestone of Wessex also includes early–middle Postglacial tufa deposits, which have offered considerable potential for landscape reconstruction: for example, at Cherhill, Evans and Smith (1983) identified early Postglacial open-ground marshy environments, which were succeeded by full woodland conditions.

Old sites, new sites

A series of new and old Palaeolithic and Mesolithic sites has been excavated and re-investigated in Wessex over the last 50 years, providing insights and contributions to a range of key research themes in early prehistoric archaeology.

At Red Barns in eastern Hampshire, this period has seen both original excavations and re-investigations. The site, located on the eastern side of a small dry valley running down the south-facing slope of Portsdown Hill, was originally investigated in 1975 by Clive Gamble and Arthur ApSimon, yielding a large lithic collection (over 8000 artefacts), dominated by the production of Lower Palaeolithic plano-convex handaxes (Gamble and ApSimon 1986).

A number of outstanding questions led to new fieldwork by Wenban-Smith in 1999. This has indicated that the site is older than previously believed, most likely dating to between OIS-11 and 9 (*c* 425–300,000 BP; Wenban-Smith *et al* 2000: 250), and Wenban-Smith *et al* (2000) have argued that the site was a locale at which handaxes were regularly made, after which they were typically removed and then used and abandoned elsewhere. Most importantly, Red Barns has been a focus for the ongoing debates in Lower Palaeolithic research about early human cognition and the impacts of raw material properties upon tool production: in particular the extent to which early humans' knapping strategies were imposed upon, or dictated to by, the available raw materials. Wenban-Smith has argued for the limited impacts of raw materials upon the knappers' decisions at Red Barns, while Shaw and White (2003) have highlighted the frost-riddled nature of the flint and suggested that the pointed handaxes are a product of this (see Ashton 2008 for the latest debates on the Red Barns handaxes).

In the extreme west of the mainland Wessex region, the Lower Palaeolithic locality at Broom has been the focus of a series of recent re-investigations, following the collection during the 19th and early 20th century of over 2000 handaxes from pits exploiting the gravels of the River Axe. Examinations of the deposits and the artefact archives by Green, Shakesby, and Stephens (Shakesby and Stephens 1984; Green 1988), Marshall (2001), and Hosfield and Chambers (2004; in press) have clarified the deposition and age of the fluvial deposits (Toms *et al* 2005 suggested an OSL age of *c* 250,000–300,000 BP), the environment (pollen analysis by James Scourse and Rob Scaife indicated a boreal, floodplain environment), and the formation and character of the artefact assemblage (Marshall 2001; Hosfield and Chambers in press).

The distinctive Broom artefacts (the handaxes are predominantly produced in chert rather than the flint which dominates the assemblages of south-eastern England and East Anglia, and the assemblage contains a significant number which are asymmetrical in plan-form: Fig 2.6) are providing new perspectives on themes central to the understanding of handaxe variability in the Lower Palaeolithic. In recent years the issue of symmetry has been explored with respect to its possible impacts on use effectiveness in butchery tasks (Machin *et al* 2007) and sexual selection behaviour (Kohn and Mithen 1999), while the impacts of re-sharpening, blank form, and raw material quality upon handaxes have been much discussed (eg Ashton and McNabb 1994; McPherron 1996; White 1998; Wenban-Smith *et al* 2000; Shaw and White 2003: see also the Red Barns discussion above). The Broom artefacts reveal the production of similar forms in both chert (of varying flaking quality) and flint, while the asymmetrical phenomenon may relate to the variable impacts of re-sharpening or to the presence of a distinctive local tradition of handaxe manufacture. The suggested OSL ages of the deposits also indicate possible contrasts between the technological traditions of south-western and south-eastern Britain during MIS 8 (see also the Harnham discussion below). Other important Lower Palaeolithic site re-investigations undertaken in the Wessex region over the last

Fig 2.6 'Asymmetrical' Broom handaxe (illustration by Margaret Matthews; © Rob Hosfield)

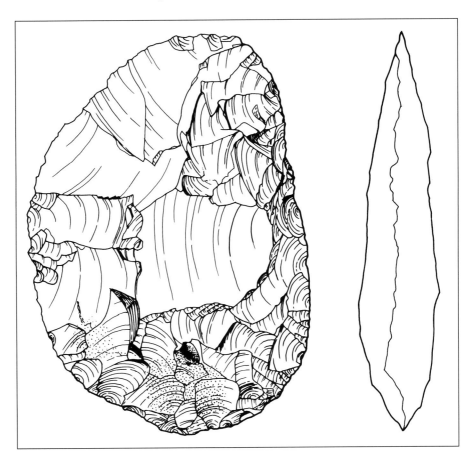

Fig 2.7 Excavations at Hengistbury Head (Barton 1992, fig 1.12)

50 years have included the work at Priory Bay (Wenban-Smith 2001; Wenban-Smith *et al* 2009), Wood Green (Bridgland and Harding 1987), and Dunbridge (Bridgland and Harding 1987; Harding 1998).

While many of the key debates in early Palaeolithic research concern lithic variability and raw material use, the theme of subsistence and its implications for understanding hominin cognition is another central element. Excavations at the Middle Palaeolithic site of La Cotte de St Brelade on Jersey have made major contributions to understanding of Neanderthal strategies for accessing large fauna. Although a number of earlier investigations had been conducted at La Cotte (eg by Christian Burdo), Charles McBurney's excavations from 1961 to 1978 have been key to current understanding (Callow and Cornford 1986; Scott 1986 and this volume, pp 16–17). Whether the site demonstrates organised or opportunistic hunting is not clear cut, but there is no doubt that La Cotte provides some of the clearest evidence for Neanderthal/mammoth interaction (see Schreve 2006 and Mussi and Villa 2008 for recent discussions of this topic), and perhaps for collaborative and co-operative hunting behaviour around 150,000 years ago.

One of the many contrasts between the early humans discussed above and the modern humans of the Upper Palaeolithic and Mesolithic (see Stringer 2006 for a recent summary of these issues) can be seen in the latter periods' evidence for activity-specific sites and differentiated use of landscapes. Work in Wessex has contributed to these issues through the excavations of the late Upper Palaeolithic and Mesolithic occupations at Hengistbury Head (Barton 1992; Fig 2.7).

The late Upper Palaeolithic site, on a high ridge overlooking the confluence of the Avon and the Stour, has been interpreted as a relatively well-sheltered and concealed residential hunting location (it is positioned near the bottom of a dry stream valley), with excellent views over the flat landscapes to the south (Barton 1992, 196). The site's assemblage (dating to *c* 12,500 BP), characterised by straight-backed blades, bladelets, and large tanged points, is in marked contrast to Britain's Creswellian assemblages and may reflect different social groups and/or contrasts between open-air and cave/rockshelter sites (*ibid*, 200, 273). The lithic artefacts have also provided evidence for the spatial separation of activities (such as the primary production of tool blanks in a peripheral zone away from the hearths), knapping and blade production sequences, and raw material procurement and use (*ibid*, 273). In parallel with continental examples, Hengistbury may have been occupied seasonally by large, aggregated groups (the camp may have been up to 2000m² in size), brought together during the spring and autumn by the opportunities to hunt migrating horse and reindeer (*ibid*, 200).

The excavations at Hengistbury Head have also been a highlight of Mesolithic investigations in Wessex in recent years. The average thermoluminescence age, 9750±950 years BP, indicates an occupation during the Boreal or pre-Boreal, when Hengistbury may have been as much as 20km inland of the contemporary coastline (Barton 1992, 273). While the majority of the raw materials (flint and non-flint) are of probable local origin, the site has also provided evidence for wider-ranging raw material mobility, with the use of sandstone from further to the west (*ibid*, 273). The narrow range of tool types (microliths, end-scrapers, and micro-denticulates) suggests a specialised activity site, probably associated with game hunting (partly based on the presence of similar tool-kits at other upland locations in the Wessex region). The presence of large numbers of proximal microburins has been interpreted by Barton (*ibid*, 274) as evidence for a primary tool production zone, while the damage to microlith tips has been interpreted as evidence of tool-use and possible re-tooling of projectile equipment. Complementary research has also been undertaken in other parts of Wessex, including at the Mesolithic site of Culverwell, near the southern tip of the Isle of Portland (Palmer 1999), and in the Langstone Harbour landscape (see comments below), while other key late Upper Palaeolithic sites have also been investigated (eg Froom 2005).

Landscape perspectives

In recent times there has been an increased emphasis upon landscape-scale projects in prehistory, integrating archaeological and sedimentary/environmental evidence to enhance understanding of site distributions, occupation histories, land-use, settlement models, and subsistence strategies. Recent examples have included an investigation of the early Palaeolithic archaeology of the Hampshire (and Sussex) coastal corridor (Bates *et al* 2004), Jacobi's (1981) discussion of

Mesolithic hunter-gatherers in Hampshire, and Green's (2000) multi-period investigation of the Cranborne Chase landscape. The multi-period landscape project in Langstone Harbour is one of the best examples of this approach in Wessex in recent years, combining survey of artefact distributions (Fig 2.8) with palaeoenvironmental sampling and re-examination of earlier artefact collections (Allen and Gardiner 2000).

The main early prehistoric evidence dates to the late Mesolithic, during which period there was considerable biodiversity, with stream valley grasslands and freshwater fens, flanked by mixed oak forests at higher elevations (Allen and Gardiner 2000, 203). The landscape was considerably different to its present day form, located *c* 30km from the contemporary coastline, with two principal streams providing routeways between the South Downs and the coast. The lithic assemblages are limited to a restricted range of tool types (adzes, picks, and scrapers), and the overall impression is of repeated, short-term visits into this landscape for the exploitation of flint (river gravel) resources, in contrast to the early Mesolithic evidence of site-use at both Hengistbury Head (above) and Bouldnor Cliff (below). Interestingly, hunting-type assemblages were not identified, and while this does not mean such activities were not undertaken, Allen and Gardiner (*ibid*, 204) concluded that any base or home camps were more likely to have been located on and around the South Downs.

Fig 2.8 Artefact survey, Langstone Harbour (Allen and Gardiner 2000, plate 9; © Wessex Archaeology and the Council for British Archaeology)

Fig 2.9 OSL sampling
by Phil Toms at
the Broom Lower
Palaeolithic locality
(© Rob Hosfield)

New techniques

One of the key developments in early prehistoric archaeology since 1958 has been
the emergence of an increasing range of absolute dating techniques. In particular
the last few years has seen the re-application of the OSL technique on Pleistocene
sediments, and two studies within Wessex, the Palaeolithic Archaeology of the
Sussex/Hampshire Coastal Corridor project (Bates *et al* 2004; Briant *et al* 2006)
and the investigations at Broom (Toms *et al* 2005; Fig 2.9), have contributed to
the increasing acceptance of this technique within the archaeological community.
In providing absolute dates for key sedimentary contexts, such techniques are
underpinning improved understanding of patterning in the artefact records of the
Palaeolithic and Mesolithic periods.

The Wessex region has also seen the development of new techniques in the
excavation of submerged landscapes. Work by the Hampshire & Wight Trust for
Maritime Archaeology at the site of Bouldnor Cliff in the Solent (Momber 2000;
2001 and this volume pp 32–33; HWTMA 2008; Momber *et al* forthcoming)
has identified early Mesolithic remains associated with a submerged forest and
eroding out of the base of an underwater cliff. Lying at -12m OD and situated
on a 10–20m wide platform, the site presented a number of logistical problems,
exacerbated by cliff and sea-bed retreat which was resulting in the exposure
and loss of rare and important archaeological evidence. The meeting of these
challenges over the last few years, in particular the need to recover the fragile

archaeological and palaeoenvironmental evidence while minimising impacts on the site's integrity, has seen notable developments in underwater excavation and survey techniques. The site's archaeology (Momber this volume) has also provided another perspective on Mesolithic land-use in Wessex, complementing the sites and landscapes of Hengistbury, Langstone Harbour, and Thatcham (discussed above and below).

Changing research contexts

The last two decades of research in Wessex have also been influenced by the introduction of the *PPG* 16 legislation in 1990, and the changing relationships between archaeology and the planning process. While the often ephemeral nature of early prehistoric archaeology has not always promoted independent identification during developer-funded fieldwork, recent work in the Wessex region has highlighted the clear potential benefits of the relationships to understanding of these periods.

To the south of Salisbury, the building of the Harnham relief road saw the identification of key river valley deposits, including up to 750m² of buried land surface. These deposits have yielded animal bones and re-fitting lithic artefacts (including 44 handaxes and thousands of waste flakes and microscopic chips) of late Lower Palaeolithic age (Whittaker *et al* 2004). The scale of the land surface, and the presence of undisturbed artefacts, is rare in the British Lower and Middle Palaeolithic, and without the current legislation it is probable that the Harnham evidence would either have been entirely lost or only identified after, rather than prior to, significant disturbance and the loss of key contextual information.

The deposits and artefacts are highly significant to current research themes: the molluscan, mammalian, and ostracod evidence all suggest an open, wet, periglacial landscape, dating to *c* 250,000 BP (the latter stages of the MIS-8 cold period), providing valuable new evidence regarding the palaeoenvironmental tolerances of Middle Pleistocene hominins. The handaxe-dominated character of the assemblage is also notable, as the dating is broadly contemporary with the first appearance in Britain of Middle Palaeolithic Levallois (prepared core) technologies, further to the east in the Thames valley (White *et al* 2006). The Harnham evidence, in combination with the suggested MIS-9 and MIS-8 OSL dates for the large handaxe assemblage further to the south-west at Broom (Toms *et al* 2005; see also above), raises the intriguing possibility of different technological traditions existing across southern Britain around a quarter of a million years ago. Such traditions may relate to the issues of Britain's cyclical settlement and abandonment during the middle and late Pleistocene (White and Schreve 2000; Ashton and Lewis 2002; Stringer 2006).

A second example of new sites and research opportunities arising through the *PPG* 16 legislation is seen at the Final Upper Palaeolithic site of La Sagesse Convent, in Romsey (Conneller and Ellis 2007). The excavation of lithic scatters by Wessex Archaeology was facilitated by the construction of a new nursing home, enabling exposure of an area *c* 35 x 57m (*ibid*, 194). The scatters were located in alluvial sediments on a low gravel terrace at the edge of the River Test, and are thought to date to the latter part of the Windermere interstadial (c 12,000–11,000 BP), during the first re-colonisation of Britain by modern humans after the Last Glacial Maximum. While the degree of post-depositional disturbance across the site varies, re-fitting has been possible, and two scatters have been respectively interpreted as a knapping locality (with core reduction sequences) and an area of tool production.

The nature of the site is in stark contrast to the example of Hengistbury Head, and suggests an open-air, short-term camp. The location is strongly suggestive of the attractions of flint, water, and animals, and the analysis of the lithic material highlights the mobility of technology during this period: Conneller and Ellis (2007, 222) suggest that the occupants introduced partially prepared cores, worked the cores further, undertook additional activities, and then left, removing at least three partly reduced cores. As a short-term occupation site, La Sagesse provides detailed evidence for individual activity patterns, in contrast to the denser occupation debris of Hengistbury Head.

However La Sagesse Convent not only highlights the contrasting and complementary settlement types and landscape behaviours occurring in southern Britain during the Final Upper Palaeolithic, but also the importance of developer-driven archaeology in permitting the controlled excavation of open-air lithic scatters:

> Most discussion [of open-air site functions and activities] has, so far, had to rely on the re-examination of existing collections and on material that has been (generally unsystematically) collected from surface exposures or very limited excavation.
>
> (Conneller and Ellis 2007, 199)

By contrast, La Sagesse illustrates that there is clear potential for the recognition and recovery of minimally disturbed late Upper Palaeolithic sites. While prediction is a dangerous exercise (see also my comments below), I happily echo the authors' concluding comments and hope that the La Sagesse excavations will go a significant way in encouraging the development of enhanced definitions for open-air Upper Palaeolithic sites, and the emergence of suitable research and mitigation strategies for the examination and protection of a key archaeological resource.

Any change?

Yet despite the many developments of the last 50 years, a return to the late 1950s highlights that the best early prehistoric archaeology of that era was pursuing many, if not all, of the questions and methods that have characterised research in Wessex since that period. The investigations led by John Wymer (1962; Fig 2.10) at Thatcham provide an excellent example, exploring questions of technology, subsistence, and settlement patterns, and integrating those investigations with

Fig 2.10 John Wymer, pictured during the Southern Rivers Palaeolithic Project (© Elaine Wakefield, Wessex Archaeology)

the contemporary stratigraphic and environmental analyses of Churchill (1962). Technological insights included the evidence for adze re-sharpening, revealing the decisions of an individual Mesolithic knapper (Wymer 1962, 344–6), while analysis of the faunal evidence indicated the hunting of red and roe deer, pig, and beaver, and the trapping of animals such as pine marten, fox, and hare (*ibid*, 337). Wymer concluded that the site was visited periodically (along with many others) by a mobile Mesolithic group, which would explain the presence of fresh chalk flint (the nearest source was almost 10km to the south) at Thatcham (*ibid*, 337).

While new interpretations of the Thatcham site, the local and regional environment, and Mesolithic settlement behaviour in and around the Kennet Valley have been proposed in the intervening years (eg Bradley 1978; Richards 1978; Healy *et al* 1992), the quality of John Wymer's original investigations remain very apparent and provide an invaluable reminder that while new sites, methods, and research contexts have emerged since 1958, the need for high-quality archaeology remains a key constant.

Conclusions and predictions

The last 50 years have seen major contributions from the Wessex region to understandings of the archaeology and behaviours of the Palaeolithic and Mesolithic periods, ranging from site use and landscape models to artefact variability and subsistence strategies. Key new approaches and techniques have been developed and tested, while the post-1990 links between archaeology and the planning process have thrown up unexpected new sites.

So where will early prehistoric research in Wessex be in 50 years time? To paraphrase my fellow contributor Dr Josh Pollard, the only safe prediction is that my predictions will very probably be wrong. I am tempted to suggest, however, that an equivalent paper written in 2058 might be assessing the impact of new dating techniques, interpreting the lithic record against an increasingly fine-grained appreciation of climatic and environmental variability, and reviewing a much-enhanced understanding of the Palaeolithic and Mesolithic periods from the perspective of submerged sites and landscapes. I'm looking forward to it!

Acknowledgements

My thanks are due first and foremost to CBA Wessex for the invitation to speak at the 50th Anniversary New Antiquarians conference. I would also like once again to acknowledge and thank all those colleagues whose excellent research is summarised here: any errors or mis-representations are of course my own. My thanks also to Julie Gardiner (Wessex Archaeology) for supplying a copy of Figure 2.8. Finally, this is inevitably a somewhat personal retrospective: my apologies to those who find their own work omitted or too briefly dealt with within the limited space of this paper.

Bouldnor Cliff: diving into the Mesolithic

Garry Momber

The submerged lands off Bouldnor Cliff on the Isle of Wight were first brought to the attention of the Island Archaeologist, Dr David Tomalin, and the palaeo-environmentalist Dr Rob Scaife in the 1980s, when local fishermen pulled up peat and trees from the seabed. A few years later the source of the peat was located by John Cross when diving as part of a seabed inspection project run by Dr Tomalin. A decade later an innovative study of sea-level rise and climate change spurred me and the Hampshire and Wight Trust for Maritime Archaeology (HWTMA) to renew examination of the submerged forest at the foot of the cliff. At that time the archaeological community believed that the rise of sea levels across old land surfaces would remove or redistribute archaeological material. The existence of whole trees on the seabed, *in situ* root systems, and deep sediment sequences in the Solent refuted that assumption. It also demonstrated that organic material could be preserved under water in an immaculate condition. The site was 11m under water, it was more than 8000 years old and it stretched for more than 1km.

Fig 2.11 A diver inspecting the submerged cliff face (© HWTMA)

Annual projects run by the HWTMA between 1998 and 2002 involved dozens of amateur archaeologists planning and sampling the seabed. During the investigations, Roy Harold and Sophia Exelby discovered flints in the up-cast of a lobster burrow. Evaluation trenches subsequently revealed hundreds of worked flints stratified within the Mesolithic land surface. This was the first time such an underwater site had been discovered and worked in the UK. In 2003, support from English Heritage enabled further excavation and full analysis of the archaeology and palaeo-environment (Momber *et al*, forthcoming).

Low visibility and the fast tides of the Solent made this a difficult working environment, so methods were developed to maximise the amount of information recovered. Air lifts, chainsaws and purpose-built sampling boxes were used to bring chunks of the seabed to the surface. The delicate archaeological horizons could then be excavated in controlled conditions.

The first investigated location (BC-II) dated from 6060–5990 cal BC to 5990–5890 cal BC. The earliest date relates to the bottom of the trench while the latest belongs to the time the site was covered by the rising sea. Flints were recovered from layers within a sand bar that had developed next to a freshwater stream over a period of 20–30 years. The stratigraphic distribution of flint tools and flakes suggests the sand bar was visited on a regular basis during that time. Research into the contemporary geomorphological evolution of the Solent shows

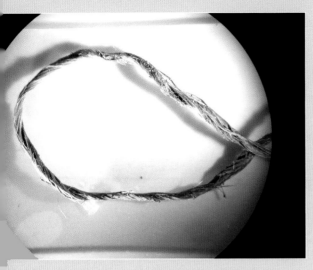

that it was a basin with substantial fresh-water wetlands before it was overwhelmed by the sea.

At the same time that work was under way at BC-II, divers were inspecting the steadily eroding edge of the peat platform. In 2004, I noticed a cluster of burnt flints eroding from the platform 420m to the west of BC-II. The flints rested in a pit that had been dug in the old land-surface. Further investigations revealed a platform-like feature, scatters of flint flakes, burnt flint and the bottom of a wooden post. In 2007, grants from the Leverhulme Trust through the University of York and from The Royal Archaeological Institute allowed the HWTMA to uncover more archaeology from the seabed. Worked timbers, twine and a piece of a possible log-boat dated to 6370–6060 cal BC were found within an archaeological horizon that was covered in charcoal, chunks of carbonised wood and burnt flints.

Fig 2.12 Organic artefacts from Bouldnor include string (width across loop: *c* 40mm) and worked timber (overall length *c* 230mm) (© HWTMA)

During 2009, extended trenching revealed an additional complex of trimmed timbers. The finds suggest a substantial structure associated with industrial activity and the possible log-boat. Coupled with the archaeological, palaeo-environmental and geomorphological data, this implies a level of sedentism not seen in any comparable southern English Mesolithic sites. As a result, it is forcing us to re-evaluate the whole of the existing archive of land-based evidence used to characterise the Mesolithic.

To interpret the discoveries we need to think about them in their wider geospatial context and to remember that the Mesolithic environment at the close of the Ice Age was markedly different from today's. Sea level was 30–40m lower than it is now, giving access to vast tracts of low-lying land suitable for human occupation. However, this was also a period of dramatic climatic change, catastrophic flooding events and persistent sea-level rise. The lowlands were being lost to the sea and all who lived there were steadily forced back upslope by

Fig 2.12

the advancing coastline. Expanding Mesolithic societies would have been continually displaced, a process that continued until sea levels stabilised and the uplands of this north-west European peninsula fragmented into islands. The inhabitants of the Solent basin may have been one such burgeoning society whose settlements and occupation areas were lost to the rising seas. To date, we have only looked at a fraction of this unique site. It has the potential to reveal a great amount about a little-known period but is being lost before our very eyes.

Real ale and handaxes: memories from Milford Hill

Phil Harding

Eventually, when someone learns that you are an archaeologist, you know that sooner or later you will face the inevitable question 'What's your best find?' It is a question that is just so predictable; as if you have only ever made one memorable find in your career. And yet I rather suspect that even the most hardened archaeologist, who claims that they only do it for the science, secretly harbours fond memories of a coin or pot sherd that they plucked from a pile of mud. I happen to love flint tools and always have done. As a child I scoured the fields picking up natural stones, taking them home, washing and loving them as tools of the 'cave men'. I subsequently learned how to identify the real thing. No matter what, my love for stone tools remains undiminished, especially Palaeolithic handaxes; absolutely iconic.

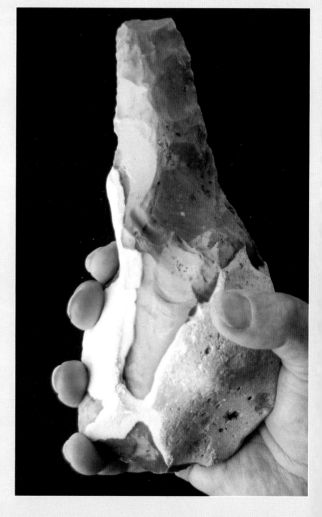

Fig 2.13 The Godolphin School handaxe, surely a worthy candidate for anyone's 'best' find (© Pat Shelley)

Dating from anywhere between 700,000 and 50,000 years ago, I still find it difficult to comprehend just how old they really are. Such stone tools from Wiltshire, my home county, are extra special, particularly when a fine discovery is rounded off with a fine pint of beer. The earliest antiquarians, who laid the foundations of archaeological science that have led to organisations such as CBA Wessex, frequently found refreshment at inns and taverns where some of their 'best' finds were discussed. Here also collections were built up from workmen who knew that they could find willing buyers for stone axes that were freshly discovered from local gravel diggings. All this awareness must have passed across my mind every time I climbed the hill to the Wyndham Arms on the lower slopes of Milford Hill and I considered how many handaxes waited to be discovered on those elevated parts of Salisbury.

Milford Hill is a spur of land forming the watershed between the rivers Avon and Bourne on the eastern side of Salisbury. In 1864 H P Blackmore, the founder of Salisbury Museum, collected a large number of flint handaxes from sections and from workmen who found them in gravel at the top of the

Fig 2.14 The pub – the Wyndham Arms, part way up Milford Hill and the scene of many discussions on the antiquity of early man (© Phil Harding)

hill. That part of Salisbury was being developed for the first time and grand Victorian villas were being built for affluent purchasers. Foundation trenches, cellars, and new roads all provided material that could be scanned for implements. The collection is one of the largest from the Salisbury Avon, numbering over 300 axes (Roe 1968), yet despite the fact that descriptions (Blackmore 1864; 1865; Reid 1885; 1903) showed that the deposits were rich in clay with some chalk, no one had been able to resolve the origin of the gravel in which the axes had been found.

The problem was that once the Victorian development had been completed virtually no new building work had taken place in the area. Then, in 1995, work began to build a new Performing Arts Centre at the Godolphin School, where 41 handaxes had been found during its construction; one of the most prolific locations on Milford Hill. The project offered the opportunity for archaeologists to look at the site for the first time in over 100 years. Funnily enough, no archaeological work had been planned because it was thought that all the gravel had been quarried away. Fortunately, discussions at the eleventh hour gained access to undertake a 'watching brief', a slightly more formal development of the methods used by antiquarian collectors to find tools and record deposits. The results were published (Harding and Bridgland 1998) in the *Wiltshire Archaeological Magazine*.

In summary, we established, by cleaning a few sections, that the deposits comprised chalky mud that had been incorporated into the river and redeposited as finely bedded, water-lain chalky gravel with flints. Over time much of the chalk had dissolved, disrupting the bedding and leaving only the clay residue which had been described by the Victorian antiquarians; however small patches of bedded material remained to testify to its water-laid origins. We were satisfied that we had finally resolved the origin of the Milford Hill deposits but we had found no handaxes.

On one occasion I maintained my surveillance as the mechanical digger dug a foundation trench for the new theatre and I noticed an elongated, larger than normal, piece of flint that bobbed up momentarily. It disappeared, just as quickly, amongst the spoil. There was a lot of loose gravel in the trench but it reappeared in the next bucket load and disappeared again, resolutely refusing to enter the bucket. It demanded attention, so on its third appearance I resolved to stop the driver and take a look. I'm glad I did. I bent down, rummaged in the spoil and found myself clutching a fine pointed handaxe, probably the first from the site for over 100 years. It was not the first handaxe I had ever found, nor the last, but it was one of the most unforgettable and its discovery is still vivid in my memory, possibly because it was from Salisbury and for the fact that I had almost resisted the urge to stop the work and take a look. I was also pleased with what I still consider is one of my better line drawings of a handaxe, which was included in the report.

Fig 2.15 Milford Hill, outlined by the Salisbury by-pass in the foreground and the Bourne valley beyond. The Wyndham Arms sits immediately beyond the trees to the left and the domed roof of the Performing Arts Centre at Godolphin School is visible immediately beyond the white house centre right (© Time Team)

As a flint knapper I could not help but admire how my Stone Age colleague had dealt with the elongated, columnar piece of flint; the rounded edges make nodules of this sort notoriously difficult to work. It was not flaked all over, just enough work to form one end into an elegant point, which had unfortunately snapped off long ago; the opposite end remained unaltered. Nice technique. The discovery of the axe caused considerable excitement; it provided good publicity not only for the school but also demonstrated that valuable scientific research could be achieved through careful co-operation with developers without stopping work. I was asked to address the pupils, many of whom had been aware of our presence but unaware of what we were doing or why, to explain the results of our work. The axe has been added to Blackmore's collection in Salisbury and South Wiltshire Museum. I now go to the pub satisfied to have contributed to the story of Salisbury, and Milford Hill in particular, and having made an unforgettable discovery in the process – now that's what I call a candidate for 'best' find.

Fig 2.16 Phil Harding, knapping his own handaxe (© Wessex Archaeology)

The Neolithic: 50 years' work on nearly two millennia

Joshua Pollard

The Neolithic of Wessex was a very different world in 1958, though one undergoing rapid transformation. Excavations at Stonehenge were continuing (the monument, at this time, placed firmly in the Bronze Age); Isobel Smith was completing the second season of work at the enclosure on Windmill Hill to facilitate the interpretation of Keiller's earlier excavations (Fig 2.17); while the extensive investigation of the West Kennet (1955–56), Fussell's Lodge, and Nutbane (both 1957) long barrows was recently completed. The assimilation of important work undertaken between the wars at sites like Windmill Hill and Maiden Castle was being combined with the results from new excavation work within a series of important syntheses. The year 1958 saw the publication of two substantive works on the region's prehistory: J F S Stone's *Wessex Before the Celts* and Leslie Grinsell's *The Archaeology of Wessex*. The previous year Grinsell had published his monumental *Archaeological Gazetteer for Wiltshire* as part of the *Victoria County History*. Much new information, and old in a different light, had been made available.

Any account of the British Neolithic at the time drew heavily on Stuart Piggott's *Neolithic Cultures of the British Isles*, published four years earlier; a volume that would remain the standard text on the period well into the 1970s (Fig 2.18). With the hindsight of 50 years' additional research, its outline sequence and understanding of causality, within the then dominant culture-history framework, makes interesting reading. Working within a 'short' and 'late' chronology prior to the full impact of radiocarbon, the region's Neolithic begins with the arrival of immigrant farming groups from the continent sometime soon after 2000 BC.

Fig 2.17 The mound of the Beckhampton Road long barrow, excavated by Isobel Smith in 1964. Work here, and by John Evans at the South Street long barrow, contributed much to our understanding of the complex architectural structure of these monuments (Reproduced by kind permission of the Prehistoric Society)

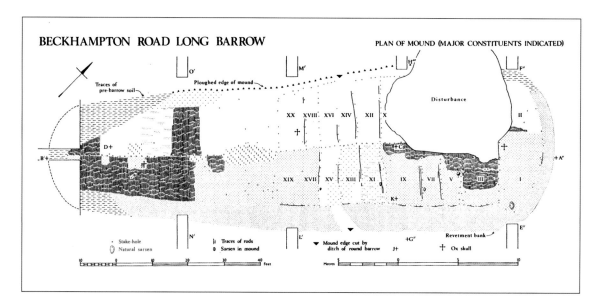

BECKHAMPTON ROAD LONG BARROW

PLAN OF MOUND (MAJOR CONSTITUENTS INDICATED)

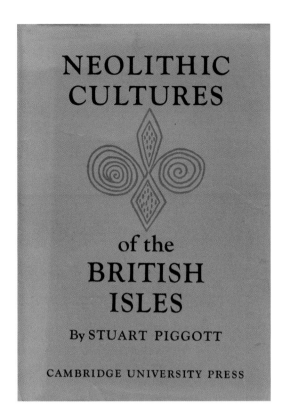

These groups rapidly coalesce to form the 'primary' Windmill Hill Culture, defined as cattle-breeders whose settlement was largely restricted to the chalk, and who constructed causewayed camps, flint mines and earthen long barrows. A 'resurgence of indigenous [and Scandinavian/north European] elements' (Piggott 1954, xviii) produced 'secondary' Neolithic cultures responsible for Peterborough and Grooved Wares, and early henge monuments, the Neolithic sequence coming to an end *c* 1500 BC, coeval with early Beakers. While the material sequence was there in broad detail, much remained hazily understood. A definable Neolithic settlement record was missing; little was understood of the contemporaneous environment; an understanding of the full distribution, chronology, and role of key monument types such as henges and cursus monuments was in its infancy; and the restricted surface visibility of Neolithic sites contributed to an image of an upland, chalk-focused pattern of settlement that avoided surrounding 'swampy river valleys' (*ibid*, 101).

What happened next?

The history of subsequent progress in understanding the region's Neolithic is one that follows a general disciplinary maturation: a story of new techniques, an enhanced scale of fieldwork and analysis, and developing theoretical sophistication. Each of these fields will be considered in turn.

Chronologies

Even by 1960, the impact of radiocarbon dating was being felt. Dates from the early Neolithic sites of Windmill Hill and Nutbane had stretched the upper end of Piggott's chronology by a millennium. A decade and a half later, calibration would have further impact, not only in pushing back both start and end dates (currently at 4000–2400/2200 BC), but in falsifying the diffusionist arguments that underpinned much of the culture-historical explanation for social and material change. Another 'radiocarbon revolution' has occurred in the last two decades, with routine application of AMS (accelerator mass spectrometry) dating, a better awareness of sample integrity and the problems of residuality, and Bayesian modelling of results. Not only do we now possess an absolute chronology for the Neolithic that could only be dreamed of in 1958, but there exists the ability to refine those chronologies (currently for individual sites, but soon for regions) to the level of generations. Though without named characters, Neolithic histories now look tangible. The work of Alex Bayliss, Alasdair Whittle, and Frances Healy on the chronology of long

Fig 2.18 The canonical text: Piggott's *Neolithic Cultures of the British Isles* (1954). Heavily influenced by the results of pre-war excavations in Wessex, it served as the standard reference work on the period for over two decades

barrows and causewayed enclosures has been key in this regard (Bayliss and Whittle 2007). It is now apparent that such monuments were characteristic of a 'developed' rather than primary Neolithic, and could be surprisingly short-lived. Across the Neolithic sequence, peaks and troughs in monument building are becoming evident: thus, a particular intensity in construction marks out the 37th and 36th, and 26th–24th centuries BC, while the 34th–32nd centuries look surprisingly quiet. It is into the second of those peaks that we can now place the greatest of monument constructions: the sarsen and bluestone phase of Stonehenge (Cleal *et al* 1995), the main earthwork and outer circle at Avebury, and the beginning of Silbury Hill. Increasingly, we are aware that this is a time of profound change, one which sees the first appearance of copper metallurgy and the end of a peculiarly 'insular' phase in British prehistory.

Analytical techniques

Wessex prehistory has a long association with the development of archaeological science. In the early decades after the war much of that work was in the field of material characterisation, and is exemplified by J F S Stone's pioneering analyses of Bronze Age faience and his contribution to stone implement petrology. In the last two decades, it has been advances in organic- and geo-chemistry that have begun to revolutionise our knowledge of past human diet, lifestyles, and mobility. Of the 'recent highlights', lipid analysis of ceramics has demonstrated widespread evidence of dairying during the early Neolithic, first hinted at by cattle sex and age patterns from sites such as Hambledon Hill. The analysis of human bone collagen stable isotopes has provided direct evidence for diet, indicating a general shift away from marine resources at the start of the Neolithic, and a significant mosaic of different subsistence practices, as indicated by varying levels of meat and plant food consumption, during the 4th millennium BC.

Other stable isotopes preserved within bone, notably strontium, oxygen, and lead, can provide signatures of individual life-time movement. Although the technique has not been applied as routinely as one might wish, the few results available are challenging the picture of uniform local residence and limited mobility. The best-known results relate to the very end of the period: isotopic signatures from early Beaker individuals from Amesbury, including the 'Amesbury Archer', show that some male individuals started their lives in continental Europe. Shorter, but still significant, middle-distance movement has also been detected. In the case of the late 4th millennium BC woman buried in the Monkton Up Wimborne pit-circle on Cranborne Chase, stable isotopes show periods of residence on geology with high lead levels, probably the Mendip Hills (French *et al* 2007). The same analyses can, and currently are, being applied to the bones of domesticated livestock. Here, because these animals were herded, the results will provide proxy data for human movement, networks of exchange, and the catchment areas from which communities gathered to participate in construction and ceremony at major monuments.

Fieldwork and excavation

The enhanced scale of fieldwork over the last 50 years is probably the one single factor that has pushed the advancement of knowledge of the period. Here, both design and serendipity come into play, both within structured research projects, often led by universities, and development-led fieldwork undertaken by contracting units. A rapid count shows that at least eighteen long barrows, ten causewayed enclosures, twelve henges, three cursus monuments, two palisaded enclosures, and sundry other Neolithic monuments within the region have been subject to some form of excavation over the last half century (Figs 2.17 and 2.19). To this should be added innumerable pits and other traces of contemporaneous settlement. New discoveries have highlighted the range of site forms belonging to the period, while the steady accumulation of data has allowed better characterisation of social, economic, and ceremonial practices, material culture and environmental regimes.

Monuments

Understanding the large public monuments of the period often requires a 'large-scale' archaeological response. Such was the approach taken by Geoff Wainwright in his campaign of excavation at the late Neolithic henge enclosures of Durrington Walls, Mount Pleasant, and Marden, between 1966 and 1971 (Fig 2.20 and see also pp 50–51). Combining a rescue imperative (a response to road construction at Durrington and ploughing at Mount Pleasant) and a clear

Fig 2.19 Excavation of the Longstones enclosure and Cove, at the end of the recently re-discovered Beckhampton Avenue, near Avebury, 2000 (© Joshua Pollard)

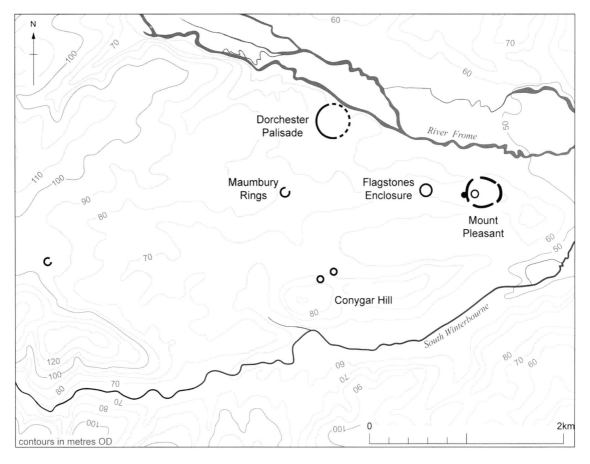

research agenda, the work involved a bold employment of machine stripping and extensive excavation that upset members of the then Wessex 'archaeological establishment'. The bold approach paid off, leading to the discovery of major timber monuments at Durrington Walls and Mount Pleasant, analogous to the multiple circles investigated 40 years earlier at Woodhenge and the Sanctuary, and by extension to the phase 3 stone settings at Stonehenge (Wainwright 1979; Wainwright and Longworth 1971). The substantial assemblages of Grooved Ware, lithics, and animal bone recovered from Durrington Walls were used by Wainwright and Longworth as the catalyst for a major re-assessment of the British later Neolithic (styled at the time as the 'Rinyo-Clacton culture'). A few years earlier, in 1965, Isobel Smith's definitive publication of the results of Alexander Keiller's work at Windmill Hill generated an equal 'sea change' in our understanding of the earlier Neolithic (Smith 1965). Work of this kind increasingly pushed Neolithic Wessex as a model or baseline for the period across southern Britain.

Smith's perceptive reading of the evidence from Windmill Hill and other causewayed enclosures has stood the test of time well. While greater variety in function is now indicated through the results of excavation at over 40 of these sites in the UK, the notion that they acted as foci for periodic aggregation and

Fig 2.20 The later Neolithic complex at Dorchester, Dorset. Little understood in the 1950s, subsequent work by Geoff Wainwright, Wessex Archaeology and others has done much to elucidate the character, extent and sequence of this major monument group (© Joshua Pollard)

deliberate deposition remains current. Further contribution to our understanding of these early monuments came from Roger Mercer's campaign of excavation on Hambledon Hill, Dorset, undertaken between 1974 and 1986 (see also pp 44–45). This massive complex, occupying the edge of the chalk, includes at least two enclosures joined by ditched and banked outworks that possess a defensive quality. The enclosures themselves were associated with very different suites of activity. Evidence for conflict, in the form of human skeletons from the ditches with embedded flint projectile points, hints at the tensions that could emerge during times of aggregation (Mercer and Healy 2008).

As knowledge of the chronology, function, and associations of familiar Neolithic monument forms continues to accumulate, an enhanced scale of fieldwork has also resulted in the detection of previously unsuspected types of construction. Without immediate parallel, the middle Neolithic shaft and pit-circle associated with a multiple burial at Monkton Up Wimborne on Cranborne Chase is a case in point. Then there are the irregular-ditched enclosures at Flagstones and Beckhampton that may, along with the first phase of Stonehenge, form an intermediary 'stage' between causewayed enclosures and henges proper. Most spectacular of all, and hidden from view until discovered through a combination of geophysical survey and aerial photography, are the massive Neolithic palisade enclosures at Mount Pleasant and West Kennet (to which can be added the analogous timber monument under Dorchester). Along with broadly contemporaneous multiple timber circles, these sites illustrate the scale of public timber architecture at a time when the earliest metal axes were in circulation, and when labour was mobilised on a previously unprecedented scale to create constructions such as the sarsen circles and trilithons at Stonehenge, Avebury's megalithic avenues, and Silbury Hill. Intriguingly, both the Mount Pleasant and West Kennet enclosures show signs of deliberate destruction through burning and post removal. While perhaps indicative of conflict, it is equally probable that their destruction was the culmination of a protracted ritual cycle (Whittle 1997).

The relationship between monuments and landscape, and a comprehension of how and why monument complexes developed, have been themes explored in a number of recent research projects. The work of Martin Green, Richard Bradley, Mike Allen, and others on Cranborne Chase, and that of Alasdair Whittle and the late John Evans around Avebury, provide good instances of projects that have worked beyond a site-based focus and integrated data on environmental change with that of constructional activity and ceremony (Barrett *et al* 1991; Whittle 1997; French *et al* 2007; Gillings *et al* 2008). Such work is always guided by a particular theoretical stance or theory-derived model, as with the current and highly ambitious Stonehenge Riverside Project (SRP). A recognition of the importance of materiality – of how the physical and metaphoric qualities of substances such as stone structured their use in ceremonial constructions – lies behind the SRP investigation of contemporaneous, mid-3rd millennium BC (cont[d] on p 46), timber and stone monuments in the Stonehenge landscape (Parker Pearson *et al* 2006). The results to date strongly support the notion that Durrington Walls, Woodhenge,

continued on p 46

Hambledon Hill, Dorset

Roger Mercer

By the beginning of the 1970s, seasonal ploughing on the cultivated part of Hambledon Hill was leading to the devastating disruption of the chalk bedrock. Great chunks of chalk were appearing, along with the odd flint implement, in the ploughsoil. Whatever remained of the dug features of Hambledon's Neolithic causewayed enclosure were clearly under imminent threat of destruction and in 1974 the decision was made to excavate. At that date there were very few permanent organisations that could carry out such a project, so I led the work in my capacity as an Inspector of Ancient Monuments in the Department of the Environment (DoE). The project was warmly encouraged by Geoffrey Wainwright, just back from his triumphant adventures with the henge enclosures of Wessex.

The excavation had to be seasonal in order to 'mesh' with the continued cultivation of the site. An excavation team was brought together and reconstituted over eight successive seasons, during which time more than 1000 people worked on the site. Weather rendered the first season a penal experience worthy of the Gulag, yet, with the help of the local villagers, and with the extraordinary dedication of the team, the date and cultural assignation of the site were established. In particular, we had begun to identify its function as a place for the ceremonial and ritual disposal of human bodies by excarnation – 'a vast reaking hilltop necropolis echoing to the cries of crows and ravens'.

But there was to be more and, in 1975, Roger Palmer joined the team, fresh from his survey of causewayed enclosures (Palmer 1976). His objective was to complete a landscape study on and around the hill, partly by aerial prospection but largely by detailed ground surface inspection. Thus began the process – excavation following survey and survey, in turn, following excavation – that elucidated the true nature of the site and its original extent. Painstakingly, it became clear that the whole hill, an area of some 60ha, had been encompassed within a colossal system of earthworks that encircled two causewayed enclosures and two long barrows, as well as other features.

Such was the importance of the emerging picture that DoE allowed the

Fig 2.21 The excavations in progress (© Roger Mercer)

Fig 2.22 Skeleton of a young man killed during another (later) phase of violence on the site
(© Roger Mercer)

excavation to continue, although with steadily diminishing support. In 1977 the Stepleton enclosure was discovered and by 1982 the whole of the southern outwork system had been established. The excavation of hundreds of metres of causewayed ditch enabled an unprecedented understanding of earthwork structure and ditch-filling processes. Given the Neolithic pre-occupation with re-cutting the ditch and burying material that was surplus from rituals, a massive, and extraordinary variety of organic (largely bone, antler, and charcoal) and inorganic (largely flint, stone, and ceramic) materials was recovered.

The Hambledon complex was, in effect, a disparate and widely spaced series of enclosures and boundaries with little or no stratigraphic linkage. It was therefore an extraordinary boon to be able to obtain some 160 reliable radiocarbon dates from across the whole span of the complex. These precision dates have produced a relative and absolute chronology for the whole site. Beginning in the 37th century BC, a great building phase saw the construction of the main and Stepleton enclosures as well as, probably, both long barrows. Later, the Shroton and Stepleton earthworks were constructed to defend the site from eastern approach. These defences were assaulted on at least three occasions in the 35th and 34th centuries BC, episodes during which three young men were certainly killed, two by arrowshot. Ultimately, in another massive effort, new defensive outworks (the Western outworks) were built along the western approaches to the hill.

Since c 3700 BC the site had been used, albeit only seasonally, as a ceremonial centre on the boundary of a territory lying mainly to the south and west. Occasionally very substantial gatherings took place. Imported materials came from great distances: surplus farm animals were driven to the site bearing supplies for several days junketings and were slaughtered there. Such a significant centre eventually became a focus of 'political' contention with the result that, c 3400 BC, its focus shifted towards 'Wessex' in the east. Episodes of organised violence were probably part of this process, whose interpretation has involved a wide range of specialised studies (Mercer and Healy 2008). Investigation on and around the Hill has also produced evidence of more or less continuous human activity from the early Bronze Age to the medieval period, making this a landscape with an exceptionally long and rich prehistory and history.

What makes Hambledon Hill so special is the length and depth of our enquiry. The scrupulous recording and dedicated management, by so many people, allowed the production of our final report to take place over decades, in many different places and, thankfully, often with techniques unforeseen at the time of excavation.

and Stonehenge, linked by avenues to the River Avon, operated as elements within a single ceremonial complex, and that Stonehenge was conceptualised as a structure for the ancestral dead of a particularly important lineage group.

No discussion of monumentality would be complete without a slight southerly diversion. Due to the inclusion of the Channel Islands within the region, CBA Wessex can claim a small part of the northern French Neolithic, and with it a site that sits at the very start of the long sequence of monument construction both in the bailiwicks and on 'mainland Wessex': Les Fouaillages on Guernsey. Ian Kinnes' excavation of the site demonstrated that not only is this long barrow one of the earliest such monuments in Europe, but its presence on the island demonstrates a maritime component to the continental European epi-Bandkeramik that was previously unsuspected (Kinnes 1998). Through a process of transmission that is still poorly understood, the region's more famous long barrows, West Kennet among them, have a distant genealogical relationship to Les Fouaillages and other northern French monuments of the early to mid-5th millennium BC. Perhaps the next 50 years will see the details of this relationship, and a convincing explanation of the chronological gap of several centuries between seemingly similar epi-Bandkeramik and British sites, properly elucidated.

Settlement

Owing to their high visibility and often spectacular scale, monuments have dominated the archaeology of Neolithic Wessex. By contrast, signatures of contemporaneous settlement are slight and often difficult to read, and so domestic life during the period has taken a backstage role in our accounts of the period. Until relatively recently, Neolithic settlement was equated with houses, domestic enclosures, and field systems, especially since the appearance of agriculture was seen as marking a transition from the mobile lifestyles of hunter-gatherers to one of sedentism and formalised landholding. However, when traces of such failed to materialise through excavation, arguments were advanced to account for their absence. These variously posited eradication of features through erosion on the chalk hilltops and burial under deep colluvial and alluvial deposits in the bottoms of valleys where archaeologists had few opportunities to look.

Subsequent and extensive excavation in a range of landscape settings, much of it in advance of development, has largely failed to uncover the anticipated houses and field systems of the Neolithic. Combined with a more critical stance on the range of practices that might characterise settlement, we can now be sure that the majority of people during the period did not live in the kinds of solidly constructed, permanent buildings that typify later prehistory (the later Bronze Age and Iron Age). Mobility, on varying scales from semi-sedentism to annual rounds, was the norm. A consequence of acknowledging settlement mobility is the recognition that ephemeral but often ubiquitous features and assemblages, notably surface lithic scatters, stake-holes, and pits, provide the common evidence for settlement. From the late 1970s, a number of landscape-scale fieldwork projects have mapped and characterised flint scatters in the region. Notable was the Stonehenge Environs Project (Richards 1990 and see also pp 64–65), which was designed explicitly to map traces of settlement as represented by lithic scatters that related to the area's major Neolithic and early Bronze Age monuments. Other programmes of surface collection such as South Dorset Ridgeway Survey and the Maddle Farm Project in Berkshire were influenced by a then current interest in long-term landscape history. At a risk of over generalising, the results of these programmes show small and/or low-density lithic scatters as characteristic of the earlier Neolithic, and much larger and denser concentrations in the late Neolithic–early Bronze Age, with concentrations around key monuments (notably causewayed enclosures and larger henges) indicative of settlement aggregation.

Houses are rare during the period and, as a consequence, the interpretation of those that have been discovered is not always straightforward. There are suggestions that some acted as communal halls, were dwellings for restricted social groups, or served special functions. It is of some interest that those examples which have recently come to light share architectural features with contemporaneous houses in distant regions. The early 4th millennium BC rectangular building at Horton, Berkshire, has parallels in Ireland, while the numerous late Neolithic houses excavated outside the eastern entrance of Durrington Walls during 2004–07

Fig 2.23 Late Neolithic houses under excavation by the Stonehenge Riverside Project at Durrington Walls, 2007, just two of many tens, if not hundreds, of structures associated with the pre-henge settlement focused on the monumental Southern Circle (© Adam Stanford, Aerial-Cam)

possess ground plans that are remarkably similar to Orcadian houses (Fig 2.23). Though solidly built with deliberately puddled chalk floors and traces of internal wooden furniture, the Durrington houses look to have been occupied seasonally as part of periodic aggregations for solstitial ceremonies and construction events (Parker Pearson *et al* 2006). Telling of recurrent links between domestic and ceremonial architecture, the plan of these buildings provided the template for a range of wooden monuments, of which the first phase of the Durrington Walls Southern Circle is an example.

Finds of charred grain and quernstones illustrate the importance of cereal cultivation during the 4th millennium BC at least. This acknowledged, there remains little evidence for field systems, suggesting that most cultivation took place in small and short-lived 'garden' plots. Ploughmarks have been discovered, under the bank at Avebury and the nearby South Street long barrow, for example, but these probably relate to the breaking-up of ground rather than repeated cultivation. It was not until the mid-2nd millennium BC that the Wessex landscape would take on an agrarian character.

Theory and interpretation

It would create an imbalanced picture if one were to argue that advancement of knowledge in the period was led solely by discovery and the application of analytical techniques. The rich quality of Wessex prehistory has long attracted scholars of international reputation (Stuart Piggott, Colin Renfrew, Richard Bradley, John Barrett, Alasdair Whittle, Mike Parker Pearson, Julian Thomas, to name a few), who have used the region's Neolithic archaeology as a 'testing ground' for theory and interpretation. Those studies of great influence include Colin Renfrew's classic 1973 model of prehistoric social evolution, which was constructed around a reading of the distribution and increasing scale of monuments in the region as a proxy for emerging social hierarchy (Renfrew 1973). Early 'post-processual' approaches which sought to emphasise ideology, structure, symbolism, and social reproduction also found the Neolithic of the region to be fertile ground for working through ideas. Two studies in particular can be highlighted. Colin Richards and Julian Thomas's reassessment of Wainwright's excavations at Durrington Walls drew attention to intentional symbolic structuring in the deposition of bone, pottery, and lithics, and transformed understanding of how the archaeological record should be understood (Richards and Thomas 1984). Though not without its problems, the concept of structured deposition now enjoys wide currency. Equally influential has been Mike Parker Pearson and Ramilisonina's use of ethnographic analogy to inform understandings of past materiality, specifically the metaphoric connections between materials such as timber and stone and different domains of existence (Parker Pearson and Ramilisonina 1998).

The next 50 years

It would be foolhardy to predict what the next 50 years might bring. We can only hope that the pace of fieldwork, analysis, and interpretation now established continues uninterrupted. There are certainly threats, including recent calls from some Druid groups for the reburial of prehistoric human remains which, if acquiesced, would virtually end the analytical work that is transforming our knowledge of individual life-histories. Current heritage management philosophies, which see excavation as essentially destructive and in need of increasing regulation and restriction, also pose difficulties in fully realising the aims of well-conceived research projects. There is certainly a need to conserve and protect, but this should always be balanced against the requirement to generate knowledge, which after all sustains academic and public interest in the past. Wessex, as ever, is in a fine position to deliver the knowledge that will further transform our understanding of prehistory. While there is growing awareness of divergent regional sequences elsewhere in Britain, the exceptional quality of evidence and history of research ensures that the Neolithic of Wessex will continue to hold a central place in our accounts of the period.

The great henge enclosures

Geoffrey Wainwright

A rich tapestry of excavations was woven in the 1960s – Barry Cunliffe at Fishbourne, Bath, Portchester, and Danebury; Leslie Alcock at South Cadbury; Martin Biddle at Winchester; Phil Barker at Hen Domen; John Hurst and Maurice Beresford at Wharram Percy. Seminal projects were being undertaken at Knowth, Jarrow, Llandegai, North Elmham, Overton Down, Usk, Wroxeter and the Somerset Levels. The excavation programme of the great henge enclosures in Wessex at Durrington Walls, Marden and Mount Pleasant arose by chance in 1966 when Wiltshire County Council decided to straighten the A345 Amesbury to Marlborough road where it crossed the interior of the large earthwork enclosure which surrounds a dry valley on the bank of the River Avon near Durrington.

The earthwork had been heavily ploughed for millennia and little remained on the surface to indicate its former importance. Nevertheless, the Ministry of Public Building and Works agreed to the expenditure of what was then a large sum of money to recruit an army of 40 contract workmen, an equivalent number of archaeologists, and a fleet of four JCB diggers and ten dumper trucks. The size of the operation – a strip of land 762m long and 18–39m wide – was predicated on the belief that similar structures to those found at Woodhenge might occur in the enclosure. If they were to be found in the bottom of the dry valley they would be well preserved by the soil having drifted down the slopes.

The most difficult practical issue was how to remove the ploughsoil, which varied in depth from 150mm on the north brim of the valley to 1.5m in the bottom. The problem was overcome by the use of JCB (3c) mechanical excavators, which have a back-actor and a front blade or bucket. By using the back-actor, the overlying ploughsoil can be removed to just above the top of the natural chalk with great accuracy and delicacy in the hands of a skilled operator. It was not the first occasion that my team, led by Peter Donaldson, had used the technique on chalk downland. Tollard Royal in Cranborne Chase had been the first in 1965 and I am reasonably confident that no structures were lost as a result of the

Fig 2.24 Durrington Walls: mechanised excavation on a grand scale (© Geoffrey Wainwright)

Fig 2.25 Marden:
the stake-holes
of a large circular
structure (© Geoffrey
Wainwright)

process. Peter was in charge of the soil-stripping throughout and undertook that role at Marden and Mount Pleasant. A team was built at Durrington Walls which stayed together for the entire five-year programme. Ian Longworth (pottery), John Evans (environment), Richard Burleigh (radiocarbon dating), Ralph Harcourt (animal bones), Tony Clark (geophysics) and Christine Boddington (published drawings) formed the team, which ensured that the project was, in a true sense, a collaborative exercise in which it was a pleasure to participate.

It was a hot summer in 1967 and the machines kicked up a thick pall of sweet-smelling chalk dust which permeated everything. We made a deliberate decision not to excavate approximately one-third of the two major timber structures uncovered. They lay outside the route of the new road and it seemed best to leave a sample unexcavated in the interests of posterity. All other deposits in the path of the new road were totally excavated and from the noise, dust, and aggravation emerged the foundations of the large circular structures that caught the professional and public imagination (Wainwright and Longworth 1971).

After Durrington Walls it was a comparatively simple matter to identify comparable enclosures in Wessex. In 1968 we all moved on to Marden in the Vale of Pewsey, where similar structures were found (Wainwright 1971), and in 1970 and 1971 to Mount Pleasant in the outskirts of Dorchester for more of the same (Wainwright 1979a). The enclosures at Avebury and Knowlton remained safe from my attentions but will reveal similar foundations of circular timber structures one day.

The five-year programme remains one of those rare projects where archaeological techniques combined with environmental sciences were able to demonstrate one aspect of life in a remarkably complex prehistoric society and opened our eyes to more possibilities. It raised these aspects of prehistoric life from the obscurity in which they had previously languished to the prominence which they receive in text-books and the media today, and the project transformed how we view the inhabitants of Britain in the 3rd millennium BC. In this context the interpretation of those great circular foundations, whether for roofed structures or free-standing circles of posts, matters not at all. What *does* matter is that they were planned and built by a remarkably complex society capable of such great public works, which culminated in the famous stone circle at Stonehenge.

It also gives me great satisfaction that 40 years on, young archaeologists are returning to investigate these great enclosures with new techniques and ideas. I am glad that we left something for them to investigate and hope that they make similar provision for their successors as well as being prepared to recall their own memories for the CBA centenary celebrations in 2058.

3

Later Prehistory

Prologue

Timothy Darvill

Throughout the last 50 years Wessex has in many ways provided the archaeology that both defines and characterises later prehistory throughout the British Isles. It is a 'happenstance' that has not pleased everyone, and is anyway both false and inappropriate given the great regional variation in settlement, economy, social organisation, and material culture that exists across the British Isles through the 3rd, 2nd, and 1st millennia BC. As a sound-track to the archaeological endeavours of later prehistorians over the last five decades there could perhaps be none better than Jerry Lee Lewis's *Great Balls of Fire* which topped the charts in January 1958 and neatly sums up the on-going debates about Wessex-centric views and competing interpretations of key monuments.

Enhanced chronologies have been the single biggest achievement in later prehistoric studies over the last 50 years. Stuart Piggott's memorable unwillingness, set forth in *Antiquity* for December 1959, to accept the first radiocarbon determinations on samples taken from a British prehistoric site now feels like the thinking of a distant era. Many samples have now been dated, levels of precision have been improved, and statistical routines for handling and interpreting determinations established to the point that later prehistory can be narrated in centuries and decades, while synchronicity within the overlapping life-spans of individuals can be postulated. There is no longer a role for the familiar labels of prehistory left over from the elaboration of the Three Age System, although no doubt the terms Neolithic, Bronze Age, and Iron Age will live on for a while in popular culture until such time as people can comfortably handle the back-projection of the familiar Gregorian Calendar into the ancient past.

Fifty years ago the world's most iconic prehistoric monument in the heartland of Wessex resembled a building site. Cranes and lifting gear had been installed at Stonehenge over the summer of 1958 in order to re-erect stones 22 and 57, re-fit stone 58, and straighten stone 21. This work created what has become a favourite view for tourists, but was just part of a long-running campaign of conservation work and associated investigations that eventually lasted through until 1964. Further small-scale works took place over the ensuing years – most notably, John Evans's re-opening of a section through the ditch in 1978, Alexander Thom and Richard Atkinson's examination of Station Stone 94 in 1978, Mike Pitts' work adjacent to the A344 in 1979–80, and the re-grassing of the interior and the construction of a circular path in 1981 – but it was another 44 years before new research excavations were allowed within the earthwork enclosure. Interestingly, both the work by the Geoffrey Wainwright and myself on the Double Bluestone Circle in April 2008, and that by Mike Parker Pearson and partners in the Stonehenge Riverside Project in August 2008, included research-funding from television companies; perhaps a sign of things to come and an indication of how the popular image that archaeology has created for itself is changing the pattern of financial support for fieldwork. Archaeological excavations are not only the outdoor laboratories in which we dissect the raw materials from which the past is fashioned; they are also arenas for a spectator sport. Back in the 1930s Sir Mortimer Wheeler recognised the power of the media to expand his audience for work at Maiden Castle, near Dorchester while, in 1968–70, the investigation of Silbury Hill was one of first extended outside broadcasts by the BBC, pioneered by David Attenborough who had recently been appointed controller of the newly created BBC2. Nowadays coverage has expanded to include not just the programmes themselves but pod-casts, blogs, downloads, discussion groups, and what is becoming known as '360-degree coverage'.

The quietude of Stonehenge from the mid-1960s through to 2008 was not repeated elsewhere. The clanking of shovels and the scraping of trowels has been heard in just about every corner of the region over the last 50 years as extensive excavations, sometimes as parts of long-term projects, have transformed understandings of later prehistory. For the 3rd millennium BC, work at Durrington Walls and Marden, and Mount Pleasant, Dorchester, by Geoffrey Wainwright between 1966 and 1971 revealed the scale and wealth of the henge-enclosures (see pp 50–51), with only Knowlton South on Cranborne Chase escaping attention until the work of John Gale and Steven Burrow from 1994. Elsewhere, work around Avebury focused not just on the great henge and associated stone circles but also on the The Sanctuary, the Beckhampton Avenue rediscovered in 1999, and the West Kennet palisaded enclosures explored and recognised for what they were between 1987 and 1992. Silbury Hill was examined in 1968–70, and again in 2007 prompted by the collapse of the earlier tunnelling. Systematic surveys around Stonehenge, Avebury, the Marlborough Downs, the Berkshire Downs, and many other areas too have set a baseline for future work, in the case of Avebury and Stonehenge consolidated as Research Frameworks that provide a context and launch-pad for further work. Chance finds and opportunistic investigations are important too, and here one thinks of discoveries such as the rich graves of the Amesbury Archer and the Boscombe Bowmen (see pp 60–61) which have both given new direction and impetus to the investigation of population movements and social organisation in the later 3rd millennium BC.

For the 2nd millennium BC, investigations on Cranborne Chase have provided new models for the relationships between settlements and burial grounds, while work in many parts of Wessex has emphasised the antiquity of the 'Celtic field systems' and the agricultural revolution that occurred here through the middle and late 2nd millennium BC. Investigations at Rams Hill, Potterne, Bestwell Quarry, All Cannings Cross, Rowden, Bucklebury, and many other sites beside now illustrate the complexity and variety of settlements across the region, in some cases challenging and breaking down familiar classifications with the recognition of whole new kinds of archaeology and further confounding traditional periodisation based on metalworking technologies.

Much the same applies for work relating to the 1st millennium BC. Work by Barry Cunliffe at and around Danebury between 1969 and 2008 shows that even familiar classes of monument such as hillforts are infinitely more complicated that imagined 50 years ago; a view confirmed by the re-investigation of Maiden Castle and work at Balksbury, Andover. The extensive investigations of non-hillfort enclosures at Gussage All Saints and Tollard Royal, and at Micheldever Wood and Winnall Down amongst others, show the diversity of these 'farmsteads', while coastal sites such as Hengistbury Head and Cleavel Point/Green Island in Poole Harbour underline the significance and scale of cross-channel and coastal trade.

Two major themes cut through the developing understanding of later prehistory in Wessex. First is the increasing contribution being made by developer-funded archaeology and the Portable Antiquities Scheme which together are enriching the database of recorded sites and material in a way quite undreamt of 50 years ago. As a result there is now a very real opportunity to consider prehistoric landscapes at both local and regional scales and the next stage is to develop innovative approaches to predictive modelling of sites and activities. Second is an increasing recognition of the wealth of material culture from later prehistory, not only in terms of physical representation but also in terms of what it can reveal about personal and group identity, the construction of both power and gender relations, and its implications for understanding prevailing cosmologies and world-views. It would be wrong to think that Wessex simply provides a microcosm of Britain's later prehistory but, in thinking about the wealth of evidence preserved in the region, it would be fair to paraphrase a sound-bite promoting a well-known brand of lager and suggest that: Archaeological work in Wessex reaches parts of the past that other areas never quite reach!

The Bronze Age: beyond the barrow mounds

Mike Parker Pearson

We like to think that there has been nothing but progress in archaeological research. Yet the heyday of early Bronze Age archaeology in Wessex was probably in the 1950s and 1960s. Since then, round barrows – the most visible surviving evidence from the period – have only been investigated in sporadic and piecemeal interventions despite an unparalleled assault upon them through ploughing and other forms of development. And we still know next to nothing about the abodes of the living either.

In contrast, our knowledge of the Later Bronze Age has mushroomed. From our limited knowledge 50 years ago, based mainly on bronze artefacts and hoards, we now have copious remains of burials, houses, settlements, field systems, hillforts, and river crossings.

The Earlier Bronze Age

Fifty years ago, round barrow research in Wessex was changing our knowledge of Bronze Age funerary practices in a way not seen since the 19th-century antiquarians. Major programmes of rescue excavation were carried out for the Ministry of Works, notably by Paul Ashbee around Amesbury (Ashbee 1960; 1975–76; 1981; 1985), by Charles Green at Shrewton (Green and Rollo-Smith 1984), by Nicholas Thomas on Snail Down (Thomas 2005), and by Faith and Lance Vatcher in Wiltshire (Gingell 1988).

Barrows and burials

In his final chapter on 'Barrows, the future and the state' in *The Bronze Age Round Barrow in Britain*, one can sense Paul Ashbee's concerns that posterity might not live up to the standards of preservation and research that he outlined (1960, 200). And sadly we have not – round barrows have continued to be ploughed out even where supposedly protected by law and on National Trust land, at Avebury, for example. Although most upstanding round barrows in Wessex are scheduled as ancient monuments, many have continued to be ploughed as a result of the Class Consent legislative loophole which allows for continuation of destructive agricultural practices after the 1979 *Ancient Monuments and Archaeological Areas Act* came into force. Whilst mapping and earthwork survey have undoubtedly improved, notably through the former RCHM(E), now amalgamated within English Heritage, the initiative for invasive, excavation-led research has been stifled.

There have been calls within recently compiled Research Frameworks for targeted excavation and re-excavation of Wessex round barrows (SWARF 2005; Wainwright 1997; Wainwright and Lawson 1995; Darvill 2005) but very little has happened. Indeed, a recent proposal by the Stonehenge Riverside Project

Fig 3.1 High Lea Farm round barrow. Whilst the primary burial, a pair of cremations, was not particularly remarkable, John Gale's team has been able to recover the complex sequence of activities – construction of a circular fence around the burial, digging out of the grave, construction of further post-circles, the Herculean labour of stripping surrounding turf, and digging of the ditch – which are generally not recoverable where barrows have since become ploughed-out ring ditches (© Mike Parker Pearson)

(SRP) to re-excavate William Stukeley's trench into a Stonehenge Cursus barrow, to provide the first-ever radiocarbon date for a Wessex I burial, was turned down by the National Trust in 2008. English Heritage's limited excavation of a badger-damaged round barrow at Figheldean, Amesbury (Last 2006), is one of the very few state-led initiatives and, even then, its main priority was to assess damage rather than address prehistoric research goals. Bournemouth University's excavation of a round barrow at High Lea Farm, near Cranborne Chase, is one example which demonstrates just how much can be learned from careful, modern excavation (Fig 3.1).

As a result of long-term institutional antipathy towards round barrow research excavations, most other excavation projects have been rescue-driven. One of the best known is Boscombe Down, Amesbury, where the famous Beaker burials of the 'Amesbury Archer' (Fitzpatrick 2002) and the 'Boscombe Bowmen' (Fitzpatrick *et al* 2004 and pp 60–61) formed part of a larger cemetery of flat graves and ploughed-out round barrows. Thomas Hardye School, Dorchester, is the site of another important barrow cemetery excavated by Wessex Archaeology but this project has remained uncompleted due to shortage of funding from the developer. The excavation of an unusual triple barrow in advance of the M3 motorway in Micheldever Wood, Hampshire, has yielded important information about mound construction and after-use (Fasham 1979).

The poverty of opportunities for new barrow excavations has, to some extent, been off-set by advances in scientific techniques for investigating the skeletons and finds from previous excavation campaigns. Birmingham University's study of heirlooms in early Bronze Age Britain is using microscopic and mineralogical analysis to find out how dress items were worn and to what extent they were already old when buried (Woodward 2002). The discovery, from oxygen and strontium isotope analysis, that the Amesbury Archer (Fig 3.2) had spent his childhood in the Alpine foothills (Evans *et al* 2006) has also led to a Britain-wide study of Beaker burials – the Beaker People Project – which is providing new insights into health, diet, mobility, and migration in the late 3rd millennium BC. Results from Wessex are still awaited but elsewhere (in Scotland and East Yorkshire) it appears that mobility was a major factor of early Bronze Age life.

Houses and settlements

If, 50 years ago, we knew about the early Bronze Age principally from the remains of the dead, the situation is virtually unchanged today. Structural remains of houses have proved almost impossible to find. Just as T C Lethbridge postulated that early Bronze Age pastoralists lived in tents, so the idea has been resuscitated (Lawson 2007, 172–3). Yet the absence of evidence is more likely due to our inability to look for the right remains in the right places. As the well-preserved house floors of Durrington Walls show so clearly, houses from *c* 2500 cal BC made remarkably little impact beneath the ground surface. Looking for them in areas subsequently cultivated or where erosion and weathering have removed the prehistoric land surface is a futile exercise. Similarly, standard field evaluation procedures of stripping small percentages of land surface are unlikely to recover the restricted scatters of small pits which are all that remain of settlement areas.

Our techniques for house-hunting have to improve. Not only should we prioritise old ground surfaces for excavation but we need to learn more about ploughzone assemblages; can we reconstruct house locations from varying artefact densities or variations in magnetic susceptibility or elements such as phosphorus in the ploughsoil? Currently, there is not one convincing early Bronze Age house plan known from Wessex.

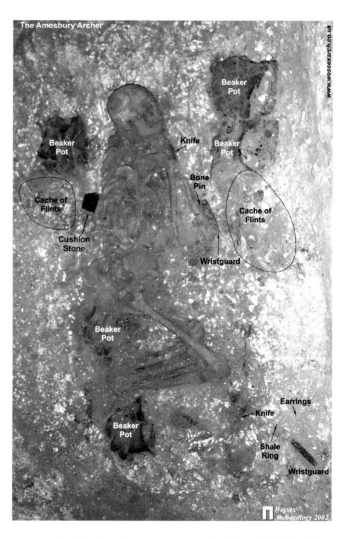

Fig 3.2 The Amesbury Archer. Not only is he the best-furnished Beaker burial in Europe but analysis of his tooth enamel indicates that he was a migrant to Britain (© Wessex Archaeology)

Agriculture and fields

It is becoming something of a misguided mantra that farming did not really take off in Britain until the middle Bronze Age. And yet there is growing evidence that Beaker-period cultivation was extensive across southern Britain (Allen 2005). Within the Stonehenge area, for example, recent excavations by the SRP have revealed deep deposits of windblown soils in the re-cut Cursus and Avenue ditches which probably accumulated during brief periods of erosion caused by breaking the surface of the surrounding grasslands. Among the dense lattice of inter-cutting field systems around Avebury, Peter Fowler considers that some of these date back to a period of agricultural expansion in the early Bronze Age (2004, 136).

At the same time, the isotopic evidence for mobility supports the evidence for a pastoralist economy, bearing out Andrew Fleming's conclusions (1971). The two modes of arable farming and pastoralism need not be seen in opposition but can indeed be sustainable within a unified economy in which tasks are divided by age and gender.

Metalworking

The concept of the Bronze Age is, of course, dependent on the adoption of tin-alloyed copper. That seems to date from c 2300/2200 BC across Britain but there is uncertainty about the date when copper was introduced. Most specialists consider that it was not adopted in Britain prior to 2450 BC (Needham 2008), a date which reflects the introduction of inhumations from which items of copper are likely to be represented among the many grave goods.

Recent excavations at Durrington Walls, however, suggest that copper might have been in use some 50 years earlier. Not only are there probable metal axe-marks in chalk dug out of the henge ditch (Fig 3.3), but the vast assemblage of 80,000 worked flints from the underlying settlement produced just one fragment of a flint axe. This raises the possibility that recyclable copper axes were in use at the beginning of the 25th century BC.

Fig 3.3 Are these metal axe marks? Chalk rubble within the henge bank at Durrington Walls, dating to 2480–2460 BC (© Shane Eales, Sheffield University)

continued on p 62

The Amesbury Archer and the Boscombe Bowmen

Andrew Fitzpatrick

The Amesbury Archer has become one of the most celebrated prehistoric discoveries in Wessex. Found in 2002 a few kilometres from Stonehenge, he lived either at the time that the temple was being built or shortly after, and he was given the richest burial of his period not just in Britain but in Europe. Isotope analysis of his teeth showing that he was an incomer has helped revive interest both in the 'Beaker folk' and how this archaeological culture spread across Europe during a distinct Copper Age (Brodie 1998; Harrison 1980; vander Linden 2006).

Fig 3.4 The Archer as he might have looked in later life (© Wessex Archaeology)

In many ways the Amesbury Archer is typical of Bell Beaker burials. The 35–45-year-old man was buried on his side as if asleep and around him were placed the accoutrements of an archer, or warrior. He had lived to a good age, but his left knee was missing, causing him to walk with a pronounced limp (Fitzpatrick in press).

The number of objects placed in his grave by his mourners is without parallel and includes what are currently the earliest objects of gold and of copper in Britain, the largest number of Beaker pots in an individual grave in Britain, and numerous flint tools and arrowheads.

His Companion, a man aged between 20 and 25, lay near by. He died shortly after the Archer and his mourners placed very similar gold ornaments in his grave. The shape of the two men's skulls suggested they were related and this is confirmed by a rare genetic trait found in their feet.

The isotopes in the enamel of human teeth store a chemical fingerprint of the environment in which the individuals lived when their permanent teeth were forming. The oxygen isotopes, which are essentially climatic indicators, showed that the Companion was raised locally but that the Amesbury Archer had lived in a much colder climate in continental Europe. The typology of his grave goods suggests this was likely to have been in Central Europe. A worked stone metalworker's tool provides part of the explanation for his journeys (Fitzpatrick 2009); if the Amesbury Archer used it, he is the earliest person yet found in Britain with the skill to work the rare and exotic metals of gold and copper.

The grave of the Boscombe Bowmen was discovered in 2003 barely a kilometre away, when a mechanical excavator cut through it during a watching brief. Unlike the single burials of the Amesbury Archer and Companion, the burial of the Boscombe Bowmen is a collective one, containing the remains of at least seven individuals – six adults and a child – dated to the Copper Age. Only two complete skeletons were found, the other individuals being represented by disarticulated remains, mainly skulls and limb bones. This does not conform to the expectation that Bell Beaker burials in Britain are single burials.

Part of the explanation again lies in the isotope analyses (Evans *et al* 2006). The strontium isotopes, which indicate the age of the underlying geological formations, demonstrate that the three adults whose teeth could be analysed had grown up in an area based on much older geological strata than those found in southern England. Again the similarities in their skulls suggest that they came from a close-knit community, though it cannot be said that they were related. Radiocarbon dating has demonstrated that the Boscombe Bowmen are the oldest Bell Beaker burials yet found in Britain.

The closest region consistent with their strontium isotopes is Wales. The first stones at Stonehenge, the bluestones, came from the Preseli Hills in Wales, more than 240km away. However, the isotopes show that the Boscombe Bowmen were in one location when they were around 5 years old and in another when aged about 13. This suggests that they made at least two journeys from one location or perhaps one longer one, and if the latter is the case it seems likely that it was from continental Europe. Although single burial became typical of Bell Beaker burials in Britain, collective burial was very common across much of France, Portugal, and Spain.

Although a definitive conclusion as to the 'homeland' of the Boscombe Bowmen is not possible, their grave and that of the Amesbury Archer represent major discoveries. Dating to between about 2425 and 2300 BC, their association with the introduction of the Bell Beaker Culture and metallurgy to Britain will make them the subject of continuing scholarly debate. Just as importantly, they provide powerful human stories to stand alongside Stonehenge, which for too long has been seen as a remote and romantic icon of a distant prehistoric past.

Fig 3.5 Flint and copper knives buried with the Amesbury Archer. Copper knife measures 107mm (© Wessex Archaeology)

Fig 3.6 The grave of the Boscombe Bowmen.
Scale = 1m (© Wessex Archaeology)

Monument building

Restorative works on Silbury Hill provided the opportunity to re-date this enigmatic monument to 2410–2390 BC (Bayliss *et al* 2007). An attempt to re-date Stonehenge's bluestones in 2008 failed because of the extent of bioturbation affecting the small charcoal samples (Fig 3.7); the sarsen circle and trilithons, however, date to around 2500 BC (Allen and Bayliss 1995, 532; Parker Pearson *et al* 2007) and were followed by a series of minor re-buildings during the last centuries of the 3rd millennium BC (and into the 2nd millennium BC in the case of the Y and Z Holes).

The cessation of major monument construction in the late 3rd millennium BC is a notable feature of the Beaker period political landscape. If Beaker pottery accompanied an influx of both people and ideas from continental Europe, as increasingly seems the case, then it is interesting that their homelands were largely devoid of the large-scale public works and monumental architecture so typical of Britain and Ireland. Instead, the earliest Beaker burials seem not to have been surmounted by large mounds. Even when mound building became common around the end of the millennium, none could be considered as monumental works beyond the capabilities of a single lineage or kin group. This devolution in monument building may have marked an important social transformation in which elites could no longer count on the corvée labour of others.

Fig 3.7 Surveying the recent excavations at Stonehenge: L–R Mike Pitts, Timothy Darvill and Geoff Wainwright. Attempts to date the bluestone arc (the Q & R Holes) in 2008 failed but the subsequent phase, when the large sarsens were erected, can be dated to *c* 2500 BC; only a few minor re-organisations of the bluestones were carried out later within the Bronze Age (© Mike Parker Pearson)

The later Bronze Age

By 1500 BC round barrow building was largely out of fashion. From c 1600 BC onwards, field systems enveloped the Wessex chalklands, and earthfast house foundations and settlement enclosure ditches fixed farmsteads in the landscape, making them ultimately more visible archaeologically.

Monument building

There are few monumental structures from this period, barring the hillforts. The Uffington White Horse has been dated by Optically Stimulated Luminescence to 1400–600 BC. At Testwood in Hampshire, the wooden uprights of three Later Bronze Age bridges have been found, together with a bronze rapier blade (Fig 3.8).

Cemeteries

Cremation burials are the most frequently recovered burial rite from this period, particularly within Deverel-Rimbury urns. They continued the tradition of inurned cremation from earlier Bronze Age times, in which Food Vessels, Collared Urns, and Biconical

Fig 3.8 Testwood Lakes. The wooden posts formed the footings for a Bronze Age bridge. Preserved organic remains such as these are a high priority for excavation in Wessex (© Wessex Archaeology)

Urns were the standard containers of ashes. Over a dozen Deverel-Rimbury cemeteries in the Wessex area have been excavated since the 1960s, notably at Kimpton (Dacre and Ellison 1981), Knighton Heath (Petersen 1981), Simon's Ground (White 1982), Twyford Down (Walker and Farwell 2000), Canford Magna (Hearne and Birbeck 1996), and Sulhamstead (Butterworth and Lobb 1992). Grave goods were sparse and, although cemeteries might be located close to an earlier barrow, graves were not marked by monumental superstructures. Deverel-Rimbury pottery was used in both settlements and cemeteries from c 1600 BC.

By 1000 BC, Post-Deverel-Rimbury (PDR) ceramics were rarely used as cremation containers and funerary rites became largely archaeologically invisible. There are a number of inhumation burials from the Later Bronze Age in Wessex. Those from Down Farm (Green 2000, 112–13), Middle Farm, Dorchester (Smith et al 1997, 72–80), and Easton Lane, near Winchester (Fasham et al 1989), are tightly contracted, indicating that they had been bound up. Similar burials from this period in the Outer Hebrides have been shown to have been mummified prior to burial (Parker Pearson et al 2005) and this remains a possibility for these individuals.

continued on p 66

Stonehenge

Julian Richards

What is special about Stonehenge? Lots. It is unique in many ways, from the distances over which its stones were transported, to their shaping, jointing and the architectural ways they are arranged. These are what make it visually unique and why it has inevitably achieved iconic status. Beyond this lies its time depth – almost one and a half millennia of construction, modification and use. These, and an enduring sense of 'mystery', are what make Stonehenge so special.

Nor does this very special monument stand in isolation. It is surrounded by a landscape rich in upstanding prehistoric remains, largely concerned with ceremony and burial, within which aerial photography and fieldwalking have added a more domestic component.

Stonehenge was excavated extensively in the 1920s and again in the 1950s and 1960s but an unfortunately consistent feature of these campaigns was the inability of the excavators to analyse and publish their work. So, until the publication in 1995 of *Stonehenge in its Landscape: 20th Century Excavations* (Cleal *et al* 1995) what we had was a Stonehenge acknowledged to be ill-dated and ill-understood.

In contrast, an understanding of the surrounding Stonehenge landscape had developed steadily from the late 1970s onwards. In 1979 the RCHME brought together all the available evidence from aerial photography and combined it with ground survey in *Stonehenge and its Environs* (RCHME 1979). In the 1980s, reflecting a developing awareness of the archaeological potential of the ploughsoil, the Stonehenge Environs Project examined in detail this overlooked resource, collecting finds and analysing the magnetic and chemical signatures of the soil itself (Richards 1990). The result of these studies was that by the end of the 1980s the Stonehenge landscape was seen as not purely one of death and ceremony, but included evidence of everyday life and industry from the time of Stonehenge.

Stonehenge sits at the centre of what is often referred to as 'the bowl', a natural amphitheatre edged with spectacular cemeteries of round barrows. This

Fig 3.9 Stonehenge
(© Julian Richards)

Fig 3.10 Stuart Piggott and Richard Atkinson planning the hole for Stone 58, 1958 (© English Heritage)

natural topography and its constituent monuments have both recently been scrutinised in novel ways. The concept of 'viewsheds', ways of 'experiencing' rather than just studying a landscape, and detailed analyses of the contents of the barrows have perhaps brought us closer to an understanding of Stonehenge's prehistoric surroundings.

The last decade has also seen rapid changes in the approaches to Stonehenge itself. The publication of previous excavations has clarified at least parts of its complex sequence of construction and finally removed the block on further investigation. Recent work by the Stonehenge Riverside Project has located an industrial stone-working zone to the north of the stones and suggested that the Avenue may have started as a natural feature within the landscape, perhaps an answer to the thorny question of why is Stonehenge where it is (Parker Pearson *et al* 2004; 2006)? And within a landscape that would not have been thought to harbour any major secrets, a new and controversial stone circle emerged in the last days of the project during the summer of 2009. Finally, after a gap of over 40 years, excavations have taken place at Stonehenge itself. The two recent (2008) excavations may have been small but they were both highly significant and engendered great debate.

Each was intended to clarify aspects of Stonehenge's sequence and dating, but also sought the answer to that most fundamental and difficult question: why was Stonehenge built? Based on their extensive fieldwork in the Preseli Hills, the source of the bluestones, Darvill and Wainwright were in search of evidence to support their theory that these stones were perceived as having healing powers. For Parker Pearson, the re-excavation of Aubrey Hole 7 with its cache of previously excavated cremated human bone would hopefully strengthen Stonehenge's association with death in contrast to the 'land of the living' identified around Durrington Walls.

So which is the answer? Welsh folklore supports Stonehenge as 'the Lourdes of ancient Wessex' while a Madagascan archaeologist is convinced that its stones mark it out as a 'place of the Ancestors' (Parker Pearson and Ramilisonina 1998). Or are the thousands who turn up to observe the movements of the sun at mid-summer and, increasingly at the winter solstice, closer to the truth? Or is everyone at least partly right and did this undeniably complex site perform a wide variety of functions over its long life, including those of cemetery, place of healing and solar calendar?

Perhaps the 19th-century antiquarian Sir Richard Colt Hoare had it summed up when he concluded his ponderings on Stonehenge with the words: 'How grand! How wonderful! How incomprehensible!'

Agriculture and fields

Perhaps the greatest revolution in understanding the later Bronze Age in the last half century has been the realisation that most of the so-called 'Celtic fields' were neither Roman nor Iron Age but Bronze Age. Peter Fowler's pioneering work on the field systems around Avebury (1983; 2000) has been followed by a range of research projects (Gingell 1992; Bradley *et al* 1994; McOmish *et al* 2002; Brown *et al* 2005) which have demonstrated the early beginnings and long-term usage of prehistoric field systems from *c* 1600 BC onwards.

Large-scale rescue excavations of late Bronze Age field systems have been carried out recently at Dunch Hill on Salisbury Plain, Horton, and Laverstock, and by the Bestwall Quarry Archaeology Project at Wareham. In such instances it is possible to examine the stratigraphic and structural relationships between house locations, droveways, and field boundaries as composite elements of the farmed landscape.

Some of the most intriguing aspects of this partitioned landscape are the long linear earthworks – 'linears' – that demarcated large land parcels. Previously thought of as 'ranch boundaries', these have been shown to divide the landscape into large rectangular blocks (Lawson 2007, 298–301). Even where they have been excavated, as in the case of the Old Ditch at Breach Hill on Salisbury Plain (*ibid*, 300–1), they are extremely difficult to date with any precision – they have little domestic material in their fills and have frequently been re-cut at later dates. Excavations by SRP in 2008 have shown that the Stonehenge Palisade was one of these Bronze Age boundaries, which underwent considerable re-cutting, from a Bronze Age palisade line to a ditch to an Iron Age pit alignment.

The Wilsford Shaft, probably dating to the 15th century BC, raises a number of issues (Ashbee *et al* 1989). Is it a secular well or a ritual shaft? Was it re-cut into a previous shaft of the 4th millennium BC? And how many more of these remain to be discovered, currently masquerading as pond barrows? However, it indicates the importance of water sources on the high chalk during the Bronze Age and also provides a window on otherwise unknown organic items of material culture from that period.

Houses and settlements

Ever since Pitt Rivers' excavation of a later Bronze Age enclosure at South Lodge Camp on Cranborne Chase a century ago, there has been an understanding of settlements of this period. Yet the explosion of knowledge about houses and settlements only took place in the last 40 years with the growth of rescue archaeology. There are now many excavated examples of enclosed and unenclosed settlements from across Wessex.

The ground plans of many roundhouses, based on surviving postholes and/ or eaves-drip gullies, have been recovered. It is worth singling out two instances where good preservation provides the ability to say something about how their interior space was used. At Bishops Cannings Down in Wiltshire, Chris Gingell recovered debris from two successive roundhouses which showed where storage

Fig 3.11 The later Bronze Age house terrace at Rowden, Dorset. This is one of the very few roundhouses from Wessex in which the house floor has survived (© Peter Woodward)

urns were placed against the inside wall (Gingell 1992). At Rowden in Dorset (Fig 3.11), Peter Woodward excavated a roundhouse whose floor had been terraced into the hillside and was thus protected from later cultivation; its floor had been kept clean but enough survived to interpret the presence of former wooden partitions (Woodward 1991).

The recognition of a new ceramic phase at the end of the Bronze Age and into the early Iron Age only came in the 1970s (Barrett 1980). Plain PDR dates to *c* 1100–900 BC whilst decorated PDR was used in the period 900–500 BC. It is associated with a variety of different sites, from hillforts to large middens. One of the latter is the site of All Cannings Cross, first excavated by Maud Cunnington nearly a century ago (Cunnington 1923). In 1984 a small part of another of these enigmatic midden sites was excavated at Potterne in Wiltshire (Lawson 2000). The deep, homogeneous layers were packed with domestic debris and extended over 3.5ha to a maximum depth of over 2m. Recent survey has revealed a dense concentration of these middens in the Vale of Pewsey, of which the most remarkable is East Chisenbury (Brown *et al* 1994). Limited test trenching revealed huge quantities of finds, indicating that the almost 50,000 cubic metres of archaeological deposits in this midden are likely to contain remains of about 255,000 adult sheep, 125,000 lambs, 60,000 cattle, and 10,000 humans. Such sites do not appear to be conventional settlements and may have accumulated over short timespans. The homogeneity of their 'dark earth' stratigraphy makes archaeological excavation very difficult and they continue to evade archaeological interpretation.

Hillforts are another element of the late Bronze Age landscape in Wessex. Two excavated examples are Rams Hill, inhabited in the period 1250–900 BC (Bradley and Ellison 1975; Needham and Ambers 1994), and the first phases of

Balksbury Camp, near Andover, dating from 900 BC onwards (Wainwright and Davies 1995; Ellis and Rawlings 2001). Whilst Balksbury appears to have been used primarily as a stock enclosure, Rams Hill contained remains of roundhouses and four-post structures.

Metalworking

Mike Rowlands' study of middle Bronze Age metalworking across southern Britain (1976) not only illustrated the wealth of bronze artefacts from this region but also identified localised zones of particular tool and ornament styles. These were used by Ann Woodward to illustrate how nodal settlements like Rams Hill were located at the intersections between style zones of metalwork and ceramics (Ellison 1980). Brendan O'Connor's study of late Bronze Age metalwork illustrates the extent to which Wessex had been eclipsed by the lower Thames valley as a deposition zone by 1000 BC (O'Connor 1980). Since these seminal studies, the quantities of Bronze Age metalwork have been increased by metal detectorists' discoveries. Within the decade to 2006, the Portable Antiquities Scheme recorded 185 new records from central southern England, of which eight were hoards (Lawson 2007, 294).

We still know relatively little about the context of bronze metallurgy and old questions remain unanswered. Was bronze cast by itinerant smiths or by specialists tied to particular communities? Why were so many hoards of non-functional axes (with excessive quantities of tin or lead added to the copper) deposited in the coastal areas of Wessex? Very occasionally, sites where metalworking was practised have been identified, as at Sigwells near South Cadbury in Somerset, where ceramic mould fragments were found in association with postholes for a building in which bronze metallurgy was practised (Tabor 2008, 61–9).

A recent find which has attracted considerable interest is a pair of late Bronze Age roundhouses at Hartshill Copse, Upper Bucklebury in Berkshire (Collard *et al* 2006). The postholes of one of these were full of hammerscale from working iron and could be dated to the 10th century BC on the basis of radiocarbon determinations and associated plain PDR ware. The results appear to indicate that ironworking was practised here in the Bronze Age, about 200 years before the beginning of the British Iron Age. The lack of iron smithing slag from this site is very odd, however, and the possibility remains that the tiny pieces of hammerscale may have been carried down into the postholes by bioturbation from a much later ironworking deposit which was removed within the topsoil prior to excavation.

Overview: the next 50 years

It is difficult to think positively about archaeology's future during a period of economic down-turn. Yet certain themes and questions look set to continue into the foreseeable future:

- Decline in university-run field projects – as universities are increasingly restricted in finances and resources, so there will be fewer university-led research projects.
- Increasing reliance on contract archaeology – lack of choice about where to dig will continue to result in haphazard discoveries regardless of the guiding hand of research frameworks.
- Loss of resource through re-burial of human remains – a small but vociferous minority campaigning for the re-burial of prehistoric human remains may well take this issue to the point where religious views outnumber those of scientific rationality.
- Maintaining the difficult balance between preservation and excavation – archaeological curators have been increasingly reticent in the last 50 years to allow research excavations on otherwise unthreatened sites. Will this continue or will a balance be struck to allow limited excavations where knowledge gain and public outreach justify them?
- Costs of fieldwork and a widening range of expensive analytical techniques – major research projects are increasingly beyond the capability and budgets of archaeological institutions.
- What, specifically, are the areas where we need to make progress in the next fifty years?
- Research questions should focus on the study of Bronze Age 'history', providing detailed accounts of regionality and sequence (rather than mere characterisation, dating and representativity).
- Where are the early Bronze Age houses? We need to look carefully in unploughed areas and buried soils under barrows and field banks.
- What are the full contexts for metalwork reported by the Portable Antiquities Scheme? Whilst there continue to be concerns by some archaeologists that metal detecting is merely government-sanctioned looting, we need to ensure that discoveries are properly followed up to restore contextual information on recovered finds.
- When, how and why was copper adopted and when, how and why was bronze replaced by iron?
- How can we develop a 'ploughzone archaeology' for traces of settlement prior to the middle Bronze Age?
- When will we get some dates for 'Wessex I' burials by re-excavating antiquarian barrow trenches (and maybe by digging an untouched one)?
- What can we find out about population and herd movements? Isotopic analyses are beginning to revolutionise our knowledge of human and animal mobility during this period.
- Opportunities must be seized to excavate priority contexts such as undisturbed house floors and waterlogged deposits, expensive though they may be.

Down (on the) Farm

Martin Green

I grew up on the chalklands of Cranborne Chase on Down Farm, near Sixpenny Handley, during the 1950s and 1960s. My family roots were firmly planted in the earth of Wessex, having farmed for generations in the region. Growing up I became fascinated by the ancient earthworks which practically surround the farm. Long and round barrows crest the ridges, the Ackling Dyke Roman road forms the farm's southern boundary, and the course of the enigmatic Dorset Cursus crosses it. Inspired by the finds of stone implements my father occasionally made during his work in the fields, I began to fieldwalk the arable areas of the farm, carefully recording my finds. Later I interested a school friend in my pursuit and together we started a systematic fieldwalking survey of the area. During our teens we volunteered on a number of excavations in the region including a re-excavation of one of the Oakley Down barrows. I well remember the excitement of watching a plaque, left by William Cunnington, being uncovered in the central burial pit! The director of this work, David White, took an interest in our field survey and published a preliminary paper in the Dorset *Proceedings* (White 1971).

Fig 3.12 Artist's impression of the north end of the Ogden Down complex as it may have appeared about 3000 years ago (© David Bennett)

As a result of the 'great drought' of 1976 my fieldwork was to expand into the realms of excavation through a chance discovery. The exceptional conditions that summer caused our wells to run dry, forcing my father to have mains water installed. Walking along the pipe trench I spotted a ditch in the section which I started to uncover during occasional free moments. By the following year I had traced the outline of a three-sided enclosure and had just started investigating the interior when I was visited by Richard Bradley from Reading University. He was most interested in the work I was undertaking and informed me of the plan by himself and his colleague, John Barrett, to undertake a major re-assessment of the prehistory of the region. This was partly instigated by the recent arrival of the Pitt Rivers' Cranborne Chase collection at Salisbury Museum where it was now available for study. It was suggested we work together on this re-appraisal which would include new, targeted excavations such as my own, a re-assessment of Pitt Rivers' work, including re-excavating the South Lodge enclosure and cemetery, incorporation of my fieldwork results, and a detailed examination of the Dorset Cursus and its environs.

This collaboration led to eight years of work in the field, with a further six for analysis and synthesis before eventual publication in 1991 (Barrett *et al* 1991a; 1991b). My principal contribution to the fieldwork consisted of completing my examination of what was, by then, clearly a middle Bronze Age settlement and its attendant cemetery, an early Bronze Age pond barrow only 40m outside the Cursus which respected its axis, and a pit-circle henge uncovered on Wyke Down. Although henge monuments were known just to the south at Knowlton, this was the first such monument to be recorded in the Cursus environs; I have subsequently recorded a further fifteen (Green 2009). After completion of their work at South Lodge, Richard and John turned their attention to the Cursus itself which, despite its enormous size and being the longest Neolithic monument in Britain, had never previously been excavated. Their excavations on Down Farm revealed its date, 3300 BC, and an area of intensive Neolithic activity within it at Chalk Pit field (Barrett *et al* 1991a).

Following the publications I re-started my fieldwork, in 1991, by examining a group of ring-ditches close to the south-western end of the Cursus at Ogden Down (Green 2000). During earlier fieldwork I had recorded these and a circular patch as soil marks. The latter I thought might be a pond barrow. Excavation soon proved the soil patch to be a natural feature but an unexpected avenue of postholes set 3.25m apart was found to be cut through the patch. This eventually led to the uncovering of an avenue 65m long which led to one of the ring-ditches. At this northern end it was integrated into a double post-circle which completely surrounded what originally would have been a barrow. The southern end terminated at another ring-ditch. This unique complex, which was laid out perpendicular to the nearby Cursus, produced radiocarbon dates which spanned the 12th–9th centuries BC making the ceremonial timber circles the latest dated in the UK mainland (Gibson 1998).

After this discovery I was once again drawn back to Down Farm where a remarkable cropmark had appeared. The cropmark had revealed the site of a deep natural shaft, which I eventually ceased digging at a depth of 13.2m (French *et al* 2007). The shaft contained a series of predominantly eroded rubble layers with silt-rich horizons filling the weathering cone (Green and Allen 1997). Within the weathering cone was a sequence of layers containing artefacts and ecofacts spanning the late Mesolithic to Beaker periods. Eventually seventeen radiocarbon determinations produced a sequence from the late 5th millennium to the late 3rd millennium BC, spanning both the Mesolithic–Neolithic and Neolithic–Bronze Age transitions. During the course of this excavation I was visited by Mike Allen, well known for his work in environmental archaeology. Mike visited me following a call from Richard Bradley suggesting he might be interested in taking samples from the section I was revealing at Down Farm. Little did Mike know that, over ten years later, he would have processed over a ton of soil from my excavations and personally identified over 150,000 microscopic snail shells! This painstaking work has contributed greatly to a high-resolution survey of environmental change in this region during a crucial time in our prehistory.

A new discovery then took me back to Wyke Down. An aerial photograph I had taken of the first henge following restoration seemed to show a possible second example nearby. Work in 1996 confirmed this hypothesis and uncovered a smaller monument of similar pit-circle construction. However, the most exciting discovery lay just outside the earthwork where part of a contemporaneous Grooved Ware settlement was revealed. Here were found groups of pits, fence lines, and two circular buildings (French *et al* 2007).

Fig 3.13 The two Richards (Bradley and Atkinson) at the Wyke Down 1 henge in 1984 (© M Green)

The postholes of the buildings contained significant finds including fragments of a fine chalk-based plaster with traces of decoration which had once adorned the walls. Radiocarbon dates centred around 2800 BC. The excavation was visited by Charly French, a specialist in ancient soils from Cambridge University, who had been talking to Mike Allen about the idea of a new project targeting sites and locations in the area that were likely to produce high-grade information on prehistoric landscape development and environmental change. With significant samples already awaiting analysis, such as those from the Down Farm shaft, he felt a new phase of work would produce dividends in the understanding of the development of chalk landscapes.

Over the next ten years excavations took place on two long barrows, four round barrows, two enclosures, three settlement areas, a dyke system, and new trenches cut across the Cursus and Ackling Dyke. In addition a major auger survey was undertaken across the Allen valley, with a number of dry valleys

Fig 3.14 Martin Green examining barrow 36 at Wyke Down in 2000 (© Salisbury Newspapers)

sectioned and open-area excavations carried out on a pond barrow and hengiform enclosure. This latter monument was composed of a most remarkable combination of features. First a ring of fourteen unevenly spaced pits 35m in diameter, broken by entrance gaps to the east and west, defined the perimeter. At the centre was a pit 10m wide by 1.5m deep. Cut through this pit were two features – a shaft 7m deep and a grave containing three children and an adult female. Isotopic analysis sponsored by the BBC during the making of a *Meet the Ancestors* television programme revealed the life movements of these individuals (Budd *et al* 2000; Montgomery *et al* 2000). Radiocarbon dating revealed that this monument was constructed at the same time as the Dorset Cursus around 3300 BC. With the full publication of this latest work by the dedicated team involved (French *et al* 2007), our goals have been realised in producing an unprecedented high-resolution survey of prehistoric landscape development and environmental change in this extraordinary region.

And now, in the next phase of investigation, I look forward to untangling more of the complex relationships which the land at Down Farm and its surroundings conceals.

An embarrassment of riches?
The Iron Age in Wessex

Andrew Fitzpatrick

An ABC of the Iron Age

In 1958 the Council for British Archaeology organised a conference at the Institute of Archaeology, University of London, on the 'Problems of the Iron Age in southern Britain'. It was a landmark conference for many reasons, not least in marking the beginning of the end of what was then the dominant interpretation of the British Iron Age: Christopher Hawkes' 'ABC' of the Iron Age (Hawkes 1931). The following 50 years have witnessed great changes in how archaeological work is undertaken and how the results of it are communicated. Throughout this time Wessex has held a pre-eminent place in the study of the Iron Age in Britain, and beyond.

Much of the evidence on which Hawkes' ABC was founded came from Wessex, reflecting on the one hand the presence of relatively abundant and well-preserved remains of this date in the region, and on the other hand what was already a long and distinguished tradition of research.

This tradition stretched back to the 19th century with excavations on Cranborne Chase by Pitt Rivers (1887–98). In Wiltshire, work by the Cunningtons who examined hillforts and settlements such as Lidbury Camp (Cunnington and Cunnington 1917), Casterley Camp (Cunnington and Cunnington 1913), and All Cannings Cross (Cunnington 1923), helped rapidly to establish Wessex as a key area for the study of the Iron Age (Collis 1994; Champion 2001).

These pioneering works were followed by Hawkes' own precocious work with fellow schoolboys J N L Myers and C E Stevens at St Catherine's Hill (Hawkes *et al* 1930) and by the swagger of Sir Mortimer Wheeler's campaigns at Maiden Castle and in Normandy, which brought both panache and the apparent clarity of a historical narrative (Wheeler 1943; Wheeler and Richardson 1957). This early importance was enhanced by Gerhard Bersu's application of open-area excavation at Little Woodbury, which revealed for the first time the post-built roundhouses and storage pits that are typical of many Iron Age settlements (Bersu 1940; Brailsford 1948; 1949; Evans 1989). Further work (for example, Chadwick Hawkes 1994) only served to underline this apparent pre-eminence.

As a result, by 1958 Iron Age Wessex could be said to be one of the best-studied regions not just of Britain but also of Europe. In 2008 the same claim might still be made, the intervening years having witnessed important excavations, field surveys, and discoveries and also sustained research, synthesis, and interpretation.

From cultures to models

In 1958 Hawkes' ABC had held sway for almost 30 years. In it, change was thought to have been caused by three main migratory invasions. In order to distinguish the British evidence from the continental European, Hawkes called these invasions A, B and C but their intellectual debt to the principal schemes for ordering and interpreting continental European material was evident.

In the ABC, the Iron Age was thought to have been introduced in the 6th century BC by Hallstatt invaders from continental Europe (Fig 3.15). These Iron Age 'A' people introduced iron, hillforts, and new styles of pottery. Three centuries later Iron Age 'B' invaders from the Marne in north-eastern France were seen as responsible for the introduction of La Tène-style material culture. They were followed in the 1st century BC by Iron Age 'C' invaders – the Belgae, also from north-eastern France – who were thought to have introduced the changes that typify the late Iron Age or Late La Tène period.

Although the basis of change in Hawkes' scheme was chronological and its cause successive invasions, the way it was applied was essentially cultural. Thus pottery might be attributed to an Iron Age 'B' culture but it might be of Iron Age 'C' date. As more excavations were undertaken across Britain, regional variation became more evident. By 1958, the need for a more flexible classificatory and interpretive system was clear.

Hawkes' response, which was published (1959) ahead of the main conference proceedings (Frere (ed) 1960), was to redefine his chronologically based ABC on a

Fig 3.15 Christopher Hawkes' 1931 'ABC of the British Iron Age': a cultural model based on waves of invasion (Source: Hawkes 1931)

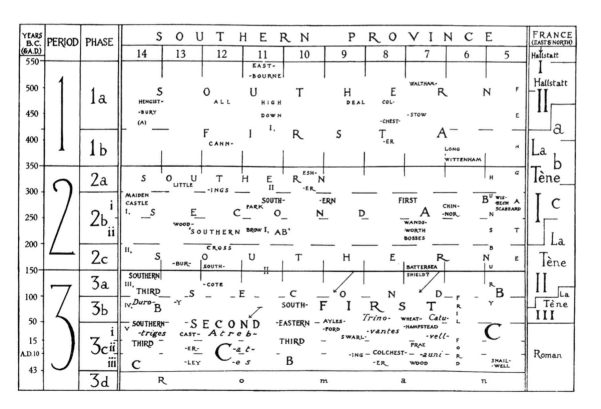

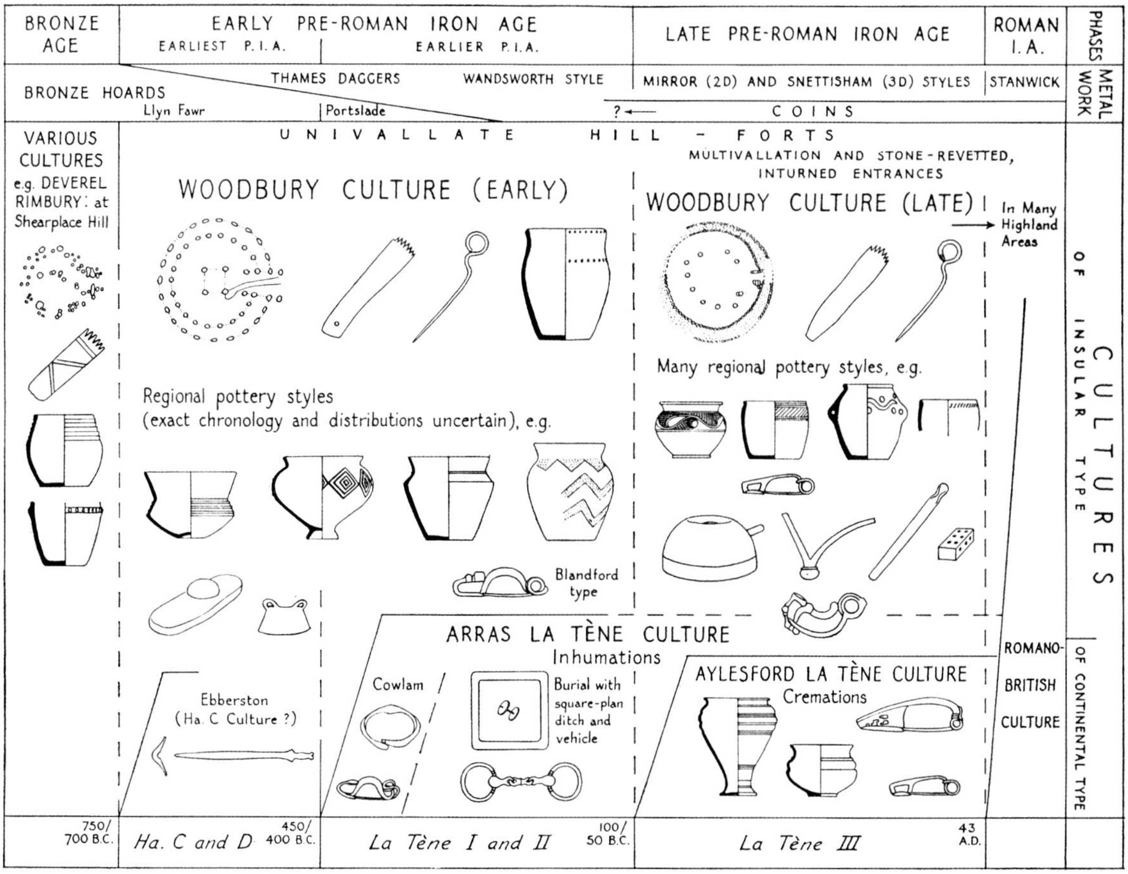
BRONZE AGE
EARLY PRE-ROMAN IRON AGE
EARLIEST P.I.A.
EARLIER P.I.A.
LATE PRE-ROMAN IRON AGE
ROMAN I.A.
PHASES
BRONZE HOARDS
THAMES DAGGERS
WANDSWORTH STYLE
MIRROR (2D) AND SNETTISHAM (3D) STYLES
STANWICK
Llyn Fawr
Portslade
COINS
METAL WORK
VARIOUS CULTURES e.g. DEVEREL RIMBURY: at Shearplace Hill
UNIVALLATE HILL-FORTS
MULTIVALLATION AND STONE-REVETTED, INTURNED ENTRANCES
WOODBURY CULTURE (EARLY)
WOODBURY CULTURE (LATE)
In Many Highland Areas
Many regional pottery styles, e.g.
Regional pottery styles (exact chronology and distributions uncertain), e.g.
Blandford type
CULTURES OF INSULAR TYPE
ARRAS LA TÈNE CULTURE
Inhumations
Cowlam
Burial with square-plan ditch and vehicle
Ebberston (Ha. C Culture ?)
AYLESFORD LA TÈNE CULTURE
Cremations
ROMANO-BRITISH CULTURE
OF CONTINENTAL TYPE
750/ 700 B.C.
Ha. C and D
450/ 400 B.C.
La Tène I and II
100/ 50 B.C.
La Tène III
43 A.D.

Fig 3.16 Roy Hodson's 1964 model of the British Iron Age in which the emphasis is shifted to insular cultural development (Source: Hodson 1964)

geographical basis. Britain was divided into provinces, which were then subdivided into numbered regions – for example, the 'Southern Province' contained ten regions. The A, B, and C were renamed as periods 1, 2, and 3, which could then be subdivided into phases – for example, Phase 2c. Despite the apparent complexity and rigidity of this alphanumeric scheme of cultural history, it was subsequently adopted and adapted for Scotland by Stuart Piggott (1966) and for the 'Irish Sea Province' by Leslie Alcock (1972).

The first challenge to this approach was made in 1960 by Roy Hodson, who questioned the quality of much of the data on which it was based (Hodson 1960), and he explored this and other issues in two subsequent key papers (Hodson 1962; 1964). The 1964 article proposed an alternative way of classifying the evidence, essentially using Gordon Childe's definition of an archaeological culture (Fig 3.16). The idea of invasions was not rejected – there were still invaders of Hallstatt, Early, and Late La Tène date – but instead the emphasis was on 'cultures of insular type', what Hodson termed the 'Little Woodbury Culture'. This emphasised the distinctively British, such as the enduring tradition of roundhouses, the number of hillforts and the complexity of their defences, and the apparent absence of burials, the latter being regarded as 'a negative-type

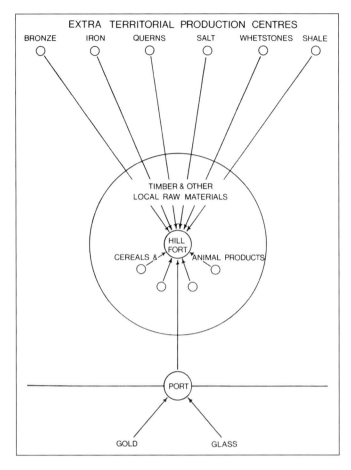

EXTRA TERRITORIAL PRODUCTION CENTRES

BRONZE   IRON   QUERNS   SALT   WHETSTONES   SHALE

TIMBER & OTHER
LOCAL RAW MATERIALS

HILL
FORT

CEREALS &   ANIMAL PRODUCTS

PORT

GOLD   GLASS

Fig 3.17 Barry Cunliffe's 1974 model of the southern British Iron Age based on economic resources and trade (Source: Cunliffe 1974)

fossil'.

By the mid-1960s the invasion hypothesis in British prehistory was coming under increasing criticism (Clark 1966) and the quantity of evidence for the Iron Age across Britain was such that it was possible for doctoral students to begin to compile well-based studies of the Iron Age both regionally (Harding 1972; 1974) and nationally (Cunliffe 1974, revised edn 2005). In these works it was now possible to see Wessex as a distinctive region, albeit one with a particularly rich record for the Iron Age, rather than an archetype for the British Iron Age (Collis (ed) 1977a).

A willingness to explore new ideas using this rich data as well as an increase in the number of archaeologists studying it could be seen in the proceedings of a conference to honour Mortimer Wheeler that was held in Southampton in 1971 (Jesson and Hill (eds) 1971). Like the meeting in London in 1958, its scope was national, but the range of interpretive frameworks was much wider. There was an emphasis on ideas derived from social and economic geography. The classificatory diagrams of Hawkes and of Hodson were replaced by flow diagrams from the 'New Geography', which set out models of trade (Fig 3.17). Thiesson polygons around hillforts were used to model their possible territories. The distribution of pottery, the origins of which could be determined by petrological analysis, was now seen not to be cultural in the Childean sense but 'socio-economic' (Collis 1977b; 1994, 129). This increased emphasis on process was called by some a 'processual' or 'new archaeology'.

From rampart to roundhouse

This change in the interpretive framework was reflected in, and partly driven by, changes in excavation strategy. For many years excavations of the numerous well-preserved hillforts in Wessex had concentrated on examining their ramparts. As the defences of many of these forts, especially those with multiple ramparts, were regularly remodelled, this strategy allowed small-scale excavations to provide valuable chronological sequences. But it was often at the expense of the examination of the interior.

The turning point was arguably the start, in 1969, of Sir Barry Cunliffe's

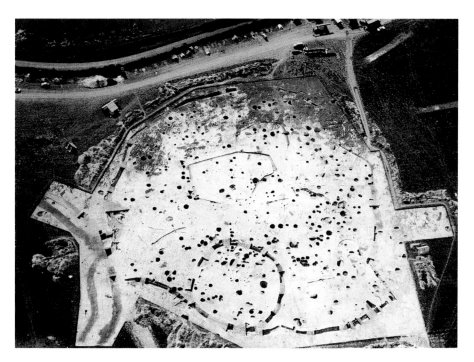

Fig 3.18 The excavations at Gussage All Saints, Dorset, in 1970 (Aerofilms collection © English Heritage)

magisterial 25-year programme of excavations at Danebury hillfort and its environs. In the cultural-historical tradition, the excavations started by examining the defences of the fort but they soon moved to the systematic excavation of large areas of the interior (Cunliffe 1984; 1993; 1995; Cunliffe and Poole 1991; see also Cunliffe this volume, pp 80–81). The value of using mechanical excavators on rural settlements had already been demonstrated in the mid-1960s, allowing much larger areas to be planned and excavated (for example, Collis 1968; 1970) and with this came changes to the subject of study.

The contrast in scale was in itself striking. All the interior of the hillfort at Winklebury and much of that at Balksbury was excavated (Smith 1977; Wainwright 1969; Wainwright and Davies 1995). Large areas of the farms at Owslebury, Tollard Royal (Wainwright 1968), and slightly later at Gussage All Saints (Wainwright 1979b) were also examined. While Owslebury was a research excavation, the work at Winklebury and Balksbury was in advance of new housing and road improvements and undertaken by a governmental Central Excavation Unit. At Gussage All Saints, the aim was to excavate completely an Iron Age farm similar to Little Woodbury using contemporary techniques (Fig 3.18; Wainwright 1979b, viii–xi; Wainwright and Spratling 1973).

As the scale of excavation increased, so did the scope of study. Settlements sited on the chalk, such as Winnall Down, yielded large and well-preserved assemblages of animal bone (Maltby 1985). Almost a quarter of a million fragments of animal bone were excavated at Danebury (Grant 1984; 1991). The use of flotation for the recovery of charred plant remains was introduced in an early form at Owslebury in the late 1960s, although it was not regularly applied until a decade later (Monk and Fasham 1980). However, it was the sheer quantity

Fig 3.19 At Danebury in Hampshire Barry Cunliffe's 25-year campaign of excavation transformed our understanding of hillfort interiors (© Institute of Archaeology, Oxford University)

of evidence from Danebury that enabled its systematic study. This rapidly moved beyond the identification of individual crop species and their relative abundance to include weeds of cultivation and the identification of different stages of crop processing. This allowed the reconstruction of habitats and farming techniques (Jones 1995; 2007). The evidence from Danebury and other Wessex sites provided some of the key data sets for a series of important Iron Age studies, whether of human remains (Whimster 1981; Wilson 1981; Wait 1985), animal bones (Hambleton 1999), metalworking (Ehrenreich 1985; Salter and Ehrenreich 1984; Foster 1980), or pottery (Morris 1994; 1996; Cunliffe 2005).

While the scale and scope of excavation changed rapidly, the quality of analytical survey remained constant. A tradition of landscape archaeology can be traced back to J P Williams Freeman and Heywood Sumner. Field survey was an integral part of Hawkes' work at Quarley Hill and the work of the Royal Commission on the Ancient and Historical Monuments bequeathed to Dorset a formidable Inventory (RCHM(E) 1952–75), and there was also work on the well-preserved landscapes of Salisbury Plain (McOmish et al 2002). Surveys of individual sites, such as Maiden Castle (see Sharples 1991), or types of site (Corney 1989), have also been undertaken. More recently these have been integrated with geophysical surveys, notably in work on hillforts (Payne et al 2006). The value of air photography on downland landscapes was demonstrated by Crawford and Keiller (1928) and surveys of cropmark evidence were used to help place Danebury in its setting (Palmer 1984). The work of the Danebury Environs Project (Cunliffe 2000) was similarly landscape based, and even if the main technique it used to examine the relationships between the hillfort, other hillforts such as Bury Hill, and a series of smaller farms, was excavation, it forms part of a long tradition.

From research to mitigation

The fundamental importance of the Danebury and the Danebury Environs projects, as well as related ones undertaken by Barry Cunliffe such as Hengistbury Head (Cunliffe 1987), can almost overshadow how rare they are. Indeed, research projects that involved excavation were becoming rare in the 1990s, and in recent years those on any scale have become scarcer still. The complete excavation at Gussage All Saints was ostensibly undertaken to examine a 'Little Woodbury type' before it was completely destroyed by ploughing, while work at Maiden Castle between 1985 and 1987 was in part undertaken as a showpiece for the World Archaeological Congress

continued on p 82

Danebury

Barry Cunliffe

The Iron Age hillfort of Danebury is one of the more impressive of the hillforts dominating the chalk downland of Hampshire, but in the 1930s, when Christopher Hawkes was exploring the Iron Age sites of the region, it was on private land and inaccessible for excavation. Tantalisingly, Danebury had to remain mysterious in its shroud of trees, its very size and complexity suggesting that it held the key to our understanding of Iron Age society in central southern Britain.

It was the forward-looking policies of Hampshire County Council in the late 1960s that finally presented the opportunity to explore the potential of Danebury. The site was acquired and opened to the public as part of their policy to make interesting areas of the countryside accessible, but this brought with it the responsibility to manage the woodland, which then engulfed the earthworks, and to provide a narrative that introduced the concept of life in the Iron Age to the visitor. It was an opportune moment, for at the time I was actively planning to excavate a hillfort within easy reach of Southampton (where I was teaching at the time), partly to serve as a training dig and partly to re-invigorate Iron Age studies, which had been rather in the doldrums for the preceding 30 years.

In the first two years (1969 and 1970) of our 20-year campaign work was concentrated on the defences and the main gate to provide an outline 'story' – one that could easily be communicated to the public – while at the same time providing a chronological framework for more detailed research. It was during this period that the county's conservation officers realised that the beech trees, which had been planted over the hillfort in the late 19th century, were rapidly dying of beech bark necrosis. The management plan was that cleared areas would be totally excavated prior to replanting. This enabled us to move into the second stage of excavation

Fig 3.20 Danebury from the air (Institute of Archaeology, Oxford University)

Fig 3.21 Barry Cunliffe unravelling the Danebury story on site (Institute of Archaeology, Oxford University)

Fig 3.22 A decorative bronze disk. Diameter: *c* 59mm (Institute of Archaeology, Oxford University)

in 1971, the systematic area excavation of the hillfort interior – something which had not been attempted before in Britain. By the end of the programme, in 1988, we had excavated more than 50 per cent of the interior and had agreed a management plan which saw the remaining unexcavated sectors preserved as an archaeological reserve. The Danebury programme, then, was an academically driven research programme led by Oxford University (to which I had moved in 1972), partially funded by English Heritage (and its predecessors) as a rescue programme, and sponsored by Hampshire County Council through the Danebury Trust. It was a co-operative venture gaining stability from its tripartite structure.

It was apparent, from the first trial trench of 1969, dug inside the ramparts, that the interior of the fort had been densely occupied, in contrast to other forts in the region like Figsbury, Balksbury and Quarley where occupation was sparse and spasmodic. To excavate totally a large percentage of the interior of such a fort was a novel undertaking. It meant dealing with huge quantities of data at a time when computers were first finding their way into archaeology. But this was the great attraction of the project. Previously most Iron Age excavations had been on a very small scale and in consequence interpretations were limited and almost anecdotal. With a very large data set we could begin to make statistically valid statements. To take two examples: it became apparent, even in the first year, that there were recurring patterns in the selection and deposition of animal bones in disused storage pits. These 'special burials', as we called them, were evidently part of a complex behaviour pattern that reflected belief systems. With some 5000 pits eventually excavated we could begin to say some meaningful things about ritual in everyday life. The other example was the dating programme, which involved taking some 50 radiocarbon samples from carefully selected contexts and analysing them statistically (the first application of Bayesian statistics to archaeology in Britain). The results, combined with a detailed study of pottery typology, allowed us to produce a chronology based on 'ceramic phases' that has proved to be a useful tool for understanding the Iron Age in the wider region.

Perhaps the greatest contribution of the Danebury excavation has been in allowing us to examine in detail almost every aspect of Iron Age society, from patterns of animal husbandry to attitudes to death and the body. Acquiring, analysing and presenting such a large dataset has involved a sustained effort from a great many people over a considerable period of time – but it has, we believe, been worth it. The Iron Age in central Wessex has emerged as an intensely fascinating period – an alien world in which the lives and aspirations of the people, pervaded by beliefs and rituals, we are now beginning to glimpse through the mists of distance. If nothing else, Danebury has given us much to stimulate our curiosity.

held in Southampton in 1986 (Wainwright and Cunliffe 1985).

Soon after the excavation of Gussage All Saints, work began to be passed from a central excavation team to regional ones. The excavations in advance of the new M3 motorway in the late 1970s were undertaken by the M3 Excavation Committee, whose work encompassed sites of many dates but, as it transpired, many of the most important ones were Iron Age – Winnall Down (Fasham 1985), Micheldever Wood (Fasham 1987b), and Easton Lane (Fasham *et al* 1989; Fasham and Whinney 1991).

The effect of *Planning Policy Guidance 16: Archaeology and Planning*, which was implemented in 1990, has been well rehearsed elsewhere, as has the development of what has been characterised as 'two cultures', one of professional practice, the other of academe (Bradley 2006). It should be noted, however, that the shift from research-led to mitigation-driven excavation was well under way before 1990 and the subsequent increase in the number of archaeological organisations and the scale of their work was, in some ways, a continuation of this trend.

As those changes in funding, scope and scale were taking place, discussion as to how the Iron Age might be interpreted continued to move on apace (Collis 2001a). The scale of the work at Danebury and sites such as Winnall Down made it clear that 'unusual' deposits of finds were far from occasional. Instead there was clear and recurrent patterning in the ways that, for example, parts of humans and animals were deliberately placed within settlements. The huge increase in data opened a series of new debates (for example, Hill 1989; 1993; 1995a; 1996; Cunliffe 1992; Fitzpatrick 1998). Alongside this, there was also a reaction against the interpretation of hillforts as central places and the use of models of Celtic society that drew on later historical evidence from Ireland (for example, Stopford 1987; Hill 1989). A renewed interest in social anthropology as an interpretive framework saw a much wider range of topics being considered. In what is sometimes called a post-processual archaeology, the topics now addressed in the study of Iron Age Wessex included the significance of enclosure (Bowden and McOmish 1987; 1989), the extent to which what had previously been considered to be everyday rubbish was instead imbued with a ritual significance (for example, Hill 1995b; Parker Pearson 1996), and whether architecture embodied cosmological referents (Parker Pearson and Richards 1994; Oswald 1997) or concepts of time (Fitzpatrick 1994; 1997).

Two conferences held in 1994 provide useful snapshots of those debates. In that year the annual meeting of the French Iron Age Studies group was held in Winchester, the first time it had been held wholly outside France. By tradition the publications associated with the meeting comprise an exhibition catalogue or guide to the region in which the meeting is held. The pre-conference publication, *The Iron Age in Wessex: Recent Work*, provided a wide-ranging review of recent excavations and current thinking (Fitzpatrick and Morris (eds) 1994), while the conference proceedings set work on settlements in Wessex in its British and continental European contexts (Collis (ed) 2001b). The 1994 meeting of the Iron Age Studies Group was held in Durham and it was decided that it would be useful to make the discussions available to a wider audience (Haselgrove and

Fig 3.23 A
reconstructed
roundhouse at the
experimental Iron
Age farm at Butser
Hill, based on an
example excavated at
Pimperne in Dorset
by Dennis Harding
and Ian Blake in the
early 1960s (©Wessex
Archaeology)

Fig 3.23 A reconstructed roundhouse at the experimental Iron Age farm at Butser Hill, based on an example excavated at Pimperne in Dorset by Dennis Harding and Ian Blake in the early 1960s (©Wessex Archaeology)

Gwilt (eds) 1997). While the scope of the volume is British, the importance of new evidence from Wessex and the use of older discoveries from it as testing grounds for new interpretations are evident. Such has been the importance of Wessex in the study of the British Iron Age that scholars of other parts of England have felt the need to achieve an 'interpretive devolution' from it (Bevan (ed) 1999).

The study of archaeology is both material and visual. While the Iron Age of Wessex has played a pivotal role in scholarly discussions, it has also provided the dominant popular images of the Iron Age in Britain. Some of these images come from the mighty hillforts of Wessex, such as Maiden Castle, but perhaps the single most influential one came from the work of the experimental farm at Butser (Reynolds 1979) and the reconstructed large roundhouse (Fig 3.23) , which was based on the plan of the house excavated at Pimperne, Dorset (Harding *et al* 1993). This has spawned a series of reconstructed roundhouses across England

and Wales (for example, Townend 2007) but perhaps more importantly, it also provided the basis of a popular and influential television series in which people lived in what was thought to approximate to Iron Age conditions (Percival 1980). As this popular image was often set in the context of a 'Celtic Iron Age', it reinforced an interpretation that scholarly debate was beginning to question, a mismatch with which subsequent discussion and interpretation has wrestled (for example, Hill 1993; James 1999; Collis 2003; Morse 2005).

Retrospect and prospect

Meantime, the Iron Age of Wessex has continued to see important work undertaken and published. This includes the evidence for the earliest ironworking in England from the late Bronze Age site of Hartshill Copse (Collard *et al*

Fig 3.24 A unique hoard of iron cauldrons excavated at Chiseldon, Wiltshire, in 2005 (© Wessex Archaeology)

2006) and the identification of a regional group of large 'middens' of late Bronze Age/early Iron Age date (McOmish 1996; Lawson 2000). A great deal of this work continues to be on settlements but even here knowledge across Wessex is quite variable. Much remains to be learnt of the Isle of Wight and the Channel Islands; even though they have yielded important Iron Age finds, these are mainly of burials or hoards (Jones and Stead 1969; Allen 1971; Burns *et al* 1988; Cunliffe and de Jersey 1997), and less is known about settlements. However, the same could also be said of west Dorset or the New Forest (cf Haselgrove *et al* 2001, 24; Papworth 2008).

Despite this, in comparison to some regions of Britain, the study of the Iron Age in Wessex might seem enviably advanced and it still provides a benchmark (cf Harding 2005). However, it also faces problems that are shared with other areas. The discipline has yet to appreciate fully that the types of research undertaken in academic-based pure research and practice-based research – Richard Bradley's 'two cultures' – while employing similar techniques create different types of knowledge that can be used in different ways. The types of pure research being undertaken in universities are also changing and the trend for the immediate future is likely to be more detailed re-examination of existing data sets (for example, Davis *et al* (eds) 2008). At the same time, the traditional mechanisms for communicating archaeological research have not expanded to cope with the greatly increased volume of work nor have they diversified to embrace fully the opportunities that the internet offers. The difficulties of knowledge transfer are now major issues but ones that are capable of being addressed quite rapidly. On a practical level, the application of scientific techniques such as radiocarbon dating or stable isotope studies (for example, Jay and Richards 2007) have yet to become mainstream in the study of Iron Age Wessex – a common problem that is again not specific to either Wessex or the Iron Age.

Despite the long history of research into the Iron Age of Wessex, new types of site continue to be recognised. These include the late Iron Age inhumation burial cemetery at Adanac Farm near Southampton, found on the site of the new Ordnance Survey offices in 2008, and unique hoards, whether comprised of miniature objects as in the Salisbury Hoard (Stead 1998) or of cauldrons as at Chiseldon, Wiltshire, excavated in 2005 (Fig 3.24). These discoveries continue to provide new materials to challenge what is all too readily assumed to be a well-understood Iron Age of Wessex. So, too, does renewed research into older finds (for example, Madgwick 2008).

All of this will ensure that for the foreseeable future Wessex will remain one of the best-studied regions of the Iron Age in Europe. In 2008, as in 1958, students of the Iron Age of Wessex were in a privileged position. That this should be so is because of the work in diverse fields by many archaeologists, some of whom have been – and are – among the most outstanding of their generation. The richness and complexity of the archaeological record of Iron Age Wessex may at times seem to be problematic but it is also an embarrassment of riches.

Going round in circles

Mike Pitts

I grew up on a farm near Chichester, and as a child was fascinated by old buildings. I loved places like Romsey Abbey or Corfe Castle – destinations on driving holidays while my father was busy with the harvest. We stayed in a cottage in the New Forest, and it was from here – on 30 July 1966 – that I first saw Stonehenge (and Woodhenge). My diary, however, suggests the main event for me then was a military tattoo at Larkhill, 'which was smashing ... found a postcard of an Abbot Self-Propelled Gun' (I was keen on Airfix models). I remember hearing announcements, over the soldiers and circling tanks, as England scored against Germany in the World Cup.

It must have been clear to my parents that I was unlikely to become a farmer, but what was I to do? What work would allow me to pursue interests in what my mother called 'castles' and my father 'rocks'? The answer, by providing me with a subject to study at university, came from Christopher Potter at Ardingly College in East Sussex. Chris became a distinguished headmaster at Old Swinford Hospital in the West Midlands, but in 1970 he was head of classics at Ardingly, where he also taught A Level archaeology (his brother, Tim, who died of flu aged only 55, was an inspiring Roman archaeologist).

Chris rearranged his timetable to make it possible for me to do archaeology after a late start. For my second-year project I chose henges (my father's secretary typed it up, turning Grooved Ware into Grooved Wart). Chris drove us to Avebury – we were a very small class, but it was still a crush in his Sunbeam Alpine – and I went on my first excavation, courtesy of the CBA's Calendar, under Geoff Wainwright's direction at Mount Pleasant. And sitting up in bed, I read the school library copy of Richard Atkinson's *Stonehenge* (Atkinson 1956). I was hooked.

Some years later, as the funding for my second degree at the London Institute of Archaeology (now UCL) ran out, I successfully applied to be curator of the Alexander Keiller Museum in Avebury. This was, I suspect for all concerned, a curious post, the only one of its kind in the Department of the Environment (DoE). Ultimately it existed as a result of Keiller opening a private museum to house finds (mostly from Windmill Hill) from his excavations at guardianship monuments in the 1920s and 1930s. My only written job description was a sentence in the advert, referring to the museum, guide lectures, and correspondence on archaeological matters. What was wanted, however, was a catalogue of the collections.

There was a Civil Service strike on my first day, 1 April 1979, so the London offices on Savile Row, where everyone else in the section worked, were picketed and in Wiltshire the museum was closed. The following day I had my first sight of the museum behind the scenes. I'd known that my predecessor, Faith Vatcher, had been ill. During my doctoral research, I had written to her hoping to study the museum's flint axes. I received a postcard telling me that she had to go to

Fig 3.25 In 1979 senior Ancient Monuments department staff were alerted to a Post Office cable being laid past the Heelstone, when they had gone to Stonehenge to receive Prince Charles as a guest. I was phoned and asked to find out what was happening. I had been at the museum for seven weeks, and mounted an emergency excavation with important results. Among the many student volunteers who came up from Southampton, almost all of whom are now archaeologists, was Mike Parker Pearson, there for half a day. Crouching on the grass are Richard Atkinson (left) and Mike Pitts; standing are Andrew Saunders and Collin Bowen; in the trench are Hilary Howard and Sue Davies (© A ApSimon)

hospital 'for this week at least', and I never made it to Avebury. Now I entered an office that looked as if Faith had just left for a walk.

But she had died the year before, and if she had been alive she could not have walked. As I learnt from a still distressed head custodian, Peter Tate, an eccentric, extrovert and very kind man who did much to help me understand the small but complex world into which I had arrived (Tate 2005), Faith was still in post when she succumbed to her cancer. Her (my) office was on the first floor (sometimes I could hear Peter singing loudly below). Towards the end she had been unable to climb the stairs, and had hauled herself up the uncarpeted wooden treads with her arms. The thick spread of paperwork over every surface of the office suggested her last work had been conducted on the floor.

All of this was unexpected, and had a profound effect on how I approached the job. As I excavated the museum's recent history I became convinced that I had a duty – to Avebury, to archaeology, to Faith Vatcher – to save, archive and record what I could of what was there. This did not endear me to those who simply wanted a catalogue, and inexperienced in the ways of organisations, I just got on with what I thought I should do.

I learned from people who knew Avebury much better than me, including people who worked with Keiller, like Stuart Piggott (who remembered a mysterious red-headed girl who lurked around the excavations, and was rumoured to have mothered a child to Keiller); Keiller's personal assistant Sorrel Taylour (then aged 80 and with a charming smile that warned me not to even think about Keiller's personal life); and Denis Grant King (who told me mostly about DGK).

The DoE owned a number of small buildings in the village, and one day a charge hand brought me a fat correspondence file he'd found in the roof of a store used for excavation equipment for the region. It contained carbon copies of typed letters between Keiller and Wallace Heaton, his photographic supplier – of considerable interest to historians of photography. It seemed odd that such a file should not have been in the museum (where it is now), and that it was so extensive compared to other files that were. The likely explanation came in a conversation I had with Isobel Smith, in her cottage at the corner of the churchyard.

Isobel had been tasked by Keiller's widow with the publication of his excavations, which she achieved with style and insight (Smith 1965; Pitts 2006). There was more to this than analysing his work, however. She and the then museum curator, William Young, had been handed all Keiller's archaeological effects, from furniture and tools to photographs and artefacts, and asked to sort and discard as they thought appropriate. Isobel and Young were private, principled people and were shocked by much of what they read in the correspondence (Keiller was an obsessive writer, frequently addressing the same recipient repeatedly in one day and filing several copies of each missive in different places). They determined that Gabrielle Keiller (who might actually have been little bothered) should be spared this revealing correspondence, and sorted it into two: letters of purely archaeological content (which were kept) and those of personal interest. The latter were sufficient to start their fires for a whole winter. The Wallace Heaton letters, it seemed, were the ones that got away.

Fig 3.26 A tidied and redecorated curator's office in 1983, with plan presses on the left made for Alexander Keiller. Behind the brown door was a water tank, and like every available space when I arrived, the cupboard had served as an archaeological store. Among its contents were rusting cans of non-safety cine film shot by Keiller in the 1920s (© Mike Pitts)

I found other things in these buildings, not least the residue of Faith's career excavating threatened sites for the Ministry of Works in the 1960s. As was the custom, she and her husband, Lance, were paid to dig but not to analyse. The inevitable result now confronted me, in the museum (stuffed into the clock tower, sprawling across shelves in the store and piled under tables in the office) and in the roof space of a small barn: here were tray upon tray of excavation finds, unwashed and unmarked (and, in the barn, decorated by birds, bats and rain).

Eventually, the bulk of this material was taken over by what became Wessex Archaeology. Then, however, it was clear that without the help of Lance Vatcher (busy at the restoration of Avebury's 'Great Barn') most of it, along with the few photos and drawings that periodically came to light (some, with more finds, at Lance's house), would remain unidentifiable. I did my best to track down the sites they had dug, some of great significance, and match finds and records to enable future study.

When I left the museum after exactly five years, I was still seeking archival storage for film and paper records, cleaning and reboxing artefacts and filing record cards. I had excavated at Avebury (Evans *et al* 1982), initiated its first radiocarbon dating programme (which Alasdair Whittle gallantly salvaged after I'd left the museum, Pitts and Whittle 1992), and dug twice at Stonehenge (Pitts 1982). As I crossed the yard to embark on a freelance career in archaeology and journalism, and to help with a new restaurant, I had little doubt that the archaeology of Avebury and Stonehenge would continue to engage me. The discovery of the skeleton of Avebury's medieval barber-surgeon that Keiller, and everyone since, had thought destroyed in the London Blitz, but which had actually survived and is now in the Natural History Museum (Pitts 2001), was but one incident in that unpredictable future.

Panel Discussion: Where next in prehistory?

Chair: Barry Cunliffe
Panel: Timothy Darvill
        Peter Fowler
        Mike Parker Pearson
        Mike Pitts

The words below are not exactly those that were spoken at the conference but are intended instead to capture the overall flavour of the discussion.

Should we still be digging at Stonehenge, or should our priority be preservation?

Fowler: I would like to divert the £4m that is being squandered each year on the Portable Antiquities Scheme to proper excavation at Stonehenge. However, we should begin by re-excavating old sites, and in particular barrows, before turning our attention to virgin deposits. In this way we can use new methods and techniques to provide a better context for old finds.

Pitts: The two small sample excavations that took place in 2008 showed that what we really need are further large-scale investigations. Too many of the old excavation reports, like those of Hawley and Atkinson, are turning out to be seriously unreliable. Our priority should be to provide ourselves with robust dating evidence from completely reliable contexts. That means that the work will need to be exemplary in the way it is planned and executed – and monitored to a higher standard than IfA (Institute for Archaeologists) rules can often manage.

Parker Pearson: The old excavation archives do still have a lot to offer. Although he may have been a poor interpreter of the data, Atkinson was a good technical excavator. This is what makes re-digging earlier barrow excavations so important, although the National Trust has sometimes been stubborn about providing the necessary permission. Another priority is to start looking more closely at what is going on outside the main Stonehenge circle and ditch – as demonstrated by the 5 x 5m excavation in 2008 of a stone-dressing area beyond the main circle.

Darvill: The entire Stonehenge research framework needs to be revisited. Aside from looking afresh at the prehistoric priorities we also need to address the previously unrecognised Roman and medieval dimensions. However, Barry Cunliffe's opening question also has a relevance beyond Stonehenge: MARS (the Monuments at Risk Survey) was predicated on the assumption that an already scarce archaeological resource is diminishing. Since then it has emerged that there is far more out there than we thought.

Cunliffe: In summary then, to keep our discipline lively we need to keep digging, but we should be willing to make the re-study of existing material and older excavations our starting point.

Do small-scale excavations have any value at all?

Fowler: Yes they do, if they are asking properly focused questions at key places – for example the use of reconnaissance excavation to resolve issues raised by non-invasive fieldwalking, aerial photography, and lidar (Light Detection And Ranging). But looking further ahead, won't we quite soon have the benefit of a new generation of remote-sensing techniques that not only provide us with a complete picture of what's under the ground but date it for us as well? Give it another 50 years and the old arguments about whether to conserve or excavate will be dead!

Pitts: I don't think Peter Fowler's vision of a totally non-invasive archaeology will ever come true. In 50 years' time the world is going to have many more important things to be worrying about than the luxury of archaeology. Meanwhile, the curatorial insistence that excavation is wholly destructive is wrong. It can actually be a very creative process, albeit with some destructive aspects. We also have to remember that excavation is about much more than the simple technical recovery of data – on the contrary, it is a complicated social and creative engagement of the present with the past.

Parker Pearson: What's *really* destructive is small holes dug into deep stratified deposits. They make it much too easy to lose sight of the big picture. The 2% contract-archaeology sample is adequate for materially rich periods like the Iron Age and Roman, but very deficient for earlier periods. Martin Green has shown *exactly* why bigger holes are so important.

Darvill: Excavation is a thinking process. I'm not sure what the difference is between a big and a small hole; it's all relative. More important is that the size is appropriate to the problem.

Cunliffe: So to summarise: the scale of our excavations should be dictated by the problems we are trying to solve.

Is the Portable Antiquities Scheme useful?

Pitts: Yes, it's not just to do with artefacts but about engaging an entirely new sector of people with archaeology in a way that has never happened before. It so happens that the range and distribution of finds is providing us with really useful information.

Parker Pearson: The existence of GPS is increasing the value of that information still further, and is a huge help in persuading the more responsible detectorists to document their work properly. We have to remember, too, that it is still only a tiny proportion of treasure hunters who are bringing the activity into disrepute: 95% of them are behaving really well, but we need to accept that the 5% of illegally operating 'nighthawks' will never co-operate.

Darvill: The nighthawks are a separate problem. The data coming from the mainstream of detectorists is enormously important in opening up the bigger landscapes between traditionally known sites. And it is at the regional level that the patterning of finds is becoming extremely interesting.

Fowler: I agree with all the previous speakers, and particularly with the democratisation arguments. However, I'm still concerned about the lack of contextualisation and the impact that this is having on the reliability of the data being documented in Historic Evironment Record Systems – some of the locational information is not simply wrong but deliberately falsified.

Is there any value in experimental archaeology?

Parker Pearson: Most certainly, and the experiments are getting better and better. Anthropology and ethno-archaeology also have a role to play. Experimental archaeology can tell us *how* people did things in the past. Anthropology helps us to understand *why* they did them.

Darvill: As well as its serious, scientific contribution to understanding *how* things were done in the past, experimental archaeology also provides people today with practical experience of what it was *like* to do those things.

Pitts: Television makes living in the past seem too easy but gaining a proper social understanding of earlier lives is more complicated than that. Making a foam henge can only tell you certain things; to really understand what is involved you need to do it with real stone and be prepared to re-learn how sarsen dressing was done.

Fowler: Unfortunately the only suitable sarsen stones for this happen to be on a stretch of the Marlborough Downs that is both a National Nature Reserve and World Heritage Site! More broadly, it's impossible to celebrate 50 years of Wessex archaeology without a discussion of experimental archaeology. The most important two examples are the Experimental Earthwork Project and Butser – the latter still sadly unpublished.

The mistake of both projects was to allow themselves to become overly institutionalised. Long-running projects of this kind need passionate people to keep them moving, although some sort of institutional structure is needed to maintain the records and archive.

Another important feature of the two experimental earthwork projects is the huge and unexpected benefit they have obtained from the emergence of archaeological science. This has raised important philosophical questions about whether it was legitimate or necessary to adapt the original research design and methodology.

4

Romans and Saxons

Prologue

Peter Fowler

One of the structural changes in Wessex archaeology in the last 50 years is that the Salisbury office of the Royal Commission on Historical Monuments (England) has flourished and disappeared. In early January 1959, innocent and ignorant, I arrived to work there, so my first view of the day-to-day reality of Wessex archaeology was conditioned by that institutional context. Romans and Saxons did not feature very largely in it: Romans in Dorset were the monopolistic territory of Ray Farrar, who dealt with them from London, and the Saxons did not leave much in the way of earthworks or buildings so were not of great moment to a monument-centred Commission, at least at that time. But almost from day one I was lecturing to adult groups so I quickly had to learn my Wessex archaeology of all periods in order to relate to a range of people who were always keen, often knowledgeable, and sometimes off the wall. They were all there at the Salisbury meeting of CBA XII in the autumn of 1959, an occasion when I first met the Group, gave a first paper, and wrongly assumed the meeting was a well-established part of the annual Wessex cycle. It wasn't, but it is now.

Basic then was the newly published L V Grinsell's *The Archaeology of Wessex* (1958). How lucky was I and others of that time to have to hand a volume which contained not just every fact but almost every interpretive view about Wessex archaeology, hoovered up into a prosaic but reliable text. Leslie was, however, no Romanist nor Saxon specialist (except numismatically), and I am sure that Michael Fulford and David Hinton (see articles below) wince at the thought that a generation acquired their first knowledge of the Roman and Saxon periods from the general accounts in Grinsell-land. But where else did you then go? – there was not a lot of choice. For Romans, Rivet's *Town and Country in Roman Britain* (1958) for the general and Boon's *Roman Silchester* (1957) for the specific, for a Wessex which, frankly, was not particularly interested in the Roman period because it did not seem very important to a region dominated by prehistory; nor was Wessex all that significant in Roman Britain. And as for the Saxons, well, apart from a few cemeteries like Petersfinger, archaeologically they were almost invisible and were best-known from documentary evidence. Amongst that, the *Anglo-Saxon Chronicle* was, for some, racially and chronologically reliable, see for example Copley's *The Conquest of Wessex in the 6th century* (1954).

How things have changed! – that was my unoriginal but accurate thought for the day. The three authoritative speakers who followed me at the Southampton conference (and whose articles appear below) left us in no doubt on that score, not least because they themselves have been major agents of that change. But I would briefly preface their profundities by highlighting what seem to me three of several significant changes in our understanding of the first millennium AD in Wessex.

First, urbanism: four of the six Roman cities/towns in Wessex have seen major excavation programmes and Professor Fulford has elaborated thereon below, including the question of the 5th and 6th centuries. Similarly, Professor Hinton expounded on how, in the last 50 years, we have virtually invented the archaeology of post-Roman urbanism by discovering early maritime and riverine trading places, by taking *burhs* seriously, and by treating the nature and function of towns literally as a matter of growing concern in the later Saxon period.

Second, rural landscape: we have now identified a number of specifically Roman and Saxon rural landscapes, in some cases documented and in estates, despite old-style 'Celtic fields' disappearing from the OS *Map of Roman Britain*. In particular, many an Anglo-Saxon land-charter is now firmly rooted by fieldwork in real-life topography, boundaries surviving and inferred, and relict features. Relevant is my own proposal, so far disappointingly uncontested, that the structure of some 'open field' systems in Wessex may well originate in the layout of preceding 'Celtic field' systems.

Third, material culture and its associated technology: we know simply so much more about THINGS throughout the first millennium AD now than we did 50 years ago, both about how they were made and how and where they were used. Major issues of, for example, technology, trade and length of use − think of pottery alone under just those three heads − are touched on more than once in the articles below.

Roman Wessex

Michael Fulford

The last 50 years of archaeology in the CBA Wessex region have seen a sea change in our knowledge and understanding of its Roman past. To a large extent this is a reflection of the huge investment made through rescue, now developer-funded, archaeology. However, 'pure' research and the efforts of county and local societies have also made a very significant contribution, to the extent that there are few topics − military, urban, rural (including landscape studies), religion and ritual (including death and burial), economy, the transitions from Iron Age to Roman and from Roman to Anglo-Saxon, as well as change within the Roman period, etc, etc − of the Roman past in Wessex which have not been deeply affected. Metal detectorists have also made their contribution.

Realisation that Roman contacts and influence on central southern England can be traced back to the 2nd and 1st centuries BC has stemmed from various sources. On the one hand, the excavations at Hengistbury Head (Dorset) have provided vital new information on contacts across the Channel to Brittany and

Normandy as well as with Italy and the Mediterranean via the Atlantic seaboard (Cunliffe 1987); on the other, the discovery of major Iron Age coins hoards such as that from near Alton (Hants) and that attributed to Waltham St Lawrence (Berks) has provided much new information on Roman relations with the dynastic houses of the Atrebates and their neighbours in the late 1st century BC and the early 1st century AD (Burnett 1990). Yet it was the military landings in south-east England in AD 43 which began the process of securing complete Roman political control over southern Britain. While the broad outlines of the military campaigns are reasonably well known from a combination of written and documentary sources, there is still comparatively little hard evidence from the Wessex region, and most of it is from Dorset and Wiltshire (Griffiths 2001; Putnam 2007). Thus the excavations by Richmond (Richmond & Brailsford 1968) at Hod Hill, published at the beginning of our 50-year review, provided indisputable evidence for conquest-period occupation of the Iron Age hillfort. The publication of the early 20th-century excavations of the amphitheatre at Maumbury Rings, Dorchester (Dorset), identified a clear military phase (Bradley 1976) and further evidence for a major military presence in south-east Dorset was provided by the discoveries at Lake (Field 1992). All of this work seemed to corroborate Suetonius' brief account (*Vesp* 4.1) of Vespasian's leadership of *legio ii Augusta* in the years immediately following the invasion, with its reference to the capture of *oppida* and the seizure of the Isle of Wight. Perspectives on the conquest of central southern Britain have been dramatically altered by the discovery of a possible legionary fortress at Alchester (Oxon), dating from AD 44, raising new questions about how the south was assimilated (Sauer 2005) and when, and over what territory, the client kingdom of Togidubnus (Cogidubnus), evidenced by an inscription from Chichester (*RIB* 91) and mentioned in Tacitus' *Agricola* (14), was established.

Important to our understanding of the 1st century AD is *Calleva* (also known today as Silchester) on the Hampshire–Berkshire border to the north-east of our region. Associated by coins carrying the abbreviated CALLE or CALLEV with the Atrebatic dynasty of Tincomarus, Eppillus and Verica, excavation has now shown evidence of a major, planned settlement, extending over some 40 hectares, which dates from the late 1st century BC (Fulford and Timby 2000; see also Fulford this volume pp 107–109). This urban community continues through to the later 1st century AD when, as ongoing excavations are showing, after a major fire and demolition of existing structures, a new, 'Roman' street grid, aligned on the cardinal points, was imposed over the pre-existing arrangement on a north-east/south-west and north-west/south-east arrangement. Evidence for a building on a palatial scale, probably constructed late in the reign of Nero, suggests a residence for the client king (Fulford 2008). This marches alongside the first 'public building' of the town, a rectangular, timber-built complex underneath the later forum basilica, the orientation of which on the cardinal points anticipates the street grid by at least a generation. The establishment of the client kingdom with a major centre, initially at *Calleva* and then subsequently also at Chichester and Winchester, also provides a context for the early (pre-Flavian) provision of public baths and amphitheatre (Fulford 1989).

Elsewhere rescue excavation has been the context through which knowledge of the early development of the Wessex Roman towns has advanced. So we can glimpse pre-Flavian occupation in *Venta* (Winchester), and, apart from the amphitheatre, in Dorchester, too, but it is the Flavian period which seems to see the firm establishment of the local unit of administration, the *civitas*, each with a single central town – *Calleva Atrebatum* (Silchester), *Durnovaria* (Dorchester) and *Venta Belgarum* (Winchester) (Wacher 1995). Hard evidence for this transition is evident at *Calleva*, where a forum basilica was constructed (in timber) in the 80s of the 1st century AD (Fulford and Timby 2000). From Dorchester, the construction of the aqueduct, studied in detail by the late Bill Putnam (2007), symbolises the establishment of the urban community there in the later 1st century. Rich burials of Flavian date from *Venta* (Biddle 1967), as also from the small town of Neatham (Alton, Hants) (Millett 1986), point to the early residences of elites.

Two projects have given significant insight into the development of town life from the later 1st century onwards: rescue excavations in the heart of *Durnovaria* and a continuing research excavation of part of insula ix in *Calleva* (Fulford *et al* 2006; Fulford and Clarke 2010; Woodward *et al* 1993). As well as documenting the development and evolution of buildings, both projects have also provided an enormous amount of detail about social and economic context through the detailed study of not only material culture but also biological remains. These suggest vibrant communities engaging in a variety of occupations from animal husbandry through to small-scale manufacture of consumer goods, and expressing their hopes and fears through a range of types of ritual deposition, some associated with the construction of buildings, others with the establishment of wells and the securing of water, as well as others still reflective of beliefs less easy to understand. Relatively low-status inhabitants appeared to have enjoyed a varied diet that included some fish and an exotic imported component through to the 4th or early 5th century.

Alongside investigations of the communities within the walls, there have also been major excavations of urban inhumation cemeteries, particularly just outside Dorchester at Poundbury (Farwell and Molleson 1993), and Winchester, notably at the Lankhills cemetery (Clarke 1979) (Fig 4.1). The chronological focus of these has been the 4th century and, apart from the very important demographic information on the age, sex and palaeopathology of the deceased, these excavations have shed important light on the social status of their respective communities. The associated grave goods, or the lack of them in the case of Poundbury, have suggested the possibility of identifying immigrant groups, on the one hand, in the late Roman town, as in the case of possible Danubians in Winchester, or of a Mediterranean origin in Dorchester (Richards *et al* 1998), and of Christian communities, on the other, as in the case of Poundbury. Debate continues over our ability to recognise different social groups, particularly as new scientific approaches to the analysis of the skeletal remains for indications of diet and of geographic origin of the deceased seem to contradict the evidence of grave goods and their particular disposition around the body within the grave

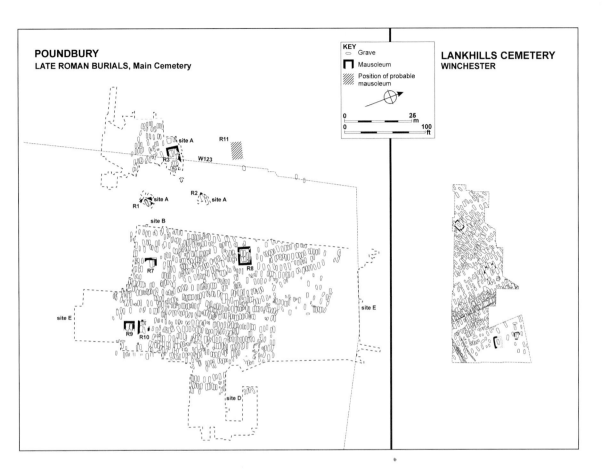

POUNDBURY
LATE ROMAN BURIALS, Main Cemetery

LANKHILLS CEMETERY
WINCHESTER

KEY
▱ Grave
◻ Mausoleum
▨ Position of probable mausoleum

0   26 m
0   100 ft

Fig 4.1 Late
Roman cemeteries
at Poundbury,
Dorchester (Dorset),
and Lankhills,
Winchester (after
Farwell and Molleson,
fig 32 and Clarke 1979,
fig 105)

(Eckardt *et al* 2009; Evans *et al* 2006). Nevertheless, even though we cannot continue to accept correlations between grave goods and their disposition within the grave as evidence of incomers without scientific support from the analysis of the skeletal remains, it seems clear that late Roman Winchester, for example, had a significant non-local population.

By contrast with a combination of work driven by development and by research in the larger towns of Roman Wessex, comparatively little has been done in the smaller towns. Excavations within the small towns of Neatham and Wanborough (Wilts), revealing a development sequence from the later 1st century onwards (Anderson *et al* 2001; Millett and Graham 1986), stand out as exceptional, while aerial reconnaissance and ground survey have shed important light on others, notably *Cunetio* (Mildenhall, Wilts) (Corney 2001). The latter is the location of the largest coin hoard ever to be recovered and recorded from Roman Britain. Dating from the 3rd century, this hoard gives a vivid insight into the bulk movement of coinage, presumably for official purposes, perhaps to pay the staff of *mansiones* and *mutationes* and/or the garrisons in south Wales (Besly and Bland 1983).

In the countryside Roman Wessex has seen extraordinary advances in knowledge, ranging from the excavation and re-excavation of individual settlements, both wealthy, such as villas for example in the Danebury Environs (Hants) (Cunliffe 2008; Cunliffe and Poole 2008) or Halstock (Dorset) (Lucas 1993), and the relatively poor, such as the village settlements so well preserved on Salisbury Plain (Fowler 2000; Fulford *et al* 2006). Much has been learnt about the transition from Iron Age to Roman, often through projects connected with major developments, such as road or motorway building (eg Fasham and Whinney 1991). While there is considerable evidence of continuities from the late pre-Roman Iron Age of the 1st century BC and 1st century AD, there is also evidence of settlement abandonment, particularly of sites occupied from the early or middle Iron Age.

The focus has not been solely on excavation of individual settlements. Whereas aerial photography was becoming well established from early in the 20th century, the last 50 years have seen the introduction and widespread use of a variety of means of non-intrusive survey from geophysics to measured earthwork survey. Fieldwalking, with varying strategies of surface collection, has given us a much more contextualised understanding of certain landscapes, including the chronology and extent of field systems and arable landscapes more generally, particularly those of the chalk. For Roman Wessex we have a remarkable transect of new evidence of settlement and land use on the chalk, from Salisbury Plain across the north Hampshire chalk to the Berkshire Downs. To a greater or lesser extent, different types of survey, along with excavation, have been used to develop a composite picture. To the east on the Berkshire Downs, the Maddle Farm survey involved extensive fieldwalking and surface collection to reveal artefact distributions consistent with widespread manuring of fields from the late 1st and early 2nd centuries onwards (Gaffney and Tingle 1989) (Fig 4.2). An intensive arable regime integrally linked with cattle husbandry was inferred; the products of both were designed to serve more distant markets. Excavation played a minor role in this project, serving to date villa and other settlement and field systems.

Westwards in north Hampshire the focus was on the individual settlement or site, rather than the associated landscape, but with geophysical survey providing local context. Cunliffe and Poole's (2008) excavations of several villas around Andover (north Hants) as part of the Danebury Environs Project have provided us with chronologies and links with the immediate, late pre-Roman Iron Age settlement, insights into the agricultural economy and into social organisation, particularly as expressed by the aisled hall, a focal point of several of the villa complexes (Fig 4.3).

Further west still we reach the higher chalklands of Salisbury Plain and the military training areas. Although subject to local damage, the larger landscape of the Plain has been largely saved from intensive agriculture through its use as a military training area. An extensive programme of earthwork survey supplemented by aerial photographic and geophysical survey has recorded this landscape with its well-preserved 'village' settlements, such as Charlton Down, Chisenbury Warren, and Knook (McOmish *et al* 2002) (Fig 4.4). Again, the picture is one of intensive arable cultivation, but with more limited cattle husbandry than further to the east. These nucleated settlements seem to be a product of the dynamic social changes of the early 1st century AD, extending

Fig 4.2 The Maddle Farm (West Berks) project, showing the distribution and density of all Romano-British pottery sherds across the landscape (after Gaffney and Tingle 1989, fig 13.1)

Fig 4.3 Danebury Environs Project: the villas at Grateley South and Dunkirt Barn, showing a relationship with Iron Age 'banjo' enclosures revealed by geophysical survey (after Cunliffe and Poole 2008, pt 2, fig 2.2 and Cunliffe and Poole 2008, pt 7, fig 7.4)

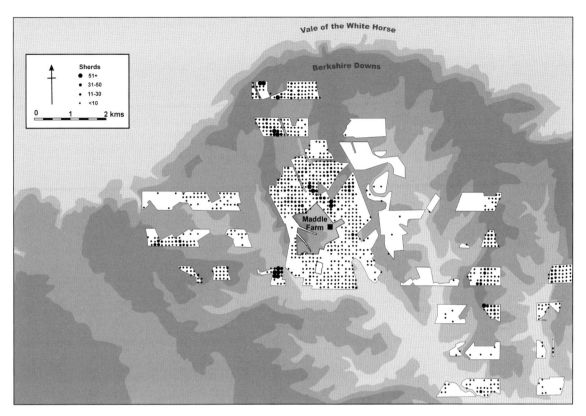

Vale of the White Horse

Berkshire Downs

Sherds
● 51+
● 31-50
• 11-30
· <10

0   1   2 kms

Maddle
Farm

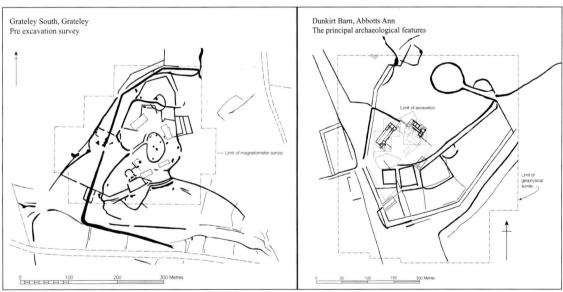

Grateley South, Grateley
Pre excavation survey

Limit of magnetometer survey

0   100   200   300 Metres

Dunkirt Barn, Abbotts Ann
The principal archaeological features

Limit of excavation

Limit of
geophysical
survey

0   50   100   150   200 Metres

into the period of formal administration by Rome, but appearing in their most developed form by the 4th century (Fulford *et al* 2006). The villas, however, appear confined to the river valleys, such as those of the Avon and the Kennet to the north, but, by contrast with examples in Hampshire, have been little explored in modern

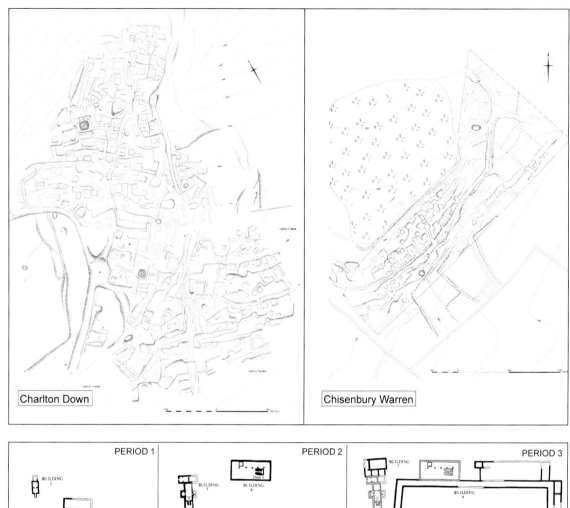

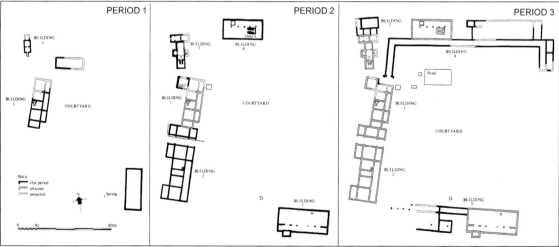

Fig 4.5 Development of the Halstock villa from c AD 140–200 (Period 1), c 175–300 (Period 2) to c 275–325 (Period 3). The villa continued in occupation through the 4th into the 5th century (adapted from Lucas 1993, figs 52–54)

NEW ANTIQUARIANS

Fig 4.4 Salisbury
Plain: earthwork
surveys of Romano-
British villages at
Charlton Down
(compact plan)
and Chisenbury
Warren (linear plan),
Wiltshire (after
McOmish *et al* 2002,
figs 4.7 and 4.13)

times. Further west still takes us into north Dorset and the villas in the hinterland of *Durnovaria* and Ilchester to the north. Here the villa at Halstock provides an excellent example of focused research through extensive excavation of a single site (Lucas 1993) (Fig 4.5).

Across the chalklands there was varying emphasis on sheep, principally for the wool, and cattle husbandry, for meat, milk and hides, with spelt wheat and barley the main crops. There was no difference between the size of sheep and cattle from the Danebury Environs sites and from the town of Winchester. Legumes, such as beans and lentils, along with a variety of fruits and seasonings, were certainly also being consumed in towns, but evidence for their cultivation in the countryside, rather than in plots in or close to the town, is quite limited.

In contrast to the Wessex chalk the picture of landscapes and settlement elsewhere is much less clear, with comparatively little recent investigation of regions like the north Wiltshire claylands or the Hampshire basin. Excavations in east Berkshire, however, have provided evidence of continuity of location and house-plan (roundhouses) from the Iron Age into the 2nd century (Roberts 1995).

Fig 4.6 Isle of
Purbeck mineral
products. Left:
Distribution of
findspots of objects
of Purbeck 'Marble';
right: distribution of
findspots of objects
of Kimmeridge shale,
including sites with
evidence for the
working of the shale
(after Allen &
Fulford 2007)

Along with agriculture, exploitation of the countryside for its mineral resources, particularly for building stone and clay (for potting), was a distinctive aspect of Roman Wessex, especially in south-west Hampshire and south-east Dorset. Work during the last 50 years has completely transformed our understanding of rural industries. While Kimmeridge shale and Purbeck marble are well-known products of the Isle of Purbeck (see Williams 2002), exploitation of the former going back into the Iron Age, it has only recently been appreciated that a much more extensive range of lithologies, including, very probably, a particular quality of chalk, was exploited from the mid-1st century AD onwards from the same locality (Fig 4.6). A range of red and yellow mudstones and a dark-grey dolomite cement stone were used in mosaics and floor and wall veneers in early villa and palatial building in the south – for example in the palatial villa at Fishbourne (West Sussex) – as well as in town houses and legionary fortress buildings

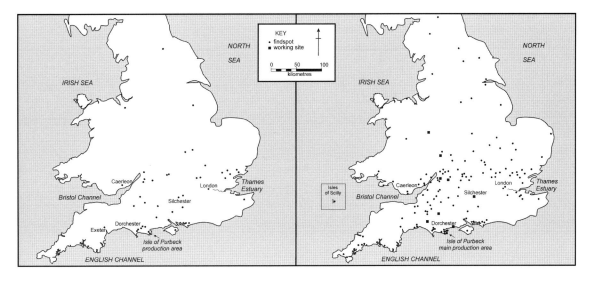

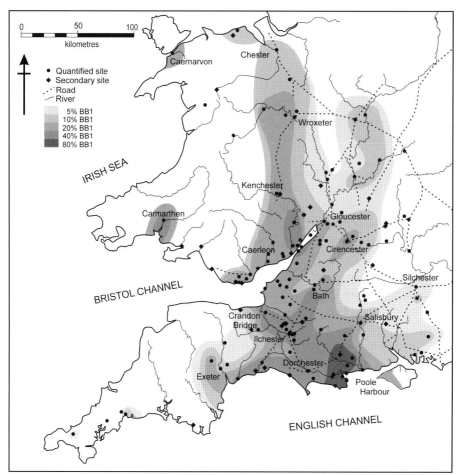

Fig 4.7 Distribution of south-east Dorset BB1 in south-western Britain (adapted from Allen and Fulford 1996, fig 8)

Fig 4.8 Distribution of New Forest slipped wares and Savernake grey wares (after Tyers 1996, figs 215 and 248)

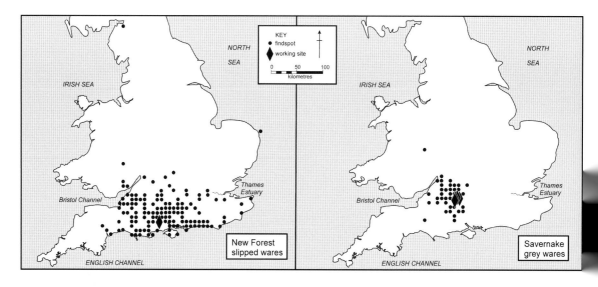

(Allen and Fulford 2004; 2007). Pottery, too, in the form of a range of cooking and kitchen wares, was manufactured around the shores of Poole Harbour and pioneering work on the heavy minerals contained within the sand used to temper the pots by David Peacock and David Williams confirmed that distant finds were indeed of south-east Dorset provenance (Peacock 1967; Williams 1977). With more systematic quantification of pottery, it is now recognised that large quantities of this Dorset pottery were traded up through western Britain. It was ubiquitous throughout the settlement hierarchy in south/south-west Britain, but also reached as far as the northern frontier of Hadrian's Wall and the Antonine Wall (Allen and Fulford 1996) (Fig 4.7). This Dorset production, surviving through to the 5th century AD, was probably the largest of Roman Britain.

Only a little distant to the east are the potteries of the New Forest, so famously explored by Heywood Sumner. More recent work on the kilns and their products, which include a complete range of drinking, table, cooking and kitchen wares, has helped to define chronologies and distributions that covered much of central southern Britain, with the very distinctive, high-fired, 'purple gloss' indented beakers travelling the furthest – as far, for example, as North Wales and Carlisle, as well as south across the Channel to northern France (Fulford 1975) (Fig 4.8). This particular product competed much more successfully with the equivalent beakers made by the major competitor, the Oxfordshire industry, to the north, than did the red-slipped bowls, imitating 2nd- and 3rd-century Gaulish terra sigillata. Supplying more local markets, still, were industries like that located in Savernake Forest (Fig 4.8) or the Rowland's Castle kilns on the Hampshire/ West Sussex border, both of which have been subjected to important research in the last 50 years (Dicks 2009; Hodder 1974a; Timby 2001). The distribution of the early Roman Savernake wares is largely confined within a radius of about 40km from the kilns, but with a greater pull extending to the north-west beyond Cirencester and Gloucester. Likewise, with Rowland's Castle, the influence of the Roman road, Stane Street, can be seen to facilitate the distribution of these wares more to the north-east, towards London (Hodder 1974b).

The comparative ease with which it can be provenanced means that pottery has always been a good proxy of local and long-distance trade. With the discovery and excavation of the wreck at the mouth of St Peter's Port, Guernsey, it has been possible to gain some insight into the connections of this particular boat (Rule and Monaghan 1993). Wares, including the south-east Dorset BB1 pottery, were found among the cargo, which otherwise revealed links along the Channel, probably to the Thames and London, and/or into the North Sea to East Anglia, as well as with the south-west of Gaul, and, through the amphoras, to the south coast of Spain and the north coast of Africa (Fig. 4.9).

In the last 50 years there have been major contributions to the study of the Roman art and architecture of the region. The documentation of Roman sculpture, which includes a number of important recent finds, such as the rare survival of a wooden figurine, the Romano-Celtic deity from Brook Street, Winchester (Cunliffe and Fulford 1982), has now been followed by the publication in two volumes of all the known mosaics from the Wessex counties (Cosh and Neal

2005; Neal and Cosh 2009). Among these are some major finds of the last 50 years, notably the remarkable pavement from Hinton St Mary (Dorset), which depicts the head of a male figure, generally believed to be that of Christ. A second pavement of major importance, depicting Orpheus, was rediscovered and subsequently restored at the Littlecote villa (Wilts). Detailed study, notably by the late David Smith, of Romano-British mosaics has succeeded in identifying a number of shared stylistic traits that he interpreted as 'signatures' of individual mosaic workshops or schools of mosaicists (Smith 1965; 1984). In Wessex these include schools focused around Dorchester (Durnovarian School) and Cirencester (Glos) (Corinian School), examples of which, including the Littlecote pavement, occur in the north of the region. In addition Johnston (1977) has proposed a Central Southern Group.

Contributions to our knowledge and understanding of ritual and religion have been made more through individual finds than through the excavation of particular structures, such as temple sites or churches. A notable exception is the temple on Hayling Island in south-east Hampshire, which originated in the late Iron Age but was constructed in masonry as early as the later 1st century AD (Downey *et al* 1980). However, much more work has been done on making sense of the more ambiguous evidence found within settlements, particularly deliberate depositions in pits, wells and ditches, extending in date from the Iron Age into the Roman period. An extraordinary example is provided by the very deep well at Oakridge near Basingstoke with its succession of fills containing concentrations of complete or partial animal and bird skeletons at different levels, as well as examples of complete, but also rare forms of samian and other artefacts (Maltby 1994; Oliver 1993) (Fig 4.10).

Much of the work of the last 50 years has illuminated the late Roman period, as evidenced by the research on villas with their associated interior decoration, on the villages of Salisbury Plain, on urban cemeteries and their associated human populations, and on industry, to select some of the outstanding contributions already commented upon above. In making the case that the

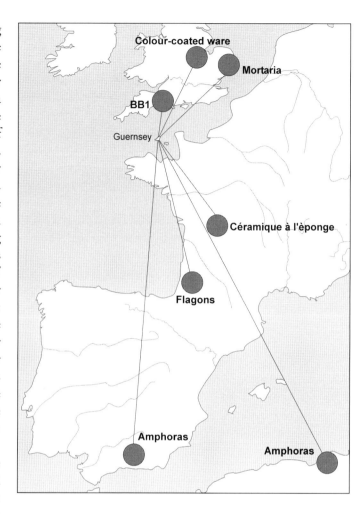

Fig 4.9 Sources of pottery in the St Peter Port (Guernsey) shipwreck, *c* AD 275–325 (after Tyers 1996, fig 43)

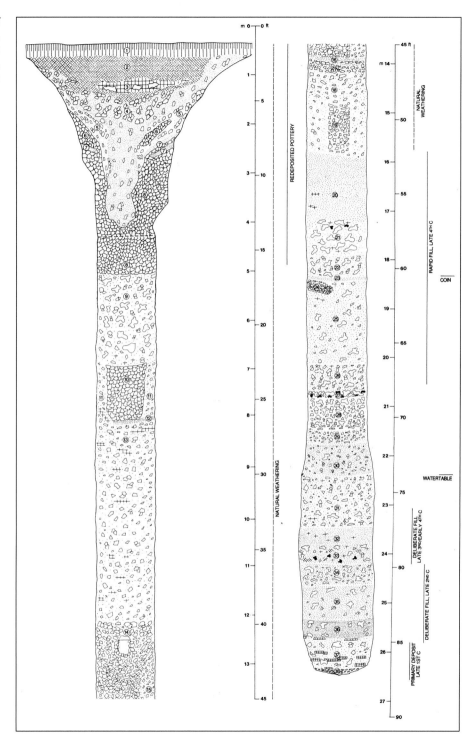

Fig 4.10 Profile of the Oakridge well, Basingstoke (Hants) (after Oliver 1993, fig 7)

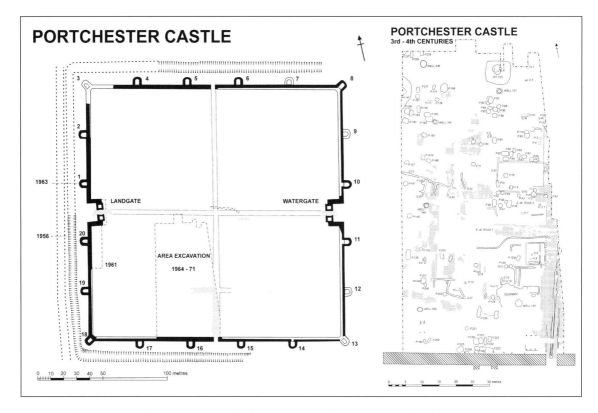

Fig 4.11 Portchester Castle (Hants) with excavated area showing details of the late Roman occupation (after Cunliffe 1975, figs 6 and 20)

Society of Antiquaries' 'Great Plan' of Silchester probably represents buildings in the town which were occupied in about AD 300–350, we can probably be more confident about the character in general of the larger Roman towns in Wessex in the late-Roman period. The large-area excavations of the 4th-century 'Saxon Shore' fort at Portchester (Hants) have also done much to demonstrate the nature of the occupation of a late Roman fortress with its timber buildings next to concentrations of pits, and to fuel the debate about whether and how it is possible to distinguish between military and civilian occupation (Cunliffe 1975) (Fig 4.11).

While a convincing narrative has yet to be written for the 5th and 6th centuries from the Romano-British perspective, there is no doubt that modern fieldwork and finds analysis has done much to illuminate this period. Occupation beyond AD 400 can be regularly demonstrated on the basis of stratigraphic sequences developing from contexts with certain associations of coins of the House of Theodosius or other independently dated material culture. However, in the absence of much well-dated, contemporary material culture or biological data, it is harder to characterise life in the 5th century, beyond the demonstration of continuing activity. The point at which sites still occupied in AD 400 are finally abandoned seems to lie more towards the 6th and 7th centuries than the 5th century, but we have come a long way from the assumption that occupation comes to an end when new issues of Roman coinage cease to be introduced into Britain in the first decade of the 5th century.

Silchester: the renaissance of an Iron Age and Roman town

Michael Fulford

The Iron Age and Roman town at Silchester in north Hampshire is important, not just because it is one of the best-preserved Roman towns in Britain, but also because, to date, it is the only one in Britain known to have evolved directly out of, and on the site of, a substantial Iron Age predecessor settlement (*Calleva*). It also remains a fascinating enigma for two principal reasons. First, why was a major settlement located there in the first place? Second, why, unlike the majority of the major towns of Roman Britain (and the only one south of the Thames) – *civitas* capitals, *coloniae* and other chartered towns – was it completely abandoned in the early medieval period? In the first place, excavations of the 1980s beneath the basilica as well as continuing excavations on insula ix have confirmed that there was a major late Iron Age settlement beneath the Roman town so that the problem of choice of location is clearly one of Iron Age dimensions rather than Roman (Fulford and Timby 2000). Second, recent excavations have shown that the town flourished like any other in the south of Roman Britain until between the 5th and the 7th centuries, when it was abandoned (Fulford *et al* 2006; Fulford and Timby 2000).

While the precise reason for the particular choice of site, which was eminently defensible and plentifully supplied with water (available through springs and shallow-dug wells), but not beside a major river such as the Thames, 16km to the north, is debatable, the broader context of the origins of the town can be seen in the developing and dynamic relations between south-east Britain and the expanding Roman world and her immediate cross-Channel neighbours in northern Gaul. Similarly, the circumstances of the abandonment of the town can be seen, on the one hand, against the broad context of the expansion of Anglo-Saxon political control in Britain, while on the other, given the unique situation of the Silchester desertion, in the particular context of the relations with the emerging kingdoms of Wessex and Mercia.

The last 50 years have also seen a remarkable restoration of the Roman town. Following substantial excavations by the Revd Joyce in the 1860s and 1870s the entirety of the walled area of the Roman town at Silchester (*Calleva Atrebatum*) was investigated by the Society of Antiquaries between 1890 and 1909 (summarised in Boon 1974). A complete plan was obtained of all the Roman masonry buildings, many

Fig 4.12 Mike Fulford and Amanda Clarke at Silchester in 2008 (© University of Reading)

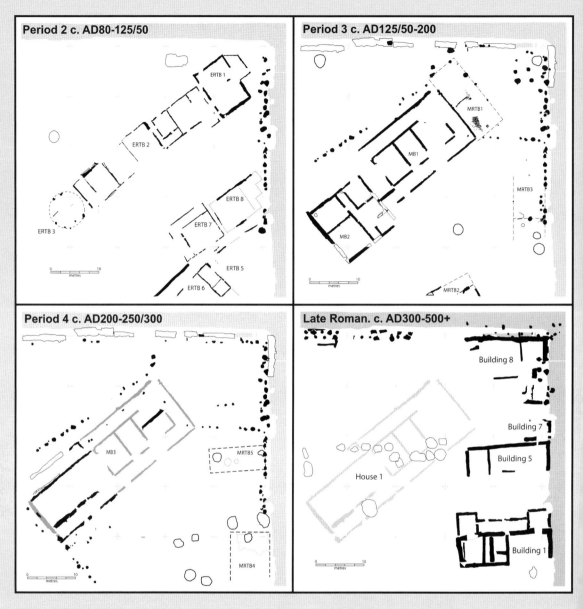

Period 2 c. AD80-125/50

ERTB 1
ERTB 2
ERTB 3
ERTB 8
ERTB 7
ERTB 5
ERTB 6

Period 3 c. AD125/50-200

MRTB1
MB1
MRTB3
MB2
MRTB2

Period 4 c. AD200-250/300

MB3
MRTB5
MRTB4

Late Roman. c. AD300-500+

Building 8
Building 7
Building 5
House 1
Building 1

Fig 4.13 Silchester: the evolution of insula ix (© University of Reading)

wells were excavated, and a large collection of artefacts was retained and curated in Reading Museum. By the end of the project it was believed that, effectively, the walled area was completely excavated. Excavations after 1909 concentrated on establishing a chronology of the town through the investigation of the Iron Age and Roman defences (Cotton 1947), including new, early arrangements lying beneath the town discovered by aerial photography (Boon 1969). The first re-investigation of any of the intramural buildings discovered by the early excavators was that of the possible church, immediately to the south of the forum, in 1961 by Sir Ian Richmond and George Boon (Frere 1976). The excavation produced disappointing results and seemed to confirm the assumption held since the completion of the Antiquaries' project that little more could be gained from the re-excavation of buildings within the walled circuit.

However, re-excavations of the south and south-east gates in the 1970s produced more positive results, suggesting that, on the contrary, much could still be gained by returning to buildings and structures within the walls which had previously been investigated (Fulford 1984). This was confirmed by a re-excavation (for the third time) of the forum basilica in the 1980s. This not only provided important new information from still-surviving late stratigraphy about the use of the space within the building in the late Roman period, but also that both late Iron Age occupation and two successive, 1st-century timber buildings, important for our understanding of the development of Roman provincial public buildings, were preserved beneath the make-ups for the great, masonry forum basilica of the early 2nd century (Fulford and Timby 2000).

A subsequent and continuing programme of excavations on insula ix, one of the residential insulae of the town, has confirmed the quality and extent of the excellent survival of archaeological deposits despite the extensive, earlier investigations. It has been estimated that more than 80 per cent of the stratigraphy within the walls which was available to the antiquarian investigators before 1909 still survives to the present day (Fulford and Clarke 2002). Besides the extramural amphitheatre investigated in the 1980s, there are all the suburbs, cemeteries and extramural environs which were not systematically investigated by the early excavators, and which remain intact. As John Creighton's geophysical survey beyond the town walls is revealing, Silchester and its environs remains a remarkable and very extensive resource for the investigation of Iron Age and Roman urbanism.

Fig 4.14 A silver minim of Verica, who ruled from Silchester in the early 1st century AD. Diameter: *c* 7mm (© University of Reading)

Developments in the early medieval archaeology of Wessex

David A Hinton

The second half of the 1950s was a formative period for medieval archaeology in Britain; a collection of essays dedicated to E T Leeds, *Dark Age Britain* (Harden 1956) was influential in showing what the discipline could achieve, and, like CBA Wessex, the Society for Medieval Archaeology has recently celebrated its 50th anniversary. Wessex did not feature significantly either in the *festschrift* or in the first volumes of the new Society's journal, although one of Leeds's own last papers, particularly relevant to the theme of this volume, was 'The growth of Wessex' (1954).

Before the 1950s

Wessex gets little attention from anyone writing about the early history of the archaeology of the 'Dark Ages' (Lucy 2000, 5–15). When opening barrows in the late 18th century, Colt Hoare and William Cunnington located many primary and secondary Anglo-Saxon burials, but they were not recognised as post-Roman until the 1850s; fortunately some of the objects from them survive. The first systematic post-Roman excavation in Wessex was by J Y Akerman in 1853 at Harnham Hill outside Salisbury, published in the same year. Much 19th-century

Fig 4.15 The massive linear bank of Bokerley Dyke looking east, its deep ditch facing towards Hampshire on the left, protecting Dorset to the right. Although the earthwork is late Roman, its use as a shire boundary shows its continued relevance. Martin Down to the left shows what much of the downland would have looked like when unenclosed and grazed by sheep, in contrast to the intensively cultivated and planted farmland to the right (© English Heritage)

work, however, was more about collecting than excavating, although General Pitt-Rivers was an exception with his investigations of Bokerley Dyke and East Wansdyke in 1888–92 (Fig 4.15). Early volumes of the *Victoria County History* reflect the limitations of the evidence (Smith 1900; 1906), though Leeds was able to begin to challenge the assumption that documentary sources provide a reliable outline that archaeology can merely serve to confirm (Leeds 1913).

Only sporadic advances were made in the study of the post-Roman period in Wessex after the First World War. One enterprise that could be considered a planned commitment was the decision by the Royal Commission on Historical Monuments (England) to create an inventory of the ancient monuments and buildings of Dorset, although few of those date to the years between AD 400 and 1100. Otherwise, work still depended upon individuals, university involvement had not begun, and the Depression of 1929 and its long aftermath did not put labour-intensive job-creation schemes to the benefit of archaeology, as happened in some other areas.

Progress

Recovery after the Second World War was slow. Bombing raids had destroyed much of medieval Southampton, which was one of the towns in which museum curators such as Maitland Muller and D M Waterman did their best to conduct at least limited excavations (Morton 1992, 10–12). Winchester gained the services of Frank Cottrill, who had trained on the building sites of London. Higher standards of excavation were developing; the Petersfinger cemetery outside Salisbury was excavated by fieldworkers who had distinguished themselves in the 1930s and 1940s, such as Professor and Mrs Stuart Piggott, who had worked at Sutton Hoo. E T Leeds combined with Hugh Shortt to publish the site (1953); Shortt was curator of the Salisbury and South Wiltshire Museum, and his other major contribution to the early medieval period was his studies of coins (Saunders 1991). 'Wessex', following revival of the term by Thomas Hardy, was by this time widely used in archaeology, covering any period and a very wide area, as epitomised by two books published in 1958, neither of which addressed the time-period when there was a definable Wessex kingdom: 'The later history of the hill-fort of Old Sarum is too involved … and is work for the historian rather than the field archaeologist' (Grinsell 1958, 305; see also Stone 1958). Grinsell in fact made many valuable contributions to medieval archaeology, notably in his barrow surveys, but also in numismatics. Old Sarum was subsequently addressed very thoroughly by the Royal Commission, though there is not, it still has to be admitted, a lot to say about the archaeology of the late Anglo-Saxon and early Norman town there (RCHM(E) 1980, 1–24; also Borthwick and Chandler 1984, 36).

Wessex featured in *Medieval Archaeology* for the first time in its 3rd (1959) volume, in two papers, both in many ways formative of much subsequent work. The first was about Silchester, and what happened to it after the end of formal Roman occupation, a topic addressed during the Second World War by one of the great figures of government-sponsored archaeology, Brian O'Neil. George Boon collected together the scatter of objects which at least showed that the place had remained some sort of focus, and he re-opened discussion of the ogam stone found in the 1890s' excavations, which remains the only thing of its kind found so far east (1959; see now Fulford *et al* 2007, 254–80). The other article in the 3rd volume of *Medieval Archaeology* was by members of the Royal Commission, which had been re-formed after the war and had resumed its work in Dorset. Its first volume, which covered the whole of the west part of the county, was published in 1952, but its format was that of the 1930s. The 1959 paper on the walls of Wareham demonstrated that the Commission was prepared to go much further in its elucidations of major monuments, as excavation had taken place through the earth rampart and ditch of the *burh*, a major undertaking (RCHM(E) 1959; such an intervention would not be sanctioned today, nor permitted by Health and Safety regulations!). Other 1950s' work included Brian Hope-Taylor's important excavation at Old Windsor, where he claimed to have found a sequence of mill structures; although this was the subject of a note in *Medieval Archaeology* (Wilson and Hurst 1958, 183–5), it remained unpublished at his death in 2001.

The Society for Medieval Archaeology also launched a monograph series, of which only one has directly concerned archaeology in Wessex. That was on the cemeteries at Winnall, outside Winchester, excavated in the late 1950s and early 1960s by Audrey Meaney and Sonia Hawkes with finance from the Ministry of Public Buildings and Works, as the sites were being developed for factories. Their principal importance was in reviving consideration of the changing nature of early medieval burial, and the changing places where it occurred, with or without Christian influence (Meaney and Hawkes 1970; for 'Final Phase' cemeteries, see recent discussion by Geake 2002). Other cemeteries excavated in that era include Alton in 1960, by which time the Ministry's archaeology service had formalised into the Ancient Monuments Inspectorate (Evison 1988).

The Royal Commission continued its long-term study of Dorset, the final volume appearing in 1975. At least as valuable, however, were the books and papers produced by its staff as individual authors. Christopher Taylor's *Dorset* (1970) includes a chapter on the post-Roman period that remains useful, not least for its demonstration of the parcelling-up of estates before the Norman Conquest, and the inter-relationship of that process with the formation of parishes. After Dorset, the Commission's attention was transferred to Wiltshire, where boundaries were a focus of the work of another member of its staff, Desmond Bonney. His argument that East Wansdyke provides evidence of the survival of some pre-Roman boundaries was stimulating, as was his work on the relationship of Anglo-Saxon charter bounds to known cemeteries, in which he argued that their proximity was meaningful. Although queried on the basis of statistics, the number of early settlements that are also close to boundaries, from which it would have been awkward to manage a community's fields, and the actual dates of some of the cemeteries in his analysis (Bonney 1966; 1976; Goodier 1984; Arnold and Wardle 1982; Draper 2004), the thesis is still upheld by many. Bonney also contributed the section on the post-Roman period in the *Victoria*

Fig 4.16 Charlton Down, Salisbury Plain. Earthworks of extensive Roman settlements and 'Celtic' fields are well preserved on parts of the High Plain. Their post-Roman abandonment was probably a steady rather than a cataclysmic process, but by the 7th century they seem to have been out of use, replaced by new settlements and field systems in the lower valleys (© English Heritage)

County History for Wiltshire (1973). Peter Fowler began his investigations of the landscape in and around West Overton while with the Commission (Fowler 2000), and Bruce Eagles has also made numerous contributions to Anglo-Saxon studies in the county (eg Eagles 2001). The final fruits of the Commission's fieldwork were to be the study of the earthwork remains on the Salisbury Plain Training Area, an area where linear Roman villages continued in use beyond AD 400 (Fig 4.16) McOmish *et al* 2002), but otherwise the series was left incomplete apart from the Salisbury volumes on the city's buildings, and the field team was disbanded, except for those members who transferred into what had become (in 1984) English Heritage.

The 1960s were the years of the Rescue movement, and those who were there are still fully capable of remembering them. They saw national and international interest in Hampshire's archaeology, and particularly its post-Roman aspects, first of all in the work of Martin Biddle at Winchester, joined during the campaigns there by Birthe Kjølbye-Biddle. The nature of the city after it ceased to be a Roman-style *civitas*, the role in its development and planning played by the kings and bishops, the great civilisation that grew around its minsters, and the range of crafts and trades carried out in its streets, markets, and suburbs, all remain fundamental issues that have set questions for many other towns (Biddle 1983; Biddle and Kjølbye-Biddle 2007). Peter Addyman collaborated with David Hill on work in *Hamwic*, publishing two seminal papers that brought the international significance of that mid-Saxon trading-place back to public notice (Addyman and Hill 1968; 1969; see Fig 4.23). Christopher Sparey Green's excavations in the 1970s on the outskirts of Dorchester at Poundbury brought to light new information on the transition of a Roman town into a post-Roman settlement (Green 1987).

The urban work in Winchester was a judicious blend of archaeological and documentary research, and of rescue and research archaeology. Rural archaeology also saw a major research project in Hampshire at Chalton, where Barry Cunliffe investigated settlement patterns through fieldwalking, and initiated excavation of the first site to show unequivocally that the early Anglo-Saxons had not lived exclusively in squalid semi-sunken huts (1972; Addyman *et al* 1972; 1973). Cunliffe's work at the Roman fort at Portchester (Fig 4.17) also encountered post-Roman evidence, in a sequence that is one of the very few to be practically unbroken throughout and indeed beyond the Anglo-Saxon period (1976). Subsequent rescue work at Old Down Farm, Andover (Davies 1979), and Cowderys Down, Basingstoke (Millett and James 1983), meant that Wessex's Anglo-Saxon settlements remained part of national and international discussion of the nature of such settlements. Peter Fasham's discovery on the line of the M3 motorway of the spread-out settlement at Abbots Worthy amplified debate with the demonstration that on the Wessex chalklands such sites might be found deeply buried by alluvium in river and stream valleys, so that the existence of many other concealed parts of the settlement pattern must be allowed for (Fasham and Whinney 1991). In Berkshire, a different complexity was revealed by Grenville Astill and Sue Lobb, who showed at Wraysbury that in some places occupation may have shifted over much smaller areas than is implied by the chalklands' total desertions, and that some present-day settlements may have much earlier, though still post-Roman, antecedents, than was beginning to be thought likely (Astill and Lobb 1989).

Concerns in the 1960s and 1970s about the destruction of archaeological material spawned a number of projects and surveys. For the early Middle Ages, both in Berkshire and in east Hampshire, the difficulty of finding sites

Fig 4.17 Portchester Castle on the south coast was a Roman fort into which a Norman castle was inserted. Excavations by Barry Cunliffe in the 1960s showed that the site was also used in the Anglo-Saxon period, perhaps continuously, sometimes for defence, sometimes for everyday occupation. In the late 9th/early 10th century the fort was one of the *burhs* used as protection against the Vikings (© English Heritage)

NEW ANTIQUARIANS

Fig 4.18 The Warminster Jewel was found in 1997 by a metal-detectorist. Made of gold and rock crystal, it is probably 9th century in date, and is similar to the Alfred and Minster Lovell Jewels (Ashmolean Museum, Oxford) and to another recent find made by a detectorist at Bowleaze Cove, Dorset (British Museum). They might have been *aestels*, objects referred to in one of King Alfred's letters that seem to have been used as manuscript pointers. Length: 44mm (© Salisbury and South Wiltshire Museum)

from fieldwalking was demonstrated owing to the friability of the pottery rather than because of absence of settlement; work in the Avon valley was much more revealing (Shennan 1985; Gaffney and Tingle 1989; Light *et al* 1995). The invaluable series of urban surveys produced in the second half of the 1970s showed what had been learnt and how much there still remained to do (Astill 1978; Haslam 1976; Hughes 1976; Penn 1980).

A different sort of archaeology emerged during the 1970s, practised by metal-detector users, not all of whom could be persuaded to report their findings. Nevertheless, the new finds that have been made known have contributed considerably to our knowledge of the early Middle Ages, with the discovery of new cemeteries, or at least of artefacts likely to derive from them, and of large numbers of things that seem to have been accidentally lost, apart from a few hoards. Numismatists have been able to argue that Wessex was part of a money-using economy in the 8th century, though less fully than further east (Metcalf 2005), a pattern that seems to be borne out by the relative paucity of 'prolific sites' and of fine 8th-century metalwork, although recognition of one of the former on the Isle of Wight has brought the island back into discussions of the mid-Saxon period, on which previously it had little to offer (Ulmschneider 1999). The picture changes somewhat for the 9th century; it was possible to write in the early 1990s that there were few exotic objects, yet within a decade two further examples of objects like the Alfred Jewel had come to light in Wessex, again from metal-detecting (Fig 4.18; compare Hinton 1994 with Hinton 2008). Wessex's prosperity, shown by such objects, enabled it to ride out the Viking threat. Vikings have left a little direct evidence of themselves, notably in the burial of a warrior at Reading, but King Alfred's resistance and his defensive system allowed the economic developments of the late Saxon period, such as the regrowth of towns and a market system.

The large amount of new material resulting from the excavations that have taken place in the last 30 years has led to new ways of investigating the post-Roman economy. Animal bones show that the quality of the domestic stock did not decline significantly, and the new towns and churches could be supplied; pasture therefore remained adequate. Less can be said about cereals, but a change to bread wheat that requires a little less labour than spelt to be processed into flour is significant, and the disappearance of grain-driers after the 4th century also shows reduced arable intensity. Similarly, the mass-producing potteries of the late Roman period generally ceased operation, although some continued at a reduced level for a generation or two in the 5th century. Not until the late Saxon period can ceramic 'industries' again be recognised in Wessex, and those are on a smaller scale.

continued on p 120

More important than life or death?
The Saxons at St Mary's Stadium, Southampton

Roland J C Smith

'Some people believe football is a matter of life and death. I'm very disappointed with that attitude. I can assure you it is much, much more important than that.' So said Bill Shankly, legendary manager of Liverpool FC in the 1960s and early 1970s. He is supposed to have said this as a flippant aside but his words have become a modern-day myth, such is the power and importance of football today. However I had the good fortune to be involved in an archaeological project that very much embraced life, death, and football when Wessex Archaeology was asked to undertake a programme of archaeological excavation in advance of construction of the new stadium for Southampton Football Club in 2000 and 2001.

The project was not only one of the most significant archaeological projects to take place within the nationally important mid-Saxon settlement of *Hamwic* but it was also important for the City of Southampton – after 100 years at The Dell, Southampton Football Club had decided to move to a new ground in the centre of the city.

Like most football grounds, The Dell had become a place of great fondness and pilgrimage to the followers of the Southampton Football Club. In its own way it had become a 'sacred' site and after the last game, fans ravaged the ground to

Fig 4.19 Southampton Gasworks in the 1940s. The gasholders in the background still exist today. The gasholder in the left centre now lies below one of the goal mouths (© National Gas Archives, Transco plc)

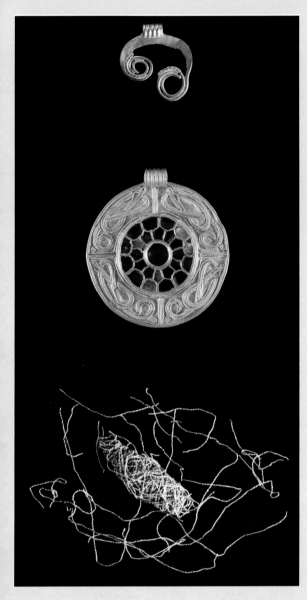

Fig 4.20 Two gold pendant grave goods from the Saxon cemetery (top, width 14mm; centre, diameter 33mm) and a knot of gold thread (20mm long) from a rubbish pit, but possibly a disturbed grave good (© Wessex Archaeology)

recover a piece of it. It was therefore a privilege to be involved in such an important project for the city, and it was also extremely apt that the new stadium should be built within the inner city, a stone's throw from St Mary's church, the mother church of Southampton. This was the place from which the football club was founded as the St Mary's Church of England Young Men's Association Football Club in 1885 … thus giving rise to Southampton FC's nickname of the 'Saints'.

Unfortunately, the area today remains relatively deprived. The construction of a new stadium for the football club was therefore an opportunity to aid the regeneration of the local area. For me, as a professional archaeologist, it was also a particular pleasure to meet and work with people I would not normally have an opportunity to encounter at close quarters. At an early stage in the project I found myself called to a meeting at The Dell. I was taken in through the main entrance and down several corridors to meet the Finance Director in the Board Room of Southampton Football Club, surrounded by the trophies and memorabilia from over 100 years of the Saints, including a replica of the FA Cup, won in 1976.

More daunting than the impressive surroundings, however, was the prospect of negotiating the finances of the project with a Finance Director more used to dealing with multimillionaire footballers and their agents. Even more daunting was the fact that the archaeology was an integral part of the construction programme. The programme was fixed and was working back from a 3.00 pm kick-off for the first game of the 2001/2 season!

In fact, the excavation turned out to be the largest single area ever excavated in *Hamwic* in one phase of excavation. An added factor was that the site was for more than a hundred years occupied by Southampton Gasworks, and photographs from the 1940s suggested little below-ground archaeology would survive (Fig 4.19). In addition, the Gasworks were seriously bombed in the Second World War (Southampton Gaslight & Coke Co 1948, 11).

As we were excavating on the site of the new stadium for Southampton Football Club, there was a strict code of conduct relating to football allegiances. The bitter rivalry and hostility between Southampton and Portsmouth Football

Clubs meant the wearing of any football attire or any item that might indicate your footballing allegiances was strictly forbidden. Indeed there was constant rumour that Portsmouth FC shirts and items were secretly being buried around the site to 'curse' it.

Wessex Archaeology's excavations in 2001 recorded much new evidence about the Saxon settlement in an area of the town previously little investigated. A gravel street, at least ten timber buildings, and over 400 pits showed that small-scale crafts and industries were taking place; most notably there was possible evidence for textiles and embroidery, including the recovery of a knot of gold thread from a rubbish pit (Fig 4.20). The accompanying environmental evidence also provided unprecedented details of the diet of the mid-Saxon residents of *Hamwic*.

Much of this evidence came from the exceptionally well-preserved contents of cess pits. The results were so impressive that the analyser of the plant remains decided to carry out an experiment on herself to find out how plant remains survive their passage through the human body (Carruthers 2005, 160). This 'experimental' work demonstrated that even present-day processed foods can contain 'contaminants' – a modern, cleanly prepared meal of wholemeal bread, tinned peas, apples, and brambles bought from the local supermarket was found to contain a stinging nettle seed.

The most significant discovery, however, was a cremation and inhumation cemetery dating to the earliest years of *Hamwic* and containing numerous late 7th- and early 8th-century grave goods of exceptional quality. As is always the way with archaeological projects, the presence of this cemetery only became apparent in the later stages of the project and as pressure on time increased. Although much of the cemetery had to be excavated in advance of construction work, it was possible to preserve part of it below the St Mary's Stadium pitch – a rare form of 'preservation *in situ*' that allows professional football matches to take place every week above one of southern England's most important Saxon cemeteries.

All of this was naturally of

Fig 4.21 Front page of the *Southern Daily Echo*, Friday 23 November 2001

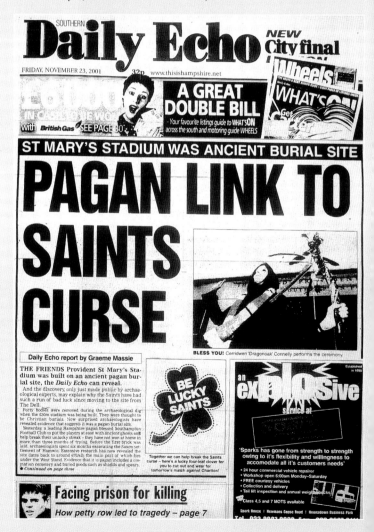

considerable interest to the local and national press which followed the work in detail. Indeed, after the Saints had failed to win any of their first five games on the new pitch there was speculation that the disturbance of these burials had contributed to the team's misfortunes. The local paper therefore called in a pagan witch, Cerridwen 'Dragonoak' Connellys to exorcise the new stadium (Fig 4.21) while dressed in purple robes (and a Saints scarf!). At the time she was quoted in the *Southern Daily Echo* as saying:

> The Saxons loved gatherings and competitions and I am sure they were the kind of people who would be delighted for a stadium like this to be built over their remains. The players should see it in that light and see it as something positive. I predict the Saints will beat Charlton Athletic.

While the archaeological profession could be dismissive of such publicity, it does highlight the special interest that the archaeology of the site generated and also the opportunities provided to promote Southampton's archaeological heritage to the local community, to the followers of Southampton Football Club, and to the residents of Hampshire generally. Wessex Archaeology therefore took the opportunity to promote the archaeology of the stadium through press releases and local TV appearances – if only our archaeological publications could achieve a similar readership!

A very successful exhibition of the finds was organised by Southampton City Council, while the Football Club displays some of the finds as part of its outreach and educational activities for local schools. A large-scale image of a Saxon coin is also now part of the artwork on the frontage of the stadium – happily visible from the Board Room and thus allowing those big footballing decisions to be inspired by the memory of an Anglo-Saxon *sceatta*.

Most rewarding for all of us involved in archaeology is that the gold jewellery and other items can now be enjoyed by the citizens of Southampton, Hampshire and Wessex in a permanent display at Southampton's Museum of Archaeology. Although we probably can't claim, like Bill Shankly, that archaeology is more important than life and death, we can at least be proud to have inspired many of its residents to learn more about the archaeology of their city through their football team – the Saints.

One industry that has produced a surprising amount of evidence is iron smelting. The complex of furnaces at Ramsbury may have been attached to the centre of a royal estate, where sculptures suggest that there was also an important church. Although the amount of iron produced cannot be assessed, the quality was good enough for some high-quality wrought iron objects to be made there by smiths (Haslam 1980). Furnaces have not been recorded, but spreads of smelting slag have been found at Gillingham and Romsey, which, like Ramsbury, seem to be mid-Saxon in date. Wider dating is suggested by radiocarbon results from Bestwall, outside Wareham, where excavations over a decade led by Lilian Ladle, a local amateur archaeologist, have produced pits with charcoal, and large amounts of smelting slag. On the other side of Wareham, at Worgret, a mill dated by dendrochronology to the end of the 7th century had a quantity of smelting slag around it, and could have been used for crushing ore. The Bestwall dates allow for production to have begun before the end of the Roman period, but the start date may have been a good deal later, though nevertheless in the first half of the 6th century (Ladle forthcoming). These ironworking sites do not seem to have continued beyond about the end of the 9th century, after which Wessex presumably became dependent on metal brought from the Weald of Kent or the Forest of Dean, but that is not yet supported by archaeological evidence. In the same way, another industry, salt production, is known only from documents such as the 11th-century *Domesday Book* (Keen 1989).

The association of royal estates and church institutions is a facet of industrial production as well as of agriculture and manorialisation. Interest in the origins and development of churches continued in the 20th century, with the Taylors' two volumes creating a firm base for consideration of the architecture (1965), and another two volumes doing the same for the region's sculpture (Fig 4.22; Tweddle *et al* 1995; Cramp 2006); there have also been several reviews of parochial administration and the early 'minster' system (eg Hase 1994; Blair 2006).

Future developments

By coincidence, this volume of essays on CBA Wessex has been prepared at the same time as a number of Strategic Research Frameworks, initiated by English Heritage, have been printed or made available online. The areas chosen for this exercise divided the CBA Wessex counties, with Dorset and Wiltshire falling

NEW ANTIQUARIANS

Fig 4.22 The Codford
Cross is one of a
number of very fine
9th-century stone
sculptures in Wessex.
The figure with short
tunic and cloak,
holding a plant-scroll
above his diademed
head, may represent
King David of the
Old Testament, who
'danced before the
Lord' after victory
in a battle. If that is
correct, he is holding
a musical instrument
in his other hand.
Height: 1.25m
(photo: K P Jukes
and D J Craig
© Corpus of
Anglo-Saxon Stone
Sculpture)

in the south-west (Webster 2007), Berkshire, Hampshire, and Wight in the 'Solent-Thames'. As far as priorities for the early medieval period are concerned, this has led to minor but interesting differences in emphasis. 'What happened to the British?' is a question that is applicable anywhere, but has different answers.

Part of the 'British' question is the ongoing debate about 'the fate of the Roman towns' and the urban network, with a new dimension added recently – the suggestion that an existing Christian presence in at least some of them could have led to the maintenance at these sites of shrines. At Silchester, this has been suggested on the basis of some window glass that could have come from a church building, possibly a saint's shrine (Fulford *et al* 2006, 280). Dorchester may have seen a site shift, to Poundbury, although the putative apsidal church there has never been wholly convincing as a single structure (Green 1980, fig 56, feature PR4). Winchester's extra-mural late Roman cemetery at Lankhills does not seem to have developed into a settlement; instead, occupation has been found within the walls of the city, datable to long before the cathedral was established (Biddle and Kjølbye-Biddle 2007). Could the 7th-century bishop have been imposing his authority over a place where some earlier cult had survived, bringing people to it? If so, why these places do not have British memorial stones, unlike Wareham which was never a *civitas* and almost certainly not even a small town, is just one of the concomitant problems.

Attention has been directed to a few burials in 'Anglo-Saxon' cemeteries of one or two men with 'Roman' culture, wearing hob-nailed footwear or shoulder-fastened cloaks (Eagles 2001, 217–18; Biddle and Kjølbye 2007, 199 n.53); these suggest more cultural overlap than traditional accounts of antagonism would allow, and lead to the posing of the question the other way round: is there 'Anglo-Saxon' influence in cemeteries thought 'British' because of the absence of grave-goods, such as some in Dorset? Recent excavations on a larger cemetery than any previously known in the north-east of the county indicate that burial could perhaps have begun while the area was still politically 'British', slowly absorbing 'Anglo-Saxon' influence, as at Somerset's Cannington (Gale *et al* 2008, 110–19). Whether DNA and isotopic studies will advance understanding of these questions, or get discredited like 'Jutish physiognomy', remains to be seen (Fig 4.20).

Another problem is that some hillforts could have had post-Roman use, but none has produced data such as that seen in Somerset and other western counties, and, perhaps not unconnectedly, post-Roman imports of Mediterranean glass and pottery have still not been found, nor of the late 6th/7th-century E ware (Campbell 2007, figs 16, 34, 39). West Wansdyke seems to be linked into some hillforts, but East Wansdyke is not. Dating these linear boundaries unfortunately remains intractable, even with more up-to-date methods than were available to Pitt-Rivers (Erskine 2007, 94). Whether some or all are frontiers in the sense of garrisoned lines with supervised entry points, or were really symbolic expressions of where a heartland began, remains uncertain, as does in most cases who built them against whom. But if hillforts were less used in Wessex than elsewhere, was it because the Roman stone-walled forts took their place? Certainly on the

Fig 4.23 A small Anglo-Saxon cemetery at Twyford, Hampshire, excavated by Wessex Archaeology in 2007. Much more information can now be obtained from well-preserved and carefully excavated skeletons than in the 1950s–1970s, when many Wessex cemeteries were investigated (© Wessex Archaeology)

coast both Portchester and Bitterne, Southampton, have suggestive evidence of ongoing use (Cunliffe 1976; Russel 2002, 20–1, 23). The small Roman towns like *Cunetio* (Mildenhall), Wiltshire (Moorhead 1997), and Neatham, Hampshire (Millett and Graham 1996), need to be drawn back into this debate: is there a contrast between those walled and those unwalled?

Radiocarbon is of enormous value when nothing else, such as pottery or coins, is found, but can give such a wide dating span that it is not very helpful, and it is sometimes inconsistent with, for instance, dendrochronology, as at Worgret mill (Hinton 1992). Without radiocarbon dating, however, the extensive ironworking and charcoal burning outside Wareham at Bestwall would not have been attributed to the later 6th century and after on the basis of the very small number of organic-tempered pot sherds found there. However, there are issues about the reliability of the radiocarbon dates, as they allow the possibility, but do not prove, that the workings began in the late 4th century, in which case they would have overlapped with the Black Burnished Ware production at the site. How long that continued to be produced there and elsewhere, albeit on a diminishing scale, has been addressed by Malcolm Lyne, who has made a strong case for it going on into the mid-5th century, but not necessarily beyond.

Rural settlement issues include the problem of the length of time that Romano-British settlements stayed in use, as they have been shown to have done for a while on Salisbury Plain. It may be that they become archaeologically invisible, but it seems still to be true that none of the excavated 'Anglo-Saxon' settlements, and very few modern villages and hamlets, have Roman antecedents. This could perhaps be tested with the 'shovel-pit' method, a technique used to good effect on a community archaeology project organised by Carenza Lewis in eastern England, but might be less fruitful because of the low level of good-quality pottery in Wessex. It should be tried, however, since traditional fieldwalking is even less likely to find scatters of early pottery in most areas. The issue of manorialisation and nucleation – possibly the final element in the shifting settlement pattern – might be put on a firmer footing with such methods, as the mid- and later Saxon pottery is more likely to survive, although even then it seems to have been less prolific than in eastern England. Or did more small sites survive than we know, creating in some areas a more dispersed settlement pattern? We still know surprisingly little of the physical form of mid- and late Saxon settlements and fields.

How the 'Anglo-Saxons' managed to exchange goods without towns, and whether gift-giving and service/tribute dues are sufficient explanation, leads to the issue in which Wessex has taken a lead: the redevelopment of urban places, at *Hamwic*, Winchester, and then at a string of places such as Wareham (Fig 4.24) and Trowbridge (Graham and Davies 1993). For the 7th to 9th centuries, there is now another aspect to this question – why Wessex appears to have had less involvement in coin exchanges than areas to the east, resulting in fewer of the newly recognised 'prolific sites' where considerable amounts of material finds indicate quite extensive trading. Continuing liaison with metal-detectorists through the Portable Antiquities Scheme is essential as a means of addressing this issue.

Much has been learnt about the early medieval period in Wessex over the last 50 years, and there is a clear agenda of questions for the future – the challenge is to maintain the progress.

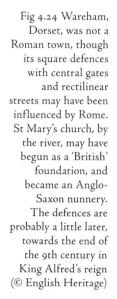

Fig 4.24 Wareham, Dorset, was not a Roman town, though its square defences with central gates and rectilinear streets may have been influenced by Rome. St Mary's church, by the river, may have begun as a 'British' foundation, and became an Anglo-Saxon nunnery. The defences are probably a little later, towards the end of the 9th century in King Alfred's reign (© English Heritage)

Mid-Saxon Southampton

Alan Morton

One must not over-emphasise Southampton's importance in the mid-Saxon economy. Despite the evidence of widespread and regular contact provided by the finds, it probably continued to exploit the relatively limited trading patterns into the Seine and along England's south coast that were already well developed by the late Iron Age. Southampton's later medieval status as a trading town partly reflected the increased importance of the Normandy traffic after 1066, and partly its value as an intercept port on the route between the Mediterranean cities and Bruges or London, but circumstances were different in the mid-Saxon period. Southampton should not, therefore, be placed in the same league as *Quentovic* (near Boulogne), Dorestad in the Netherlands, or London, places that contemporaries dignified as *emporia*. What distinguishes the archaeology of mid-Saxon Southampton is simply its great abundance and coherence.

In today's terminology, mid-Saxon Southampton (or *Hamwic* as it is sometimes referred to by archaeologists) was a 'productive site' for much of the 19th century, notable for the large quantities of coins and other material that were recovered. Proper archaeological excavations began in 1946 – the earliest in England to be targeted at a large Saxon settlement and a shift from the previous obsession with Saxon burial grounds. Work continued in sporadic bursts until 1968, since when investigation has continued steadily year on year. As a result, mid-Saxon Southampton has provided far more data than any other English site of its type. Nearly a tenth of the settlement has now been investigated, revealing significant variations in the type and density of occupation. Today, metal-detecting at other 'productive sites' around the country is bringing to light assemblages comparable in size to those recovered from Southampton, but it is our local excavations that continue to provide the most rounded English context in which to understand such material – and it is a picture that alters regularly as more evidence accumulates.

By the early years of the 7th century a small settlement had been established on a spur of gently rising ground inland of the river, with its cemetery on the same spur, closer to the river. Although there is indirect evidence for the

Fig 4.25 The mid-Saxon site today, almost flat to the river. A: the focus of lay occupation. B: St Mary's church (© Alan Morton)

Fig 4.26 Two sites compared: the north-west of the town (left) with its abundant evidence for buildings and its many deep rubbish pits packed with debris; and the south-west (right) with little evidence for buildings, and where considerably less rubbish has been thrown into the smaller pits (© Southampton City Council)

existence of a landing shore at a creek close by, the complex should be interpreted as a Jutish 'palace' site rather than a trading settlement. The cemetery is unusual for comprising inhumation and cremation burials, the best part of a century after that mix had disappeared from elsewhere in the country. However, the Jutish kingdoms of the Isle of Wight and the adjacent mainland were the last to be converted to Christianity. The conversion was a violent affair, and we should include mid-Saxon Southampton in Bede's account of the conquest of the Isle of Wight in AD 686 by the West-Saxon king Cædwalla, and his attempt to replace the population with people from his own region.

Cædwalla gave a quarter of the island to the Church, and presumably a similar thing happened at Southampton. By c AD 700, a minster had been established on a slight natural rise of land to the south of the earlier settlement, with its own landing shore along the river. Only one of the two churches that were there throughout the Middle Ages remains today, and the original enclosure has been considerably reduced to a small rectangular churchyard, but the nucleus survives as Southampton's mother church, St Mary's.

The lay settlement that emerged during the 8th and 9th centuries developed out of the earlier centre of settlement. One should therefore picture adjacent lay and ecclesiastical settlements, each on a low rise set back from the river and each with its own landing shore; the density of lay occupation was on average about seven times greater than that within the minster enclosure.

The wider picture that is emerging as a result of the last fifteen years' investigations in the rest of Southampton is unusual (Andrews 1997; Birbeck *et al* 2005). Where one would expect to find a relatively large number of smaller satellite settlements (mills, farms, hamlets and so on), these are almost wholly invisible in the mid-Saxon period. Instead, apart from some continued occupation of the Roman walled town, nearly all of the outlying occupation clusters within a 250m-wide fringe around the settlement. This could simply demonstrate how difficult it can be to identify mid-Saxon evidence, but the balance of probability

Fig 4.27 Saxon Southampton symbolised. Right: one of the 'pecking-bird' sceattas minted in 8th-century Southampton (diameter: c 10mm) (© Southampton City Council); left: a lead-alloy brooch with the same motif (© Wessex Archaeology)

is that the general picture is correct, and that mid-Saxon Southampton developed in a way not seen in a typical town. It was a royal vill and appears to have been maintained as a specialist estate, provisioned from the king's nearby rural estates.

For more than six decades, many hundreds of people have been associated with the excavations at mid-Saxon Southampton, both in the field and in the laboratory. While most have to remain anonymous here, it would be unfair not to remember the following: the great O G S Crawford, who re-awakened interest in Saxon Southampton; Denis Waterman, the 'fiery dragon', who was a driving force behind the early excavations; a young M R Maitland Muller, who carried out most of those early excavations; an equally young Alan Aberg, whose energy and fieldcraft ensured the success of the excavations in the mid-1960s; Peter Addyman, without whom there may never have been an organisation able to carry out a thorough investigation of the settlement; and Councillor John Barr, who did so much to give that organisation political credibility.

5

Medieval and Recent

Prologue

Martin Biddle

In the half century before 1958 British archaeology in the modern sense was born in Wessex. From Hadrian Allcroft's *Earthwork of England* (1908), Williams-Freeman's *Field Archaeology as Illustrated by Hampshire* (1915), and Crawford and Keiller's *Wessex from the Air* (1928), via the excavations of Hawkes, Myres, and Stevens at *St Catharine's Hill, Winchester* (1930), and Hawkes and his contemporaries at a clutch of other Hampshire hillforts, to Wheeler's *Maiden Castle* (1943) and Crawford's *Archaeology in the Field* (1953), the idea of an archaeological landscape and its investigation from above, on, and below the ground had come into being.

I first saw the grey ship of Winchester cathedral from my parents' car on the by-pass in 1949, but did not visit the city until driven through the West Gate for the first and last time on the day of my demobilisation from the Royal Tank Regiment in February 1958. Sent by the Ancient Monuments Inspectorate to excavate part of a Roman villa at Twyford the following summer, I lodged in Winchester and saw something of the personalities of Winchester and Hampshire archaeology. So it was that the call to dig the site of the proposed Wessex Hotel north of the cathedral, just after coming down from Cambridge in the summer of 1961, was not unwelcome.

What followed was the idea of an archaeology of a city as an urban phenomenon through time, from the Iron Age to the Victorian Age, across the whole social scale from cottage to cathedral, using all the available evidence, from written sources, topography, archaeology, and the natural sciences, the last a direct result of reading archaeology at Cambridge under Graham Clark, author of *Prehistoric Europe: the Economic Basis* (1952).

What we did not attempt, what has still not been attempted, was to set the city in the fullest context of its hinterland through 2000 years, as knowable both from archaeology and from the written sources. The example of Danebury has shown us what can be achieved for the undocumented Iron Age and Roman centuries. How much more could be done by combining the evidence of field archaeology with the vastly rich documentary evidence readily available, not least for many parts of Wessex, in the pipe rolls of the bishopric of Winchester, now long since returned from London to the Hampshire Record Office in Winchester.

A huge step forward in the last decade, in the archaeological study of all periods from the Bronze Age onwards, has been the recording by Finds Liaison

Officers through the Portable Antiquities Scheme (PAS) of the thousands of finds recovered by metal-detecting. Whatever one may think of this generally deplorable hobby, it would be madness to ignore the tremendous value, if properly recorded, of the finds being made – the dubious moral equivalent of 'if you can't beat them, join them'. The distribution maps now available, although difficult to construct without the expert and willing help of the PAS staff at the British Museum, can be used to raise and address questions both general and particular.

In Hampshire, for example, what is the real meaning or explanation of the almost total lack of recorded finds of any period from the Tertiary sands and gravels of the Hampshire Basin? Lack of metal-detecting? Absence of settlement? Both are unlikely to be the complete answer. On a more detailed level, the thorny problem in the Itchen Valley of the relationship of Winchester and *Hamwic* has been greatly clarified by the now rich evidence for at least thirteen pagan Anglo-Saxon cemeteries clustered around Winchester.

The study of the rural economy of medieval Wessex needs an investment of effort comparable to that given to earlier periods. There are big problems to address. One is the purpose and effect of droving vast numbers of cattle on the hoof from the North and the Midlands via 'Oxen ford'. Another is the question of whether or not, and from what date, sheep were bred primarily for wool rather than meat. The over-wintering of sheep may be the key to the emerging role of Wessex and England in the growth of the wool trade which, long before the days of the *Domesday Book* and the first pipe rolls of the mid- and later 12th century, lies behind the wealth of Anglo-Saxon England. A third question is why the victualling of towns should have been more successful in maintaining the health of the Anglo-Saxon inhabitants of Winchester than that of its later medieval inhabitants – for this is what the evidence of the skeletal remains from the city seems to suggest.

Here lies part of an agenda for the next half century in the archaeology of the medieval recent past of Wessex.

Developments in the later medieval archaeology of Wessex

David A Hinton

The five counties that now constitute the CBA Wessex region had no administrative unity within the English kingdom after the Norman Conquest. Geologically, they had some similarities, as all had chalk belts that provided arable and grazing land, but also agriculturally unprofitable clays, sands and gravels. In contrast to the Roman period, these were hardly exploited for making pots, and bricks and tiles were not commercial products. Nor does anywhere in Wessex have the deposits of metals that helped to create settlements on the moors of the south-west or in the iron-ore rich forests like Dean or the Weald. The only natural resources worth exploiting in any significant quantity were stone, notably Purbeck marble and Quarr limestone, and salt from the sea. Agriculture, including timber exploitation, was therefore the main economic driver, with cloth production the only craft that offered significant opportunities for growth.

For the Isle of Wight, southern Hampshire and Dorset, the sea was a primary element in the development of trade and of ports, some already established like Wareham and Southampton, others new foundations in the 12th and 13th centuries, like Poole and Portsmouth. Fishing, however, seems never to have had a significant economic role, unlike Yarmouth or Dover.

Before the 1950s

The later medieval archaeology of Wessex attracted relatively more attention in the 19th and early 20th centuries than did the Anglo-Saxon period. The recovery of 13th-century and later artefacts from the open drains of New Salisbury in the 1850s was a remarkably prescient enterprise that led to the establishment of what is now the Salisbury and South Wiltshire Museum (Saunders, P, 1986). Also pioneering was General Pitt-Rivers' investigation of 'King John's House' on his Cranborne estate – an architectural survey combined with excavation, from which came descriptions and drawings of artefacts, and analysis of animal bone (Pitt-Rivers 1890). The excavation at Old Sarum castle and cathedral before the First World War typically focused on major monuments, and was funded partly by the Society of Antiquaries and partly by donations which the Wiltshire Archaeological and Natural History Society collected both from individuals and from Salisbury's municipal corporation; the subscription list shows a high level of public interest (St John Hope 1910; Hawley 1912). In the 1930s, the Society of Antiquaries funded excavation at nearby Clarendon Palace, another site important in the nation's history and therefore then perceived as of greater interest than common-place towns and villages (James and Robinson 1988, 30–1).

Ecclesiological focus meant attention paid to churches, and romantic views of monastic ruins (Hare 1993); a different sort of attention was paid by the American tycoon W R Hearst, who had substantial parts of Wiltshire's Bradenstoke Priory demolished and shipped across the Atlantic in the 1920s (Gerrard 2003, 77). Happier efforts at conservation included the purchase and preservation in the 1880s of the late 15th-/early 16th-century 'Tudor House' and the Norman 'King John's Palace' by a wealthy Southampton citizen who established a private museum and subsequently sold them to the City 'at a price very much below his outlay' (Leonard 1987).

Wessex did not otherwise feature much in the naissance of the archaeology of the later Middle Ages that was stirring before the Second World War, although the decision of the Royal Commission on Historical Monuments to compile an Inventory for Dorset was to have a major impact subsequently. Such developments were put on hold in 1939, although in its sad way the war was to be a major factor in subsequent work, because of the destruction wrought on the port of Southampton, and O G S Crawford's record of the way that the bombs revealed the town's Norman and later lay-out (Hauser 2008).

Progress

Urban redevelopment after 1945 led to work in Southampton and Winchester, but it was the 1960s that made the latter into a focus of international attention with the programme that integrated excavation of rescue and research sites with documentary investigation led by Martin Biddle and the late Birthe Kjølbye-Biddle (Fig 5.1); they had had predecessors in Frank Cottrill, Barry Cunliffe and John Collis. In Southampton, the 10th-century and later town was investigated by Alan Aberg and then by Colin Platt, whose book (1973) synthesised its archaeology and documentary history in a way still hardly achieved for most

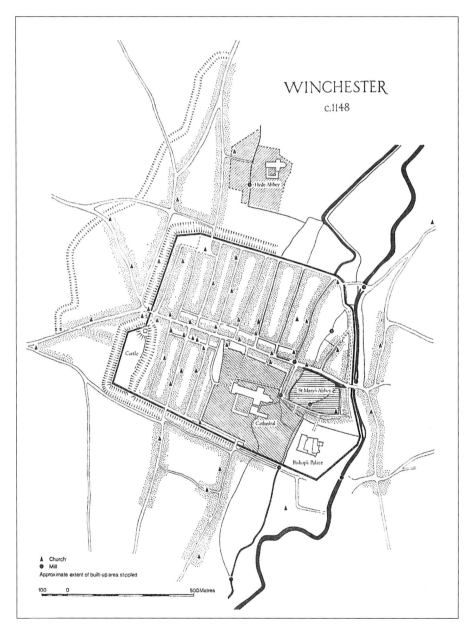

WINCHESTER
c.1148

Hyde Abbey

Castle

St Mary's Abbey

Cathedral

Bishop's Palace

▲ Church
● Mill
Approximate extent of built-up area stippled

100   0   500 Metres

Fig 5.1 Winchester in 1148 (from fig 27 in *Winchester Studies 1*, Oxford, 1976), showing the location of churches and the likely spread of occupation both intra- and extra-mural. Mills on the braids of the River Itchen are also shown; these were for grinding grain, but running water led to various crafts such as dyeing and fulling clustering in the Brooks. This area was upstream of both the New Minster and St Mary's Abbey. To get away from the smelly and dirty water was one reason given for the former's relocation to Hyde Abbey; the nuns had to put up with it (© Winchester Excavations Committee)

other towns; it was followed by two volumes of excavation reports that showed just how wealthy and widely connected some of the citizens had been, an aspect of urban culture that is still having an impact on assessments of the period (Platt and Coleman-Smith 1975).

Some other towns, such as Reading, sought also to have their archaeology taken seriously, but the interest shown by local authorities varied, and it was partly to try to achieve a balance that the Inspectorate of Ancient Monuments commissioned reports in the 1970s on the implications for archaeology of development. Apart from the Isle of Wight, which combined rural and urban survey (Basford 1980), all the counties produced urban implication reports. These included what are still useful historical and documentary summaries, particularly for the large number of smaller market towns that had until then tended to be neglected (Astill 1978; Haslam 1976; Hughes 1976; Penn 1980). They were not exclusively about the Middle Ages, as some towns were Roman or at least had a Roman background; but the main emphasis inevitably was medieval, which caused some disquiet amongst archaeologists of earlier periods or with rural interests, who felt that too much attention was being paid to what was only a small fragment of the overall study of the past. A sense that the archaeology of medieval towns was something separate can be seen in Ann Ellison's enormously thoughtful implications report (1981), in which urban archaeology had a section by a different author (Stephen Dunmore, who soon afterwards left archaeology but eventually became more influential to it as a senior executive involved in the distribution of money from the National Lottery).

The rural archaeology of later medieval Wessex was not neglected. An early example of an excavation of a deserted medieval village site was undertaken at Holworth in Dorset in the 1950s by Philip Rahtz (Fig 5.2), who was to become one of the best-known post-Roman archaeologists, and a pioneer of open-area excavation. This work was funded by a private individual for training, an enlightened act of sponsorship (Rahtz 1959; 2001, 78). Another early excavation was by John Musty and David Algar at Gomeldon, Wiltshire, still the only such site to have yielded a gold coin, though the interpretation of the main structure as a long-house has been called in question on practical grounds – an internal drain may mean a dairy, not a cow-shed – and cultural; this form of housing is not simply something found in any grazing area, but seems geographically specific to the west (Musty and Algar 1986; Gardiner 2000, 163–5). Peter Fowler's motorway work included the M4 in Wiltshire, and publicity from the destruction caused by such developments was a major spur to action, with Peter Fasham's work on the M3 in Hampshire a noteworthy 1970s' example; that road ploughed through part of a medieval site at Popham (Fasham 1987) and a surprisingly rare example of a late Saxon/early Norman rural structure outside Winchester (Fasham, Farwell and Whinney 1989, 75–8). Attrition by the plough was not so eye-catching as destruction by earth-scraping, and it was much more difficult to find funding for sites in the countryside that were not immediately threatened with total obliteration.

Fig 5.2 Surviving earthworks of the deserted medieval village at Holworth, Dorset, looking west. The square earthworks are the sites of individual houses and outbuildings, one of which was excavated by Philip Rahtz in the 1950s. Each property had a croft on which midden rubbish could be spread, vegetables grown, and a pig tethered. The crofts are carefully hedged off from the valuable meadow along either side of the stream on the right (© English Heritage)

Rural investigation by fieldwork other than excavation was promoted by the Royal Commission's work in Dorset, their splendidly produced inventory volumes containing many earthwork surveys of deserted and shrunken medieval sites. A summary by Christopher Taylor showed how landscape history could throw light on settlement and prosperity (1970). The Commission's transfer to Wiltshire led to work on Salisbury Plain that revealed how much survived within the army ranges; whole plans of sites such as Imber, blocks of strip lynchets, and isolated downland barns and sheep-pens were recorded, reflecting changing population pressures and economic circumstances, as 12th-/13th-century expansion demanded more arable, and 14th-/15th-century contraction favoured grazing (McOmish, Field and Brown 2002, 109–34). Fieldwalking programmes produced comparable results from the collection of pottery scatters; most of this work with late medieval relevance has been done in Hampshire (Shennan 1985, 91–103; Light, Schofield and Shennan 1995), but has been taken up by Stephen Clarke and a group from the Berkshire Archaeological Society.

Recent work

For better or worse, later medieval archaeology is concerned with a period in which documents are informative about many aspects of life, particularly politics, religion and the law. As these were dominated by the wealthy and powerful, later medieval archaeology has been criticised for dealing too much with the grand monuments that they created. Yet a better understanding of these leads to a better understanding of their place in society and the impact that they had. At New Salisbury, for instance, the cathedral was intended in the first half of the 13th century to have no more than a low central tower; the upper part and the great spire came in the next century, necessitating internal changes affecting the sense of space (Tatton-Brown 1991). It includes adaptation and addition, just as does the plan of the new town grafted on to it, which archaeology has also shown to be more piece-meal than it might at first appear (Cave-Penney 2005). The effect of another major church, Reading Abbey, upon the town which served it has been explored in waterfront excavations (Hawkes and Fasham 1997). Old Sarum's predecessor, Sherborne, became an abbey; a fundamentally late-Saxon building was transformed, by extension and adaptation rather than by wholesale demolition, into a Gothic and Perpendicular one (Keen and Ellis 2005). The Romsey nunnery has also had its later history amplified by archaeology – its nave was extended in the later Norman period and a new east end subsequently replaced separate Norman chapels, creating a unitary Lady Chapel, but with its great Norman crossing retained (Scott 1996).

Studies of various lesser religious houses have been undertaken, both of their churches and of other buildings in their precincts (eg at Wherwell; Roberts 1998). Some work has been done on hospitals, and Simon Roffey made good use of Wessex examples in his studies of chantry chapels (2007). Wessex has fared less well in consideration of burials, however, as it provided almost no examples to the fine study of medieval practice by Roberta Gilchrist and Barney Sloane (2005).

The great churches in Wessex reflect the ambitions of its bishops, abbots and priors; parish churches tend to reflect lay priorities and therefore the wealth of the people. As that was not great, and few sons of the counties prospered in London and lavished patronage on their birthplaces, it is urban churches such as St John's, Devizes, St Thomas', Salisbury, St Nicholas', Newbury, and Holy Cross chapel, Basingstoke (Hare 2007), that generally had the most money spent on them.

The archaeology of lesser urban churches was pioneered in post-war London (Grimes 1968, 182–209), which the Biddles' work in Winchester on St Pancras and St Mary developed into an exemplary demonstration of the way in which excavation could recover sequences of expansion and retraction, and adaptation for new liturgical requirements (Biddle 1972, 104–15). A minor church excavated in Trowbridge, Wiltshire, had its parochial function extinguished by the imposition of the 12th-century castle; this site had the extra dimension of a graveyard, initially reduced in size and then also closed by the castle, that has provided information about people's health, life expectancy and burial practices (Fig 5.3; Graham and Davies 1993, 37–41, 63–74 and 120–7, report by V Jenkins).

In the countryside, Hatch Warren church and its surrounding graveyard – and other settlement traces – were investigated as part of the expansion of modern Basingstoke (Fig 5.4; Fasham and Keevill 1995, 76–148). This church and Otterbourne (Hinton 1990) typify a number of rural churches that did not grow in plan after the end of the 12th century, despite population growth, although Hatch Warren had its small chancel replaced with a much larger

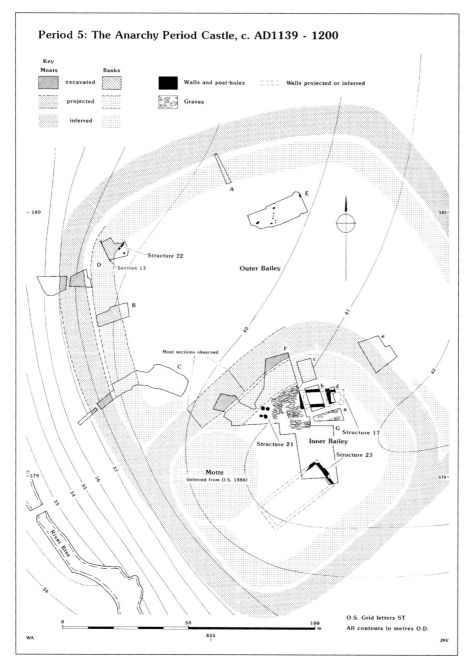

Fig 5.3 Plan of excavations in Trowbridge, Wiltshire, by Wessex Archaeology in the 1980s. The nave and chancel of a small late-Saxon church are shown in solid black, with its surrounding graveyard. Originally outside the entrance to a manorial enclosure, the church came to be incorporated into the bailey of a Norman castle. The building's function was changed, but for a time part of the graveyard stayed in use (© Wessex Archaeology)

one, probably to allow the altar to be placed at the east end and to give the congregation a view of the priest elevating the Host, reflecting liturgical changes and new Eucharist practices. Yateley, in contrast, saw a series of expansions despite technically being a chapel, including the building of a bell-tower (Hinton and Oake 1983), a common late medieval addition as heavier bells regularly tolled the Church's message further across the fields and hopefully deeper into people's minds.

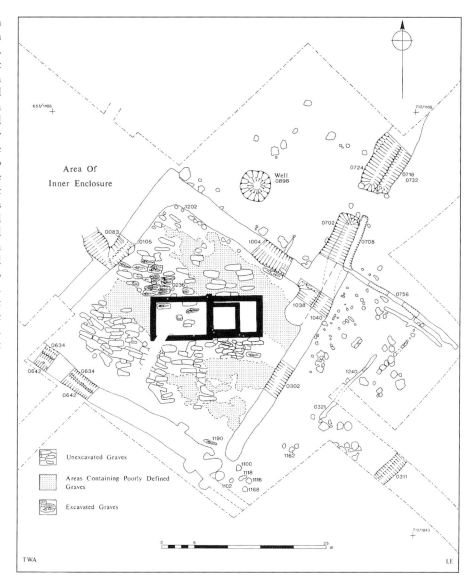

Fig 5.4 Hatch Warren church and graveyard, excavated by Wessex Archaeology in 1987–90. The original small late Saxon chancel was replaced by a much larger one at the end of the 12th century, but no other changes were made before it lost its parochial status in 1380. The small square graveyard was aligned with buildings, and presumably also streets and paths, outside it, not liturgically east–west like the church and graves (© Wessex Archaeology)

Reconciling archaeological evidence with documentary is not always straightforward: at Trowbridge, the easy assumption that the castle was a product of the Anarchy could be neither denied nor confirmed – the de Bohun family may have started work on it before King Stephen's reign. Similarly, Carisbrooke on the Isle of Wight is not documented as a defensive place before the Conquest, but seems in fact to have been a substantial 11th-century enclosure, and the assumption that its motte represents the first fortification was shown to be incorrect (Young 2000, 191–5). Portchester's keep-tower has been shown to have a more complex architectural history than had been thought, developing from a single-skin structure to a double-thickness stone tower of only two storeys – unless it had a timber superstructure – that was raised to its present height in the later 12th century (Munby and Renn 1985, 72–87). Again, adaptation and

Fig 5.5 Ludgershall Castle, Wiltshire, reconstruction by Peter Dunn of the inner enclosure as it would have looked in the mid-14th century. The stone tower was built c 1200–10 by King John across the line of an existing bank, and was therefore not primarily defensive; instead, it gave views out across the adjoining hunting grounds. Adjacent to it were royal chambers and a chapel, making it a comfortable royal residence rather than a castle. In the centre is the grand hall built by Henry III in 1244 (© English Heritage)

alteration suggest changing ideas about the need for an imposing and dominating focal point.

Hampshire was one of the first counties in which castles were reviewed in relation to their landscape rather than just to their owners and defences (Hughes 1989). Ludgershall Castle, Wiltshire, with its park and adjacent town, became a 13th-century country house, castle only in name and by dint of having a tower, its earthworks designed to give pleasant walks and views of the surrounding park and distant hills (Fig 5.5; Ellis 2000). In Berkshire, Windsor's remodelling over a long period of time was also associated with its great park. The discovery of traces of the building intended by Edward III for the chivalric Round Table which he was planning to establish after the great feast of 1344, followed by his abandonment of it as political circumstances changed and the Order of the Garter knights gave him a better guarantee of support, shows how such buildings played their part in the development of the state (Munby *et al* 2007). Berkshire's other main contribution to castle studies is Donnington, now dominated by its twin-towered, five-storey gate tower built by a courtier at the end of the 14th century and part of the debate about the extent to which such grand late medieval houses were seriously defensive (Emery 2006, 83–5).

The French raids of the 1330s and 1380s meant that defence was a serious issue. Even if Donnington, well inland, was not likely to last for long against a determined siege, new problems are shown at Portchester, where Assheton's Tower, built 1376–81, is claimed as the first to have been constructed in England with provision for all-round cover by the 'gunnes' (Munby and Renn 1985, 95). Another early artillery tower was built in or before the 1420s as an external extension to Southampton's city walls. This provided for heavier guns than were allowed for in the 1360s' emergency, which was probably when blocked-up warehouse entrances had a line of gun-loops set into them. On the Isle of Wight, Quarr Abbey may have built a sea-facing wall with gun loops at much the same time. Piecemeal defences were seen to be inadequate, however, and Henry V's *Grace Dieu*, now trapped in the mud in the River Hamble, is the first sign of a Royal Navy; it was not maintained, and the *Mary Rose* represents its revival by the Tudors, seen also in the choice of Portsmouth for the first royal dry dock in the 1490s and in the royal forts – the south coast could not bear the costs of such new systems on its own, and the role of the state increased proportionately (Saunders, A, 1989, 15–52).

Great houses did not all have even the semblance of being defensive; the bishop of Winchester's palace at Waltham (Hare 1988), and the king's Clarendon (James and Robinson 1988), spread liberally because they did not need to be confined within high towered walls. A lesser royal house, the Tidgrove of 1170s' documents, is currently being investigated (Fig 5.6; eg CBA Wessex *Newsletter*, autumn 2009, 19); it was used for a much shorter time than the comparable site at Faccombe Netherton, where a sequence from the 10th to the 15th centuries has shown not only building changes but also social and economic trends (Fairbrother 1990). Still-standing structures include 'King John's House' at Romsey, now known

Fig 5.6 The royal wine cellar excavated at Tidgrove by Kristian Strutt for the University of Southampton and the Kingsclere Heritage Association. Royal accounts of expenditure refer to work at Tidgrove only in the 1170s, but the site was certainly used for longer than a mere decade (© University of Southampton)

Fig 5.7 Glazed jugs of the 13th and early 14th century excavated at the kilns at Laverstock, outside Salisbury, by David Algar and John Musty in the 1960s. As well as being close to the major market in the city, the Laverstock potters had the advantage of an occasional bulk order; at least two loads of 1000 vessels each were delivered to the royal kitchen at Winchester Castle in the 1260s (© Salisbury and South Wiltshire Museum)

to be a misnomer because precise dating by dendrochronology of its principal tie-beam to 1256 establishes that it cannot be the building referred to in earlier documents (Allen 1999). Many of these houses, if royal, were associated with forests. If maintained, they became associated with deer parks, which occur in all the Wessex counties; the balance between their social and their economic roles is a current topic (Bond 1994; Mileson 2009). Fishponds were another status symbol, and the origin of such well-known open waters as Fleet and Alresford ponds (Roberts 1986); so too, of course, were moats.

Parks, ponds and moats often took up land that could have been used for agriculture, and the extent to which they therefore reduced the ability of the peasantry to lease small holdings from their lords is one of the topics that explores the relationships between the different social levels; in some areas, moated sites were probably constructed by better-off peasants rather than by their lords. Investment in fields, crops and stock is not easily explored by archaeology, though consumption of animals at least can be investigated through surviving bone deposits. More obvious evidence of consumption is provided by pottery; a small medieval rural site such as Wroughton Copse, near Marlborough, Wiltshire, has a much more limited range than urban or castle sites, but it may be more important that its peasants could exercise some degree of choice between different jugs and cooking-pots at the local market, as they had the wherewithal to buy such things (Fig 5.7; Brown 1997; Hinton 2010). Although Gomeldon remains the only excavated site from which a gold coin has been recovered, the large numbers of coins now being found and reported by metal-detector users shows that no later than the early 13th century, peasants were part of an active currency-using economy.

Rahtz's excavation at Holworth showed one way in which peasants could exercise choice, by investment in building (1959). The demonstration of a change in the 13th century to buildings that had drystone footings, and therefore greater potential for durable timber-framing to be set on them, has proved to be a national trend. Rahtz also showed that earthworks are not a direct guide to structural evidence below, and that considerable time and patience, and therefore money, are needed for the open-area excavation that he demonstrated to be necessary for such sites. Consequently most subsequent work has resulted from rescue, such as Popham on the M3 (Fasham 1987); other large-scale rural excavations have been a consequence of urban expansion, such as Basingstoke's over Hatch Warren, where traces of 12th-century structures with timbers set in the ground showed how non-durable they would have been (Fasham and Keevill 1995, 83–108). From the 13th century, survival of rural structures becomes a possibility, not just of manorial buildings, but of crucks and box-frame farmhouses, with dendrochronology again giving dating precision (eg Roberts 2003). This feeds into vexed discussions of the impact of the Black Death and other 14th- and 15th-century problems, their effect on the economy and the changes that resulted, such as desertions and shrinkage of settlements, and the sheep-driven rise in Wiltshire's prosperity relative to other counties, and Hampshire's virtual stagnation despite rabbit husbandry (Hare 1994).

Towns were fed by the countryside, and in return supplied pottery, clothes, boots and shoes, and petty luxuries; they provided opportunities for work, and the ambitious could hope to thrive in them. They also have to be viewed as different sorts of space. Somewhere like Salisbury may have had a metaphysical element in its planning, geometry reflecting God's design – but the failure to achieve perfect rectangles equally reflects Man's imperfections (Lilley 2002, 163–7 for the concept)! Excavations show how close-packed people were, with one of Winchester's richest citizens establishing his courtyard house deep into what modern senses would see as the squalor of the damp, craft-focused Brooks (Scobie et al 1991, 40–54).

Future developments

It is fifteen years since a book with 'Wessex' in its title last focused on the medieval period (Aston and Lewis (eds) 1994). Some of the contributions in it opened debates that are still running, such as the extent to which desertion and shrinkage of rural sites are a facet of the 14th and 15th centuries, or the result of subsequent emparking – though it has been pointed out that villages weakened at the end of the Middle Ages would not have been robust enough to offer much resistance to subsequent land-owners' pressure on them (Hughes 1994; Hare 1994). Lewis' paper (1994) on Wiltshire raised the difficult matter of the different sizes and shapes of medieval settlements, and how they reflect topography and agriculture; her method has been criticised for not taking into account changes in the two hundred years before the first reasonably reliable county-wide maps were produced (Chandler 1996, 154–5). Rather similarly, a country-wide attempt

Fig 5.8 Great Chalfield manor house already had a moat and buildings when acquired by Thomas Tropenell. In 1452 he began to build the great T-plan hall, with kitchen and other services in the range to its right, and parlour and chambers to its left. To the left is an outer court, for stables and farm buildings. On the right, the existing parish church could be viewed as though it were a private chapel (Neosnaps via Wikimedia Commons)

to categorise areas of dispersion and nucleation has been challenged because its 'zones' are too arbitrary, and underestimate the cohesiveness of linear settlements (Hinton 2005). These are certainly topics that need further consideration and refinement. Dorset and Berkshire could also usefully have new overall surveys, to put into perspective work such as that by Taylor for the former, recognising regular plot widths in the Winterbourne valley (1994), or to put an archaeological dimension on the work by Yates on the latter (1999). How did different landlords affect settlements and farming, for instance?

Voices have been raised recently to say that late medieval archaeology has focused too much on economic questions, and it is certainly the case that studies of social relations and people's use of their built space and their expression of ownership of fields and property could be extended. Studies of churches to show people's attitudes to the places in which they worshipped and where they might hope to be buried could be explored in Wessex as they have been in Devon and Norfolk (Graves 2000). Economic issues are part and parcel of other questions, however, such as the ambitions of the peasantry. Their ability to influence their own lives through production of small surpluses that they could sell would have given them some degree of flexibility, even in the 13th century. The proliferation of reported finds made by metal-detector users needs to be taken into consideration in this context, as it is not only coins that are proving more common than had been realised.

Tied to the nature of peasants' prosperity is their ability to use the market, and the expanding network of towns. Here, more publication of results is needed in some of the biggest towns, though good work has been achieved, for instance in Salisbury (summary by Cave-Penney 2005), in Poole (Horsey 1992; Watkins 1994) and many others; indeed the point has been reached where so many small excavations have been done in so many small towns that an assessment of what has been achieved overall would be useful. Just how important the small towns were as motors of the economy is a national issue (eg Dyer 2003), and their proliferation in Wessex should be viewed in relationship to great towns and estates, to routeways, and to local specialisation in dairying as compared to sheep-rearing.

Prosperity in the late Middle Ages could take a successful man (a deliberate choice of gender) a long way, and more studies of how a career in law and administration, or in royal campaigning, could make a fortune would be useful. That of the 'perilous, covetous' Thomas Tropenell of Great Chalfield, Wiltshire, was particularly welcome as so much of the evidence about his aspirations derives from the physical survival of his chantry chapel as well as of substantial parts of his manor house (Fig 5.8; Driver 2000; Emery 2006, 569–74). The gentry and their fates was tied up with the great lords, though baronial and ducal interest in Wessex was less overbearing than in some other parts of England, probably because there were too many prelates and abbots to stop them from creating fiefdoms. Such matters are national issues, to be explored at local level.

Discovering industrial Wessex

Peter Stanier

CBA and Industrial Archaeology

CBA Wessex and industrial archaeology (IA) grew up together over the last half century. During his time at the Ordnance Survey, O G S Crawford saw that archaeological techniques could be used at sites of the 19th and 20th centuries. There were already practitioners, although the term 'industrial archaeology' was not devised until the 1950s. It came to mean the recording, even excavation, and, if necessary, preservation of industrial monuments that elucidated something of our more recent social and technological past.

In 1958 a first CBA Industrial Archaeology Research Committee was established under the chairmanship of Prof W F (Peter) Grimes, Director of the Institute of Archaeology and a former assistant of Crawford. There was then no real idea of the extent or variety of industrial monuments surviving in Britain, nor how rapidly this resource was being lost. The CBA's initiative led to the creation of the National Record of Industrial Monuments, with record cards to be filled in mostly by volunteers. It was a start, but the survey was soon found to be inadequate and responses from around the country were patchy. The CBA arranged a first national conference in 1959 to give industrial archaeology an official launch. The birth of this new subject was not without its critics, nor was it helped by the unfortunate combination of 'archaeology' and 'industry'. The subject meant different things to different people and Kenneth Hudson, author of the first handbook on industrial archaeology, wrote mischievously that it could be an academic subject or 'an agreeable hobby' (Hudson 1963, 34).

The national development of industrial archaeology has been summarised elsewhere (eg Cossons 2000) but in Wessex its rapid rise in popularity during the 1960s was accompanied by the formation of local or county societies, drawing on a strong amateur base with abundant enthusiasm for recording and preservation. By the end of the decade the main societies included the Berkshire Archaeology Society IA Group, Poole (WEA) IA Group, Salisbury and South Wiltshire IA Society, Portsmouth Polytechnic IA Society, Southampton University IA Group and the Wiltshire Archaeology and Natural History Society IA Sub Committee. Only Dorset remained without a county society until the late 1980s and now there is a society on the Isle of Wight. The results of early research projects and surveys appeared in county archaeological journals before some societies took on their own publishing.

The industrial world of 1958

Fifty years ago the *Queen Mary* still docked regularly in Southampton on transatlantic voyages, but her days were numbered because the Boeing 707 jet airliner was then being introduced. Steam trains still ran in many places and Dr Richard Beeching had not yet been heard of. For better or worse, the Beeching 'axe' unintentionally made available miles of potential routes for the railway preservation movement and the Mid-Hants Railway, or Watercress Line as it is popularly known, and the shorter Swanage Railway in Dorset are two Wessex region successes re-opened by volunteers. To the archaeologist's eye, Beeching also created a new swathe of interesting linear earthworks in the field.

Away from the railways, canals such as the Kennet and Avon were woefully derelict in 1958. Volunteers with a mission and support from British Waterways eventually restored its whole length to a working waterway, officially opened by the Queen in August 1990. The canal's famous Crofton beam engines were only retired in 1959 but the Kennet and Avon Canal Trust got them both steaming again by 1971 (see Corfield, this volume pp 150–152). The 1812 engine is the world's oldest Boulton and Watt pumping engine still doing its original job at its original site. Of additional interest nearby, the Wilton windmill of 1821 was restored to working order by the Wiltshire Buildings Trust and Wiltshire County Council in 1976 (Fig 5.9).

Fig 5.9 Wilton
Windmill in
Wiltshire is the
superb outcome of
a restoration project
in the early 1970s
(© Peter Stanier)

Changing perceptions

Fifty years ago Victorian buildings were generally deemed 'ugly' and most industrial sites were even worse. Perceptions change and 'industrial heritage' is now an important part of our early 21st-century culture. Wessex boasts spectacular industrial monuments of national importance, notably I K Brunel's Great Western Railway with the Maidenhead Bridge, Box Tunnel, and the railway village and engineering works in Swindon. The latter, still a major employer in 1958, was run down and closed like so many other industries but large historic buildings survive as a shopping centre, railway museum, and English Heritage's headquarters. Such 'adaptive re-use' or 'constructive conservation' works well if done sensitively. In Hampshire the value of Portsmouth's historic dockyard is fully recognised, where HMS *Victory* has been joined by the salvaged *Mary Rose* (see Hamer, this volume pp 172–173) and the restored HMS *Warrior*, a ship of the industrial age. The encircling Victorian fortifications, such as Fort Nelson on Portsdown Hill, were built on a truly impressive industrial scale. The growth of industrial collections in museums reflects the popularity of exhibits to which visitors can relate. For example, Milestones at Basingstoke, with its recreated street scenes, can now show large items from Tasker & Co and other transport manufacturers previously held in storage by Hampshire County Council. Trowbridge Museum has a fine collection relating to woollen textiles, while many other museums have something of industrial interest. There are restored corn mills open to the public, while utility companies have museums in a Victorian water pumping station near Weymouth and an Edwardian electricity power station at Christchurch.

Professional archaeologists became increasingly involved, for example on the Kennet and Avon Canal, where recording included the excavation of an unusual turf-sided lock on the Kennet Navigation section at Monkey Marsh, Thatcham, in 1989–90 (Harding and Newman 1997). Phil Harding, 'generally a specialist in the Palaeolithic', confessed to having 'developed an expertise in the archaeology of turf-sided locks.' A budding industrial archaeologist perhaps? Professional and amateur specialists have worked together on many sites and a good example is the Town Mill at Lyme Regis, Dorset, which was restored carefully using the combined expertise of an archaeologist, historian, and millwright (Graham *et al* 2005).

Focus on Hampshire

Hampshire, the host county for the CBA Wessex 50th anniversary conference, has been especially active since the early years. The University of Southampton's Extra-Mural Department offered an industrial archaeology programme from 1965 and within three years the Southampton University IA Group (SUIAG) was formed under the guidance of Edwin Course. The Hampshire Field Club's *Proceedings* soon included summaries of surveys of Hampshire mills, roads, breweries, brickworks, and aerodromes. Later surveys published by SUIAG itself included ice houses, the Itchen Navigation, farm buildings, and gazetteers covering Hampshire and the Isle of Wight (Ellis 1975; Moore 1984) as well as newsletters and an annual journal. Renamed the Hampshire IA Society since 2001, there remain close links with the Hampshire Mills Group, Twyford Waterworks Trust, the Tram 57 project, and SS Shieldhall Group.

A highlight of the society's volunteer work was the restoration of the *Golden Lion* Brewhouse at Southwick (Fig 5.10), culminating in a special brew in June

Fig 5.10 Southampton University Industrial Archaeology Group restored Southwick's Golden Lion brewhouse to brewing condition in 1982. Work included refurbishing the mash tun (seen here), vertical boiler, horizontal steam engine and pump (© Tony Yoward)

Fig 5.11 Volunteers from the Hampshire Mills Group at work restoring a waterwheel for pumping water at Timsbury in July 2006 (© Nigel Smith)

1985. Lord Asa Briggs drew the first pint and, because Customs and Excise forbade the beer to be sold, a very willing gathering was delighted to indulge in its appreciation (Moore 1992). The Hampshire Mills Group has been involved in recording and restoration at over 50 sites (Fig 5.11) including the Bursledon Windmill and Eling Tide Mill near Southampton. An unusual project was the restoration in 2002 of a 100-year-old wind engine used for water pumping at Crux Easton (Fig 5.12; Gregory 2003), while more recent work has been the

Fig 5.12 The Crux
Easton wind engine,
erected in the 1890s
for pumping water,
was restored from a
derelict state in 2002
by the Hampshire
Mills Group (© Tony
Yoward)

inspection of the fire-damaged tide mill at Beaulieu. These hands-on industrial
archaeologists and the Hampshire Buildings Preservation Trust were also active
in saving the working Whitchurch Silk Mill and establishing the Burseldon
Brickworks Industrial Museum.

Kimmeridge, fieldwork, and CBA Wessex

Fieldwork can reveal more low-key but nevertheless important industrial sites
in the Wessex landscape. Personally, having investigated extractive industries in
Dorset (eg Stanier 1993; 1996; 2000), my choice for a site with some connection
with CBA Wessex would be Kimmeridge Bay, for its oil well was discovered
exactly 50 years ago and the descendant of its original nodding donkey is still
pumping away. Visitors come here to enjoy superb scenery, explore the shoreline,
or perhaps admire the cliff-top Clavell Tower, moved to a safer position in 2008.
Yet this spot on the World Heritage 'Jurassic Coast' may be described as an
industrial landscape. Kimmeridge is a name familiar to archaeologists and there

is something here for most specialists, not forgetting abandoned medieval fields and farms or shipwrecks out on the Ledges. Kimmeridge shale was exploited for ornaments in prehistory, and even items of furniture in Roman times.

Archaeologists dug at Rope Lake Hole in 1979 (Woodward 1987) and in the following year excavations began on the site of Sir William Clavell's short-lived glassworks of 1618–23 (Crossley 1987). Clavell built a sturdy pier, now destroyed, and the cove here also saw alum and salt production, all three industries using the local oil shale or 'Kimmeridge Coal' as fuel. All went quiet until the Blackstone shale was exploited commercially for its oil content between 1848 and 1890 when it was shipped for refining in retorts at Weymouth and then Wareham. A high sulphur content meant that the three main enterprises quickly failed, but not before one firm exported shale to Paris, New York, and Australia. They left behind evidence of tramways, pier foundations, collapsed shafts and levels along the cliffs to Clavell's Hard (Fig 5.13), and a terrace of workers' cottages. Even a limestone band was quarried from the cliffs and shipped to the Isle of Wight for making cement. Completing the picture, Second World War dragons' teeth and pillboxes defend landing places, and there are remains of target ranges too (Fig 5.14). Fifty years ago such structures were not even considered as archaeology. After all, they were then only eighteen years old but today their national significance is accepted alongside earlier Great War features.

Fig 5.13 Seen from the cliff above, the foundations of old piers and other structures can be discerned amongst the foreshore rocks at Kimmeridge Bay (© Peter Stanier)

Bill Putnam and his observant fieldwork

It is gratifying that practical fieldwork can still uncover something new from the industrial past. Discovering industrial Wessex was the late Bill Putnam's planned title for his talk to the conference and I am certain that he would have spoken about the chance discovery of his 'Puddletown Tramway' while surveying the Roman road through Puddletown Forest in Dorset with students some years ago. Having finished investigating Dorchester's Roman aqueduct, Bill returned to the forest in 2004 to make sense of his discovery (Fig 5.15). The result appears to be a 7km narrow gauge tramway course with cuttings, embankments, and inclines perhaps linking sand pits and brickworks and constructed between 1839 and 1857 (Putnam 2004; 2005). Perhaps the mystery tramway failed before rails could be laid along the completed earthworks, for there are no apparent historical references and even the Ordnance Survey missed it off its maps.

Fig 5.14 Anti-tank blocks and a small Type 25 pillbox defend a landing point at Gaulter Gap in Kimmeridge Bay (© Peter Stanier)

Fig 5.15 Bill Putnam investigating a tramway embankment surrounded by trees in Puddletown Forest near Dorchester in March 2004 (© Peter Stanier)

The future

Future discoveries will almost certainly be made, while reassessments of industrial monuments will lead to new interpretations. We will see further constructive conservation, while more traditional restoration work gathers apace on the long-abandoned Wilts and Berks Canal. The modern period is providing a steady stream of new industrial sites which will continue to be endangered, risking the valuable work undertaken in the past. There are major issues regarding the recording of very large structures which are clearly beyond the expertise of amateurs, like Fawley Power Station or the Esso oil refinery next door (we may not wish to preserve them!).

Over the past 50 years industrial archaeology has been driven forward largely by amateur volunteer groups, with the significant benefit that many members had actual working experience and understanding of the industries they were trying to record or restore. There was also a wide range of expertise to draw upon, from engineers to surveyors. Industrial archaeology groups in all the Wessex counties including the Isle of Wight have done valuable work but we cannot ignore the fact that average ages are rising and the recruitment of younger members is a nationwide problem. We must ask who will be the volunteers out there discovering our industrial Wessex in 2058?

The Kennet and Avon Canal

Mike Corfield

Although Wessex is primarily renowned for its prehistory it is also the home of notable monuments of the Industrial Revolution. Chief among these is the Kennet and Avon Canal Navigation (K&A), an amalgam of three separate waterways. The Kennet Navigation from Reading to Newbury was opened in 1723, the Avon Navigation from Bath to Bristol in 1727, and the linking canal in 1810. The River Kennet in Reading was from early medieval times a safe haven off the Thames, and to bring the navigation to Newbury involved the construction of 22 locks and 18km of artificial cuts in its 29-km length. The Avon, which had been navigable to Bath since time immemorial, was a much larger river than the Kennet and needed only six locks and no artificial cuts. The canal was first proposed at a meeting in Hungerford in 1788, but its Act of Parliament was not approved until 1794.

The new cross-country route was a great success and regular dividends were paid to investors. However, in 1841 the railway from London to Bristol was opened and merchants switched to this more reliable method of transport. The K&A nevertheless survived, though after the Second World War it was in a very poor state, its swan-song being the transport of materials to build a line of wartime defences. Happily, the post-war years saw the rise of the Inland Waterways Association, whose aim was to re-open abandoned canals for commercial traffic and pleasure boating. An offshoot of this was the Kennet and Avon Canal Association (later Trust), which spent most of the 1950s fighting to prevent the

Fig 5.16 This crane at the Marquis of Ailesbury's wharf at Burbage was the last survivor of many of its type on the wharves along the canal. It was first rescued from dereliction by the Salisbury and South Wiltshire Industrial Archaeology Group in the 1970s and is now undergoing further restoration by the Claverton Pumping Station team (© Kennet and Avon Canal Trust)

Fig 5.17 The Kennet and Avon Canal re-born – the magnificent Caen Hill flight of fourteen locks at Devizes after its re-opening in 1994 (© Kennet and Avon Canal Trust)

Inland Waterways Executive and its successors from legally abandoning the canal. The climate changed yet again in the 1960s with the creation of the British Waterways Board (BWB), which took a more positive attitude to restoration, though still constrained by a shortage of money and power.

Through these early years the Association had carried out valuable work to prevent further decline: dredging in Reading using an old spoon dredger that by rights should have been in a museum, digging out the notorious dry section of the canal between the Dundas and Avoncliff aqueducts, clearing weed using a waterborne mechanical cutter designed and built by an Association member, and clearing the locks on the Caen Hill flight at Devizes. With support from the Trust a team of enthusiasts restored the inoperative Crofton pumping station to working condition. At Claverton a team of volunteers, primarily from Bath University, set about restoring the unique waterwheel and pumps, which had become unusable in the early 1950s because the job of pump keeper had been considered unnecessary by the new owners.

An early initiative was the creation of a team of lengthsmen (and women), each responsible for a length of the canal; they sent in regular reports on its condition and by 1963 there was a card index of every structure on the canal. These records were primarily concerned with condition and risk but inevitably important

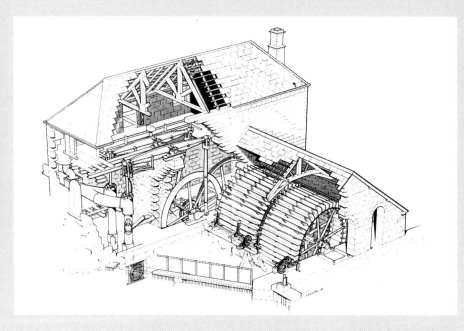

Fig 5.18 This isometric drawing of the Claverton pumping house near Bath typifies the high standard of recording used to document the canal's surviving historic structures (© Kennet and Avon Canal Trust)

historical information was documented too. Another Trust member carried out a detailed survey of the canal and its structures, which was first published in map form in 1969. As BWB became more reconciled to the restoration of the canal it was prepared to carry out work on derelict structures, but only at the Trust's expense. Volunteers were still able to help by preparing locks for gate fitting and were even allowed to restore Bull's Lock east of Newbury in its entirety. Sadly, however, all volunteer work on the canal ended in 1978 when BWB union members refused to co-operate with Trust working parties.

Research into the physical remains of the K&A has been regularly reported in the pages of *The Butty* (the Trust's official magazine). The significance of the remains was assessed in the 1970s as part of the CBA's Industrial Monument Survey, but only a handful of key sites was scheduled or listed. In 1966 the Trust leased the last of the buildings of the Newbury Wharf for use as a museum, and in the 1970s it leased the warehouse on Devizes Wharf for conversion by Trust volunteers into an interpretation centre. This and the need to provide interpretation at other sites along the canal led to a major effort to collect historical materials both for display and to create a historical archive. The resulting exhibition, with its focus on the people of the canal, won numerous awards and its archive has grown into a major source of information for researchers.

Today, when the restoration of industrial sites is often used as a focus for the regeneration of neglected urban areas, volunteers too often find themselves on the sidelines. In the case of the K&A, however, they still have a vital role to play in ensuring that the magnificent canal that they brought back to life is not swamped by inappropriate development. That now must be the key priority for the Kennet and Avon Canal Trust.

Post-medieval Wessex: breaking new ground

Richard Osgood

Unusually for this volume, many of the protagonists who were responsible for the creation of the top-most layers of the archaeological palimpsest are still alive. We shall consider here the material legacy of the 20th century – a century of conflict, of collapse of empires, of heightened archaeological awareness, both of the state and individual. 1958 was not simply the founding year of CBA Wessex; it was also the time of much political upheaval and event. Wessex would experience the first of many anti-nuclear marches – to the Atomic Weapons Establishment of Aldermaston – while further afield it was the year when bodies of unknown soldiers from the Great War and Korean Wars were repatriated to the National Cemetery at Arlington in Virginia. Although one might think that there is little to be gained from archaeological studies of an age within living memory, for which there is so much documentation, our discipline can still add hugely. For example, few people would now be surprised at a news bulletin which discussed the employment of 'forensic archaeologists' by the police force investigating a crime scene. Nor do the techniques of geophysical survey and forensic anthropological study coupled with DNA analysis seem alien – such is the coverage of our subject by the mass media.

In the later years of the 20th century, English Heritage recommended statutory protection for increasing numbers of near-contemporary monuments – Flying Corps headquarters and military badges carved into chalk hillsides in Wiltshire, practice trenches from the Great War in Pembrokeshire, RAF fighter pens in Kent, rocket testing sites in Cumbria are all now scheduled. During the same

Fig 5.19 This .303 cartridge case was recovered from the excavations at the Bustard Practice trenches on Salisbury Plain. Both live and blank rounds from the Great War were excavated. Unusually for Salisbury Plain, no ordnance was recovered that was later in date than the First World War (© Richard Osgood)

period the CBA's own Defence of Britain project showed just how vulnerable the archaeology of the contemporary past can be – as witnessed for example by the decline in the number of monuments such as pillboxes.

Along with my colleague and co-director, Martin Brown, I have had the good fortune to undertake research into one fragile collection of traces of the Great War in Wessex, the training of the Australian 3rd Division on Salisbury Plain in 1916 (Brown and Osgood 2009). We have excavated elements of the 'Bustard' practice trenches, finding the remnants of the training regime, with spent live ammunition, empty food packaging, traces of 'life in the trenches', and trench architecture (Fig 5.19). All this goes some way to dispel some myths of the Great War, of troops sent to their deaths in huge numbers with only the minimum of military doctrine inculcated within them. Here the Australian soldiers had practised hard for a specific event, the battle of Messines in 1917, even going as far as blowing up mines and capturing them in readiness for the main feature of this attack in Belgium. Messines was a colossal success and this was in no small part due to the training on the Plain.

Smaller vignettes were also illustrated by the material culture such as an 'Anzora' bottle found nearby – this a viola-scented hair tonic, far removed from the stereotype of the Australian soldier!

Perhaps most powerful, however, are some nearby carvings. A search through the woodland around the Bustard trenches also showed traces of the Australians. Carved into the wood of the beech trees of Halfmoon Copse to the north-west of the practice trenches is a series of names. A number of these are of Canadians and Americans from the period of the Second World War, some with addresses and even the names of sweethearts. In addition to these are names of men from Australia carved a quarter of a century earlier. Given that they are carved into a living surface which grows and stretches, these names are slightly less clear than their Second War counterparts, and slightly more lichen-covered. Nevertheless they can still be read and perhaps indicate a certain amount of quiet time for soldiers even when in their practice front-line positions.

Units as well as individuals are commemorated; one such is the 10th A I F (Australian Imperial Forces). One individual can be traced from his initials 'A.T.' in conjunction with the associated carved elements of 'Vic', '10' 'A.I.F.' and 'Orbost' (Fig 5.20). This man was Service Number 398 Lance Corporal Alexander Todd of the 38th AIF (10th Brigade, 3rd Division), a labourer from Orbost, Victoria. Alexander was wounded in the shoulder on 7 June 1917 at the Battle of Messines. He was later to be awarded the Military Medal before dying of wounds on 3 October 1918 after a shell hit his dugout. Some of his comrades complained that they should not have been in this dugout; they had been held up waiting for the Americans to join their advance in front of the Hindenburg Line. Alexander Todd now lies in Doingt Communal Cemetery extension in France; the carving is an incredibly poignant inscription.

References of this kind become especially intriguing if they can be associated with the remains of a soldier recovered from the battlefield or a makeshift

Fig 5.20 Tree carved by Alexander Todd at Halfmoon Copse on Salisbury Plain, close to the Bustard Practice trenches. Pte Todd trained here in 1916, his first major action being the Battle of Messines in 1917. He was killed in October 1918 in front of the Hindenburg Line (© Richard Osgood)

grave. This is something we felt when, on discovering the body of an Australian soldier at St Yvon, Belgium (part of the battle front of Messines), we excavated a wallet, coins, a knife, and other personal possessions. Although we have not yet been able to give him a name, he was probably one of those who had trained on Salisbury Plain, probably at the Bustard. With scientific breakthroughs into isotope analysis and DNA research, the chances of identifying the man have manifestly increased. Techniques that can be applied as readily to Beaker burials as to soldiers of the Great War perhaps show that the 20th century, although immediate, is still a period which can be regarded 'archaeologically'.

Whatever the motivation for these young men, so very far from home, to carve their names into the trees of an English training area, these small traces draw us as close to them as any diary account. As the trees die, so too will the surviving legacies of the soldiers – for archaeologists it is important that we record these messages before they fade. We can record such aborglyphs through such standard archaeological techniques as a photographic survey, and also through the same laser-scanning methodology used to record the dagger carvings at Stonehenge.

Carving on trees was not an activity limited to the Australians. Another set of beech trees on a series of round barrows at Tidworth, also on Salisbury Plain, has revealed many American names and a date of 1944 cut into their trunks – perhaps in the days and weeks leading up to Operation Overlord. Laser scanning has also been used to record the American graffiti within the barracks at Tidworth – names, places, armoured unit insignia, and even a depiction of an armoured car have all been found.

The Stonehenge Riverside Project is best known for its advancement of our understanding of the Neolithic and early Bronze Age communities of Wessex, yet this prehistoric landscape has an altogether more modern element draped over it. In the course of carrying out an extensive geophysical search for Neolithic deposits the survey team identified a large area to the west of Durrington Walls that looked not dissimilar in form to a Roman marching camp (Kate Welham, pers comm). Subsequent excavation showed that this had nothing to do with either Roman or prehistoric activity but instead was the brick footings and service trenches of a long-demolished army camp of Great War vintage – the barracks of amongst others the Australian 3rd Division whose soldiers had carved their names in the trees of Halfmoon Copse (Fig 5.21).

Aside from these survivals of the First and Second World Wars, Salisbury Plain has other more exotic landscapes to explore. There are East German (and now Middle Eastern) villages, Normandy (or Northern Irish) hedgerows, Russian entrenchments, and even a copy of the Siegfried Line (Fig 5.22). All this is part of what the French philosopher, Baudrillard, refers to as a 'simulacrum' of landscape (Baudrillard 1994).

One must not forget that Wessex also includes an incredibly important seascape. The work of Wessex Archaeology's maritime team (Anthony Firth, this volume) highlights the wonderful preservation of much of this material. Included within this are military aircraft, subject to the Protection of Military Remains Act, and wrecks from the 20th century too. In the next 50 years more and more work will need to be carried out on this material, whether in advance

Fig 5.21 Great War soldiers of the 2nd Australian Division in barracks. Such hut camps were a familiar sight throughout the UK in the Great War and leave strong archaeological traces (source: author's collection)

of dredging activities, renewable energy construction, or research in its own right.

Much of this may well be connected to important events from the recent past – association with a famous event can, after all, be an important consideration in selecting sites for designated protection. And do those events need only to be confined to our 20th-century military past? What about events connected with the suffrage movement, or with festival sites like Glastonbury? And could that ultimate in simulacrum, the film or television set, not yield material of interest to a society with such a vigorous appetite for nostalgia? As John Schofield has illustrated through his archaeological examination of the Peace Camp at Greenham Common (Schofield *et al* 2003), archaeology is about people, be they prehistoric, Roman, medieval, or those who lived in the recent past or are even still alive. The name carved in a tree,

Fig 5.22 Siegfried line – a series of anti-tank 'Dragon's Teeth' on Salisbury Plain representing German defensive positions (© Richard Osgood)

the camp site used by a protestor, the midden of food waste from an army barracks are no different to the evidence we use to reveal our more distant past. Perhaps we have come full circle. Although archaeology is a finite resource, new material culture and contemporary heritage is being added all the time.

Documenting the past

John Chandler

I think that my first encounter with the annual conferences of CBA Wessex was about 30 years ago, and it was not entirely auspicious. I was, for a few years, secretary of the South Wiltshire Industrial Archaeology Society, and had to present a brief report of the society's work. And very brief it was too. The conferences in those days tended to be arranged chronologically, which meant that industrial archaeology came at the end, when the late running of earlier speakers, and a certain disregard of industrial archaeology by so-called 'mainstream' archaeologists, exerted a palpable pressure on a young and inexperienced speaker to get it over with as quickly as possible. (I am told, though I was not there, that one such report, by an IA group restoring a brewery in the Portsmouth area, concluded by explaining that when they had finished they passed water through it.) Undeterred I was invited back, to a Winchester conference in 1996 to explain, as I recall, the history of the Wessex landscape from the Saxons to the 18th century – a rather tall order for 45 minutes – much of which turned on the observations of John Leland, the perfect travelling companion for such an occasion.

Indirectly my involvement with CBA Wessex was as editor's assistant and agitator's accomplice. Alison Borthwick, who would have been the life and soul of this conference, died as the result of a diabetic coma in 2001 at the age of 49. We were together from 1982, married in 1986 and separated in 1998. From 1984 to 2000 (with a brief gap) she was a committee member, and for two spells (1986–89, 1996–97) the CBA Wessex newsletter editor. A tireless champion of archaeological causes, she put phenomenal effort into enquiries, reports, consultative documents, and the like, and was always conscientiously working on things up to and beyond the last minute. My role in such circumstances generally involved proof reading, multiple photocopying, coffee-making, and rushing to the post (once catching a train to Birmingham to deliver something needed the same day).

Although she has no string of publications to her name, nor ever held an academic post, I do think that (aside from her CBA work) Alison's contribution to the development of archaeological practice in Wessex was significant. As Roy Canham's assistant in Wiltshire during the 1970s and 1980s she negotiated persistently and successfully with developers, archaeological units, and central and local government departments, using her considerable powers of persuasion in the service of her beloved archaeology. I meanwhile was Wiltshire's Local Studies librarian, a role which included developing an archaeological library, and for a time Roy and I sat at adjacent desks at Trowbridge. Alison and I collaborated on a 1984 report on Salisbury's archaeology, *Our Chequered Past*, which opened our eyes to how the historian's approach, and particularly the local history sources dispensed by people like me, and my colleagues in archives departments, could be exploited in the service of the day-to-day archaeological planning process.

Fig 5.23 Alison Borthwick, mid-1980s (© John Chandler)

Alison went freelance as an archaeological consultant in 1986, recognising that in a professional world that was becoming more civilized and regulated (no longer the 'Stonehenge in a bulldozer bucket' of the Rescue years) there was a role for someone with her particular skills. Employed by housebuilders, supermarket chains, planning consultants, and others, she helped them steer their way through the archaeological aspects of the planning process, interpreted for them local authority requirements, and engaged and monitored units working on excavations, surveys, and watching briefs. After 1990, following *Planning Policy Guidance* Note 16, a pattern of desktop assessments emerged. I was still supplying her with the documentary and cartographic elements of such assessments at the time of her death, and have also, for nearly twenty years, worked in this and similar roles with units, especially AC Archaeology and Wessex, on many hundreds of sites in the region and beyond.

For a local historian this has been a charmed life. Most of us are concerned with a single place, or at most a single county – perhaps two or three in the course of a career (as archivist or librarian, for instance). *PPG* 16 assessments require one to perform keyhole local history, as it were (just a few fields or a couple of burgage plots), anywhere, and so to experience the idiosyncrasies of the historical record and the way it is accessed all over the place.

When I first began this work archivists found my pursuit a novelty and I had to explain what I was trying to achieve. Now it is commonplace and understood, although I still run up against an old Catch 22. My brief, you see, from a local authority archaeologist, usually requires me to include copies of relevant manuscript maps in my report, but the rules, imposed by staff in the same authority, generally prohibit such copying except for private research, which patently mine is not. I have therefore spent my professional career signing pieces of paper assuring local authorities that I shall not supply copies to a third party – the very thing that I am being employed to do. And usually that third party, ultimately, is the local authority itself.

But much has changed for the better, in local history as in archaeology, since I began. New and commodious record offices and libraries almost everywhere; internet searching of online catalogues; digital photography of manuscript maps – to mention just three revolutions. And there has been an intellectual change too. When CBA Wessex began 50 years ago there was just emerging into popular consciousness the work of the so-called Leicester school of local history, with its integration of archaeology, landscape studies, fieldwork, place-names, and documentary research. Gradually during my career this approach has become the norm.

The historian's instinct is to couch research in terms of questions, the simpler the better. Maybe the simplest historical question of all is to stand

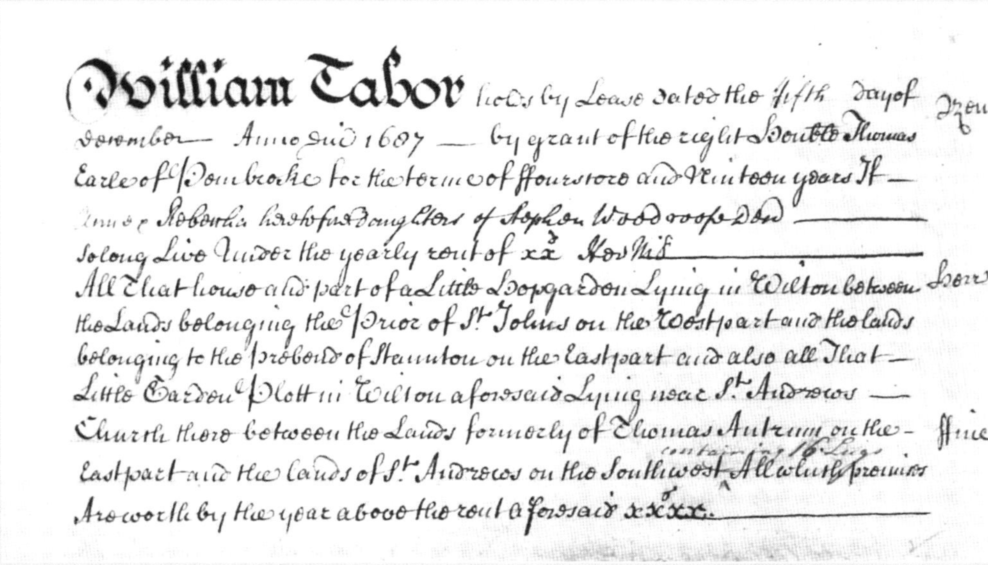

William Tabor holds by Lease dated the fifth day of

November — Anno dni 1607 — by grant of the right honble Thomas

Earle of Pembroke for the terme of ffourscore and Nineteen years If

Anne & Roberthe his two Daughters of Stephen Woodroofe Decd

Solong Live Under the yearly rent of xx Nov Mic

All That house and part of a Little Hoppgarden Lyeing in Wilton betweene

the Lands belonging the Prior of St Johns on the West part and the Lands

belonging to the Probend of Staunton on the East part and also all That

Little Garden Plott in Wilton aforesaid Lyeing neare St Andrews

Church there betweene the Lands formerly of Thomas Antrum on the

East part and the Lands of St Andrews on the Southwest All which premises

Are worth by the year above the rent aforesaid xxxx.

in a field, garden, or lane, and ask 'What has happened here?'. Precisely, of course, what archaeological excavation aims to discover, but it can also be attempted by the documentary historian, using a now well-trodden range of regular and, with a little lateral thinking, irregular sources. Every week, it seems, I go off to some record office briefed only with a coloured-in photocopy of a bit of a map. Often I am not sure why a routine study is being done – windfarm, supermarket, powerline, housing estate – but sometimes the research is more exotic. Timber for repairing a medieval church spire, documented in churchwardens' accounts; the dentist who filled a nobleman's teeth, sought in his household receipts; a hanged murderer's skeleton, identified from gaol records; the medieval extent of Melcombe Regis quay when the plague-carrying rat landed – they are all there to be discovered, when the archaeologist and historian work together.

Fig 5.24 Extract from a Wilton estate survey, *c* 1750 (Wilts & Swindon Archives 2057/S37). This and similar documents established that burials excavated by Wessex Archaeology in 2007–08 were associated with the 'lost' church of St Andrew, Ditchampton (Reproduced by kind permission of the Earl of Pembroke)

6

Exploring New Frontiers

Prologue

Charles French

Formative times

My first impressions of Wessex were shaped as a small boy of eight visiting Stonehenge for the very first time with my parents in 1962, and subsequently as a Cardiff undergraduate through the teaching of Prof Richard Atkinson and an especially memorable field-trip before finals in May 1975. But I was then diverted to the East Anglian fens and its associated river valleys with my first digging job, which ended up as a 25+ year engagement with that landscape. Nonetheless, in the last decade I have been enticed back to Wessex through conducting a geoarchaeological investigation of landscape change during the Mesolithic to Bronze Age periods of the upper Allen valley of Cranborne Chase, and more recently as a team member of both the Sheffield and Bournemouth University-led projects at Durrington Walls and Stonehenge.

Important developments

Four major things have stood out from my more recent engagement with the chalk downlands of Wessex. First, despite, the calcareous groundwater system and the associated pressures of urban development, groundwater abstraction, and intensive arable agriculture, well-preserved peat deposits containing pretty full sequences of Holocene landscape and vegetational development are still to be found, primarily in palaeo-channels in the river valleys dissecting the downland. Second, soil erosion, especially hillwash sequences in the dry valleys and on the lower slopes of the larger river valley, is both much less frequent and much more variable in its presence than had been expected. So for example in the upper Allen valley, the thickest hillwash deposit was no more than 0.50m, and almost non-existent in Stonehenge Bottom. In contrast, much greater thicknesses of eroded soil have been observed locally within Durrington Walls henge and outside its eastern entranceway where there were several metres of post-Roman calcareous silt hillwash deposits. Indeed, much of the Wessex downland colluvial record seems to be of historic and recent periods. Third, where we do find buried soils of pre-Neolithic and pre-Bronze Age date in the Stonehenge/Durrington Walls/Avon and upper Allen valley/Cranborne Chase study areas, whether beneath monuments or subsequent erosion deposits, they are all thin grassland or rendzina soils. There are only the vaguest of hints of these palaeosols once having been better developed and thicker woodland soils. Thus evidence for the conventional model of climax soil and vegetational development of the earlier Holocene requiring the formation of thick well-structured brown soils under dense mixed deciduous woodland in the Mesolithic and earlier Neolithic periods is patchy at best. There is little doubt that both the upper Allen valley and Stonehenge–Durrington downland landscapes were ostensibly open grassland by the middle of the 4th millennium BC, with woodland and marsh survival only along the floodplain fringes and perhaps small pockets of woodland survival in limited places on the downs. Certainly by the latter part of the 3rd millennium BC, both areas were predominantly open grassland.

Perhaps more important than all of these landscape developments is the recent discovery of definitive evidence of prehistoric settlement. This comprises the remarkably well-preserved, middle Neolithic structures outside the eastern entranceway of Durrington Walls as well as later Neolithic examples from Wyke Down in the upper Allen valley. The Durrington structures take the form of sub-square chalk slurry floors with central hearths within stake and/or post outer walls, and there are at least two later Neolithic circular structures with cob walling material at Wyke Down (Green in French *et al* 2007, 83–94 & 307–35). These discoveries are a quantum leap forward in the elucidation of the earlier prehistoric settlement record for the area.

Where to from here?

Despite these exciting discoveries of new data which have led to nuanced ideas of landscape development and human activities within this chalk downland landscape, there remain many gaps in our knowledge regarding its development and change, especially in the Mesolithic and Neolithic periods. How well developed was Mesolithic–earlier Neolithic woodland on the chalk? What were the trajectories of clearance and soil change? How did early clearances occur – by fire, slash and burn, game management, shifting agriculture, or what? And over what spatial dynamic did they occur? – ubiquitously, or only in certain places (such as around Durrington Walls, Stonehenge, Wyke Down, Knowlton) as important or pre-conditioned places in the pre-existing landscape, or patchily, driven by unknown cultural and environmental factors. Are there any areas of definitive and recognisable earlier prehistoric field systems? If not, where might we look for these? In future, both greater resolution of prospection techniques, better spatial resolution, interrogation and modelling of palaeo-environmental data (see Allen, this volume), the introduction of new techniques such as lidar, geoarchaeological survey and the micromorphology of palaeosols (cf French *et al* 2007), and the investigation of drowned near-shore and estuarine environments (see Firth, this volume) may help in the identification of such processes and human engagement with them and response to them. Importantly also, developer-funded investigations will uncover unexpected and new sources of data capable of high-resolution interpretation by virtue of looking in many different and new places in the landscape.

I am also convinced that we will be able to find both field systems and habitation structures of the Neolithic and earlier Bronze Age in due course, both through the application of some better sets of techniques and by investigating parts of the landscape that have not yet seen much archaeological activity. This direction of investigation really does require some focused work over the next decade if we are to discern the non-monumental aspects of life. Developer-funded projects investigating large swathes of chalk downland landscapes will certainly help, but targeted explorations of lower foot-slopes beneath colluvium and floodplain edge zones beneath alluvial flood deposits are also needed. We already possess some geoprospection techniques which will enable the identification of human habitations and their rubbish, namely fine-grained geophysical survey techniques such as caesium magnetometer (Gaffney and Gator 2003, 38–42), magnetic susceptibility, and phosphate analyses of ploughsoils (Gurney 1985; Crowther 1997), and multi-element geo-chemical survey (Linderholm 2007). The latter technique has proved successful in other parts of the world in identifying settlements and the use of built space (Cavanagh *et al* 2005; Linderholm 2007; Wilson *et al* 2008), but does require testing in the Wessex landscape, especially on plough-denuded downland.

Thus, future applications of both scientific and palaeo-environmental techniques of data retrieval will be able to contribute significantly to future archaeological discoveries in Wessex, elucidating different trajectories of human development on the downland and in the riverine valley landscapes through time.

The marine zone: archaeology offshore

Antony Firth

Introduction

The marine zone of Wessex – taken here to encompass the coast from Chichester Harbour to Lyme Bay, out to the limits of the UK Continental Shelf – has been at the heart of the development of marine archaeology over the last 50 years, both in the UK and internationally.

Unlike most of the other contributions to this volume, which have reasonably discrete and confined periods to address, this paper must cover the entire span of human history – from more than 700,000 years ago to the very recent past. This task is made a little easier because it is certainly the case that the level of knowledge and understanding arising from marine archaeology for any one period is still very sparse. By itself, marine archaeology still provides little basis – within Wessex and elsewhere – for making confident, general inferences about the main themes and questions of any particular period. Happily, increasing levels of investigation, complemented by technological advances, are enabling archaeologists to start framing more thematic syntheses arising directly from coastal and marine data (eg Centre for Maritime Archaeology 2009). In this paper I hope to show how developments in approaches and methods that have taken place in Wessex have contributed to this movement, with reference to three basic themes: wreck investigations, coastal archaeology and submerged prehistory.

What follows is necessarily a personal view of marine archaeology and this region. Although I am not from around here, the vast majority of my career as a marine archaeologist has taken place in the region. I came into archaeology as a volunteer diver on the Isle of Wight; surveyed designated wrecks in the region whilst working for the Archaeological Diving Unit; studied for a doctorate at the University of Southampton; helped out with the Hampshire and Wight Trust for Maritime Archaeology in its earliest days and wound up as Head of Coastal and Marine Projects for Wessex Archaeology. I am by no means a disinterested observer, but I hope to draw out some generally recognisable trends nonetheless.

That there have been significant changes over the last 50 years in marine archaeology can hardly be doubted. Put simply, marine archaeology did not really exist in 1958, whereas today it is thriving.

While earlier roots can be discerned, marine archaeology as a discipline more-or-less related to archaeology on land only emerged in the UK during the late 1960s and early 1970s. For the next 25 years or so through to the mid-1990s, marine archaeology, both in the region and the UK, seems to have stayed somewhat separate from archaeology on land. Convergence of the two disciplines gathered pace in the 1990s, although progress has not been consistent. It might even be contended that marine archaeology became fully comparable with its

Fig 6.1 The Swash Channel wreck, off Poole, was found in 2004 during a geophysical survey in advance of dredging to deepen the navigation channel. The survey indicated a large wooden ship. Diving later that year confirmed the presence of a wreck site about 40m long; a sherd of Rhenish pottery suggested an early 17th-century date. The site has since been subject to extensive investigations (© Wessex Archaeology)

terrestrial counterpart when responsibility for it was formally vested in English Heritage in 2002. The role of local authorities and museums beyond the low-water mark continues to be ambiguous.

Despite marine archaeology having only a very brief history, the historic environment of Wessex has a marine component every bit as ancient as its terrestrial component. There have been old things off the coast of Wessex for a lot longer than there have been marine archaeologists to consider them. Some of the country's most important historic wrecks have been found in the region, including the 15th-century *Grace Dieu* (Friel 1993), the 16th-century Studland Bay wreck (Thomsen 2000), the *Mary Rose* (Marsden 2003), the 18th-century *Invincible* (Bingeman 1985), and the recently discovered Swash Channel wreck (Fig 6.1). The presence of prehistoric material below sea level in the region has also long been known, especially in the catchment of the palaeo-Solent, as evidenced by 19th-century discoveries in the docks of Southampton (Shore and Elwes 1889) and elsewhere. A walk along any shore in the region would also quickly highlight the intensive use of the present coast and seascape for all manner of purposes during more recent millennia. In short, the marine and coastal historic environment of the Wessex region is rich, diverse and representative of the entire range of archaeological periods, bearing comparison with any other coastline in England.

Institutions and people

With a marine historic environment as abundant as this, how could Wessex be anything other than centre-stage? However, marine archaeological innovation in the Wessex region has not arisen simply from the particularities of the historic environment that we are so lucky to inhabit. There are other regions of the UK where the marine historic environment is just as rich and where equally important innovations have been – and continue to be – developed. Notwithstanding, the Wessex region appears to have earned an extraordinary profile.

As well as having a marine historic environment that is rich and diverse, our region has been fortunate to host a very productive mix of individuals and institutions over the last half century. Without taking anything away from those based elsewhere, many of the most influential organisations over the last 20–30 years – covering the whole spectrum of interests in marine archaeology – have been based in Wessex. The roll call includes national and local curatorial agencies, tertiary educational and research institutions, voluntary groups and societies, museums and contracting units. English Heritage's maritime team in Portsmouth was preceded by the RCHME's marine team in Southampton and later Swindon. Local authorities in Isle of Wight, Hampshire and Dorset have played a very important role in coastal and intertidal archaeology, pushing seawards whenever possible. The University of Southampton is internationally recognised for its post-graduate teaching in marine archaeology, joined more recently by Bournemouth University. Both of these universities, alongside other regional institutes such as the National Oceanography Centre, the University of Reading and the University of Portsmouth, have developed their capacity to carry out coastal and marine archaeological research. The Wessex region also hosts important international organisations such as the Nautical Archaeology Society in Portsmouth, organisations that pioneered underwater investigations such as the Mary Rose Trust and the Poole Maritime Museum, and community-focused organisations like the Hampshire and Wight Trust for Maritime Archaeology (HWTMA). Wessex Archaeology started to carry out coastal/marine projects in the mid-1990s and has rapidly become one of the main providers of marine archaeological services in the UK.

Amongst all these institutions, I would like to recall one that is now defunct – the Isle of Wight Maritime Heritage Project (IWMHP) – a Manpower Services Commission (MSC) scheme that ran from 1984 to 1989. As I explain below, the Maritime Heritage Project gave impetus to a range of ideas that have gained momentum over the years and, incidentally, provided my own introduction to marine archaeology.

It is not just institutions that innovate but people too, and there are numerous names that I could mention across the avocational and professional spectrum. In particular, I would like to honour David Tomalin, former County Archaeologist of the Isle of Wight, and Alan Aberg formerly of the RCHME who – by drawing marine archaeology into the sphere of archaeology as a whole – typify the way in which people in the region have had an influence that has spread far beyond Wessex.

Wreck investigations

Looking back, the investigation of wrecks in the region was – as elsewhere – typified by a focus on single – often historically documented – wreck sites that were either sought proactively or investigated in reactive response to their discovery. Often, the aim was pursuit of the minutiae of the individual ship's history for public edification, usually by way of extensive excavation and recovery. Although the *Mary Rose* might be archetypal, single-ship studies have tended to dominate research on many sites (Firth 2002).

Important innovative strands in the region, which were evident in earlier work and remain focal, include the development of technical methods of investigation (Fig 6.2) and research into the processes affecting the survival and preservation of wreck material (see for example Tomalin, Simpson and Bingeman 2000; Momber and Geen 2000; Plets, Dix and Best 2008; Plets *et al* 2009). Equally significant has been a move to consider individual wrecks within the context of an overall resource. This innovation accompanied the development of the Isle of Wight Maritime Sites and Monuments Record, a county-based record of wrecks (and other marine sites) structured in a manner entirely comparable with the terrestrial sites and monuments records (SMRs, now known as historic environment records, HERs) that were gaining in importance in the late 20th century. The Isle of Wight MSMR became the model for the maritime section of the English National Monuments Record (NMR) and, in turn, the national records of the other home countries, as well as an inspiration for the development of marine elements to SMRs in various other counties (JNAPC 1989, 26–7; Williams 1991, 65).

More than 20 years on, it is unfortunate that the potential of this Wessex-region innovation has not been fully realised nationally, as HER provision for marine areas is still patchy. It is especially frustrating that when the need to place HERs on a statutory basis was finally recognised in the 2008 draft Heritage Protection Bill, extension to marine areas was regarded as desirable but optional (DCMS 2008, 10).

The emergence of regional and national recording of wrecks had an effect, from the start, on how their investigation should be framed. Specifically, the Isle of Wight MSMR provided an explicit context for the methodologies adopted in investigating the Yarmouth Roads Wreck in the late 1980s. Prompted by the MSMR to address how it might be possible to manage numerous shipwrecks, Yarmouth Roads provided both methodological feedback and a framework for site assessment (Watson and Gale 1990).

The paradigm introduced by the Isle of Wight MSMR has strongly influenced the way in which Wessex Archaeology has sought to draw up schemes and methods that can be applied consistently to all manner of wrecks – including aircraft as well as ships (Fig 6.3). As on the Isle of Wight, we have pursued the development of practical field-based approaches to wreck assessment in ways that enable local and national records to be easily enhanced with results, and approaches to wreck assessment that allow the character and importance

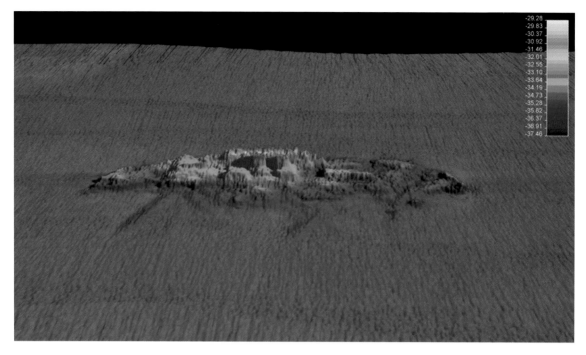

of individual sites to be compared in a systematic and transparent manner. Methods and levels of wreck recording that emerged during development-led investigations in the Wessex region were further explored through the *Wrecks on the Seabed* project funded by the Aggregates Levy Sustainability Fund (Wessex Archaeology 2007) and became the general operational model for assessing wrecks that are subject to – or candidates for – designation under the Protection of Wrecks Act 1973. Simultaneously, projects such as 'England's Shipping' (Wessex Archaeology 2004a), 'On the Importance of Shipwrecks' (Wessex Archaeology 2006) and 'Assessing Boats and Ships' (Wessex Archaeology 2010) are providing frameworks within which such assessments can acquire broader relevance and meaning.

Some people might feel that the introduction of heritage management systems into underwater archaeology has replaced the romance of shipwreck adventures with mechanistic detachment, but I take a different view. Moving away from site-specific modes of investigation is instead allowing archaeologists to re-focus upon the great themes to which wreck archaeology provides access. With technical issues increasingly overcome (or at least capable of being overcome), wrecks can cease to be regarded primarily as 'maritime' sites. Perhaps for the first time, we are free to consider them in terms of the contemporary social, industrial, commercial or military themes of which they are part, rather than separating them away on the basis of the environment in which they happen to have been preserved. Advances made in the Wessex region are at last starting to allow the stories of the ships to outshine the escapades of maritime archaeologists.

Fig 6.2 Multibeam image of the remains of the steamship *Mendi*, off the Isle of Wight. Launched on the Clyde in 1905, the *Mendi* carried mail and cargo between Liverpool and West Africa before being converted to a troop ship. Carrying men from the South African Native Labour Corps to France, almost 650 died when the *Mendi* was run down by another ship in thick fog in February 1917. The *Mendi* is highly significant in South Africa, and just one example of the internationally important wrecks lying off the Wessex coast (© Wessex Archaeology)

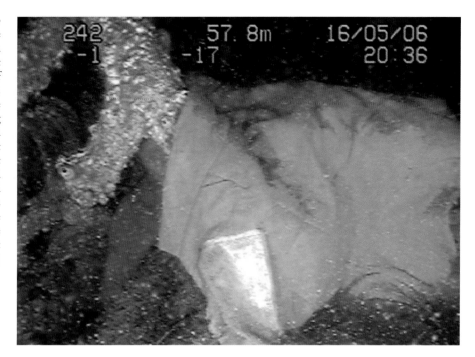

Fig 6.3 Close-up of the label on the orange lining of a Snorkel parka caught in the remains of a B-24 Liberator, presumed to have been lost during the Second World War. The aircraft wreck lies in about 56m of water and was investigated by archaeologists using a Remote Operated Vehicle (ROV) (© Wessex Archaeology)

Coastal survey

Coastal survey, especially the investigation of intertidal areas, has been a key component of the development of marine archaeology in the region. Other regions have developed a very strong tradition of intertidal archaeology over the same period: investigations in Essex (Wilkinson and Murphy 1995) and in the Severn estuary (SELRC 1992) immediately spring to mind. Notwithstanding, intertidal initiatives in Wessex have been very influential. Major investigations at Wootton Creek (Tomalin 1993) on the Isle of Wight demonstrated not only the presence of rich prehistoric material and important evidence for the history of sea-level change, but also presented very clearly the degree of threat posed by coastal erosion associated with future sea-level change.

Questions raised by the Wootton-Quarr project about the quality and quantity of archaeological material under threat in intertidal areas, and about the resource implications of offering some form of mitigation, reinforced the need for a strategic review of coastal heritage. The *England's Coastal Heritage* project, though national in scope, was conducted primarily by the Wessex universities of Southampton and Reading. As well as resulting in a published survey of coastal archaeology (Fulford, Champion and Long 1997) it provided the basis for a policy statement (English Heritage 1996), demonstrating again the influence of activities in Wessex far beyond its boundaries.

At around the same time, Hampshire County Council's Langstone Harbour Project had a tremendous practical impact in demonstrating seamless investigation of the geomorphological history of the harbour. Seamless meant having an integrated approach to archaeology irrespective of its environment – above high water, in intertidal areas, or fully submerged. The project integrated desk-based research, geoarchaeological investigations, fieldwalking, excavation and diver-based survey, resulting in an overarching account of the physical, environmental and social development of the harbour in prehistoric and early historic periods (Allen and Gardiner 2000).

Another strand of coastal survey has been the smaller, generally site-specific investigations that continue to build up a detailed patchwork along the Wessex coast. Intertidal survey is a very effective means of introducing people both to maritime archaeology and to the health, safety and logistical considerations of working with the sea, but without the additional complications of diving. Consequently, intertidal survey has featured strongly in training courses, both for students and for members of the public with an avocational interest. The University of Southampton, Hampshire and Wight Trust for Maritime Archaeology, and Nautical Archaeology Society have all made substantial contributions to coastal archaeology in Wessex, frequently in collaboration with each other and often blending public outreach with training (HWTMA/NAS 2009).

Development-led work at the coast is also site-specific, but leads occasionally to broader thematic and strategic investigations. One good example is the investigation of the remains of early salt-making industries on the north shore of the western Solent around Lymington. The later post-medieval salt industry was largely responsible for the current form of a coast that, despite its industrial roots, is now important for nature conservation. A little further inland, limited intervention in the course of aggregate extraction and landfill revealed the remains of earlier, probably medieval, saltmaking preceded by Iron Age settlement activity that also displayed evidence of saltmaking (Powell 2009). The need to understand the wider context of the Lymington industry prompted work to trace historic cartographic evidence of saltmaking along the whole of the Hampshire coast (Wessex Archaeology 2002a). A parallel exercise to map changes to the coastlines confirmed, in particular, the degree of intertidal erosion that has taken place (Wessex Archaeology 2002b).

A characteristic of the Wessex coastline is that its archaeological remains are capable of revealing a great deal about the past while simultaneously being at tremendous risk. This was a key message of Wootton-Quarr, developed through *England's Coastal Heritage* that prompted the series of Rapid Coastal Zone Assessment Surveys (RCZAS) funded by English Heritage, and which bring this brief survey of Wessex coastal archaeology up to date. The desk-based phase of the Dorset RCZAS was completed in 2004, with fieldwork expected to take place in conjunction with a wider South West RCZAS in due course. In parallel, the Wessex coastline from Sussex to Redbridge is being studied as part of the South East RCZAS, while a complementary New Forest RCZAS is covering the coast from Redbridge to the Dorset border. With the Isle of Wight already the subject of comprehensive surveys that took place following the Wootton-Quarr project, the entire coast of Wessex has now been – or is in the process of being – comprehensively reviewed.

Submerged prehistory

The Solent has played a very major role in stimulating interest in submerged prehistoric sites both prior and subsequent to the Devensian Late Glacial Maximum (LGM), about 18,000 years ago.

Prior to the LGM, the understanding of Palaeolithic archaeology in the region is closely related to the terrace systems associated with the palaeo-Solent and its tributaries, whose gradients lead offshore (Bridgland 1996). Subsequent to the LGM a clear relationship between Holocene climate, sea-level change and prehistoric landscape was demonstrated by the mapping in the mid-1980s off Bouldnor, in the western Solent, by the Isle of Wight Maritime Heritage Project of an underwater cliff comprising a sediment sequence of evident palaeo-environmental interest (Momber *et al*, forthcoming; and Momber, this volume pp 32–33).

In the mid-1990s submerged prehistory was still largely an 'in principle' argument, not only off Wessex but around the UK and much of the world. General accounts of sea-level change, underwater topographies hinted at by bathymetric charts, recoveries of peat in marine cores and accounts of artefacts discovered in trawls or during harbour construction all pointed to the presence of archaeological material offshore. Beyond the intertidal strip, however, most evidence was fortuitous rather than a result of systematic investigations directed by archaeologists.

The discovery of *in situ* artefactual material at Bouldnor from 1998 onwards (Momber 2000) was therefore very significant, providing the 'proof' to support more speculative environmentally-based investigations beyond the region as well as within it. The timing was especially favourable as it coincided with the emergence of development-led archaeology at sea, bringing previously unimagined levels of capability and resource into the discipline, especially with respect to seabed prehistory.

Starting with Environmental Statements in support of marine aggregate dredging proposals, such as those for Areas 471 and 407 in the palaeo-Solent, development-led marine archaeology grew to encompass proposed developments in ports and estuaries in the region. Port investigations generated archaeological results and methodological improvements that have spread very widely, even if – like Dibden Terminal in Southampton Water – the proposed developments themselves have not taken place. Marine aggregates have continued to be critical both for the industry's encouragement of strategic solutions and regional assessments, and for the funding and technical innovations enabled by the Aggregate Levy Sustainability Fund (ALSF).

ALSF-funded investigations of submerged prehistory within or close to the region have included desk-based reviews (Westley, Dix and Quinn 2004), record enhancement including cataloguing artefacts found by fishermen (Wessex Archaeology 2004b; 2004c), methodological developments in the coastal strip (Bates, Bates and Dix 2009), extensive geophysical investigations (Gupta *et al* 2004) and detailed geophysics combined with coring and sampling (Wessex Archaeology 2008). The ALSF-funded historic seascape projects are also drawing

continued on p 174

The *Mary Rose*

Alison Hamer

The *Mary Rose* has iconic status within maritime archaeology as one of only a small number of wrecks raised and the only 16th-century warship on display anywhere in the world. Millions watched the television on the day in October 1982 when the ship emerged from beneath the waves for the first time since she sank in July 1545. This became a seminal moment in the history of maritime archaeology and has influenced the very nature of the discipline and inspired many of those involved today. Locating, excavating, raising, conserving and studying the *Mary Rose* has been a major undertaking and an outstanding achievement (McKee 1982; Rule 1982; Marsden 2003). Nearly 29,000 artefacts, timbers and other items have been carefully recorded and are being conserved and analysed to solve the mysteries of this great ship. It represents a massive commitment both in time and finances; prior to the raising of the *Mary Rose*, more than 27,000 dives covering nearly twelve man-years were spent on the seabed excavating the site. In the subsequent decades many more hours have been spent on the site and on analysis, conservation and publication.

The *Mary Rose* was built by Henry VIII in response to the ever-present threat of attack by the French navy and served for 34 years; her design incorporated the most advanced ship-building technology of the time. On 19 July 1545, while the king watched from the shore, *Mary Rose* sank off Southsea Castle, during a battle to defend Portsmouth from the gathered French fleet.

The late Alexander McKee began the search for Henry VIII's ship in 1965. McKee was keen to utilise new techniques and embraced the developing technology of side-scan sonar. Archaeologist Margaret Rule had been involved in the project from the early days and she and McKee started diving on the site with their team to investigate the buried anomaly. Working on a small budget, the team began finding fragments of timber and then uncovered an iron gun. They soon realised they had located the remains of the *Mary Rose*.

The project set an important precedent for sports divers working alongside archaeologists and represented a step away from commercial salvage of historic wreck sites. Excavating the *Mary Rose* provided a real test for archaeologists; the site was located in 12m of water, which posed many challenges for working safely. The team even had to design and build their own equipment and develop techniques to cope with the new challenges of working on a three-dimensional underwater site. Since planning frames were only effective on flat surfaces, a Direct Survey Method was developed to record

Fig 6.4 The ship, which has been sprayed with wax since she was recovered in 1982, is now entering a new phase of air-drying before being moved to the new museum (© Mary Rose Trust)

Fig 6.5 Wooden combs such as these have survived remarkably well and offer a personal link to the sailors who were on board the ship (© Mary Rose Trust)

Fig 6.6 The anaerobic burial conditions of the ship have allowed a high degree of preservation of organic remains, as shown by this magnificent wooden tankard (© Mary Rose Trust)

quickly and accurately the positions of artefacts within the ship. The new method allowed depths to be taken in low-visibility environments where other methods were unreliable.

The culmination of all this work was the ambitious plan to raise the ship for display and further recording. Many plans for the recovery of the wreck were considered and it was eventually decided to attach an underwater lifting frame to the hull. The frame and wreck were then transferred to a lifting cradle ready to be raised. Archaeologists and divers spent months preparing the *Mary Rose* to be lifted and finally it was possible to raise the frame, lifting cradle and its important contents.

The anaerobic burial conditions of the site had allowed the survival of many unique artefacts that would not have survived on land. From armaments such as longbows and arrows to personal items such as combs, shoes and tools belonging to the ship's carpenters, the wreck provides a wealth of information about the sea-going world of the 16th century. The ship itself also provides important evidence of early ship construction and has been meticulously studied and drawn. The *Mary Rose* project has not only greatly enhanced our knowledge of life and warfare in the Tudor period but the conservation of the ship and artefacts has led to the development of many new procedures and techniques for dealing with waterlogged finds.

The raised section of the hull currently lies in a purpose-built but temporary ship hall in a dry dock at Portsmouth Historic Dockyard. Conservation is almost complete and the ship is now in the final phases of spraying with wax followed by air-drying. The museum has an active education programme that engages and enthuses thousands of schoolchildren and other visitors each year. In September 2009 building work started on a major new museum that will eventually provide the *Mary Rose* with a permanent and impressive home, surrounded by the objects that were discovered within her. Although the ship hall will be closed during the construction period, the current museum containing the artefacts and telling the stories will remain open to the public. This remarkable ship, and the artefacts she contained, will thus continue to provide evidence for archaeologists and historians and delight the public for years to come.

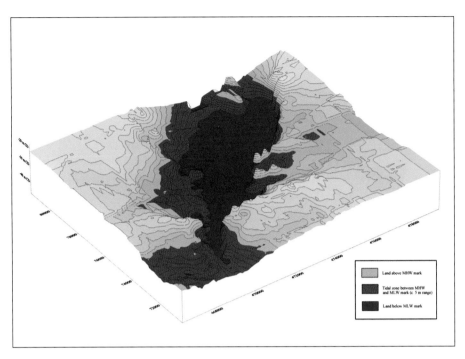

Fig 6.7 Digital model of a postulated topography in the lower reaches of the palaeo-Solent prepared in 1998 to supplement an Environmental Impact Assessment accompanying a marine aggregate licence application. Sea level is presented as 35m lower than today. High points on the relatively steep shoulder of the eastern shore might have presented favourable occupation sites in the late Upper Palaeolithic and early Mesolithic (© Wessex Archaeology)

in information about submerged prehistory (HWTMA *et al* 2007). Lastly, an extensive multi-disciplinary 'Regional Environmental Characterisation' (REC) survey of the south coast from Dorset to Sussex is taking place, again funded by the ALSF, the archaeological elements of which will help to provide an overall framework for considering offshore prehistory in the region (BGS *et al* 2010).

The combined effect of ALSF projects, development-led investigations for aggregates and ports, and a range of research projects and coastal investigations is that the empirical basis for postulating the presence of significant prehistoric material offshore has grown considerably in the last 10–15 years (Fig 6.7). At various times in early prehistory Wessex landscapes encompassed an extensive lowland plain flanking a more distant coast. As remarked by other authors (eg Wymer 1996), our understanding of Wessex may change significantly as we start to reconsider what we know on land in the light of glimpses into the past obtained offshore.

Looking ahead

Marine archaeology as a discipline comparable to archaeology on land has only come into being within the later half of the period that is the subject of this volume. Developments in Wessex have been influential far beyond the region, helped by a rich marine historic environment. It is, however, a Wessex-based infrastructure of individuals and organisations with marine archaeological interests that has been especially important in narrowing the gap between land-based and marine research. That gap between land and sea is nevertheless still considerable. There is no fundamental reason for our subject matter to be riven by differences in the environments in which artefacts and features are situated. Methodological seamlessness can be attained, as investigations in the region have repeatedly demonstrated. However, there seems yet to be little sign of real seamlessness of interpretation – whether in prehistoric or later periods.

A part of this failing can undoubtedly be attributed to the specific experience, working practices and technical specialisation of marine archaeologists. However, I also feel that many land-based archaeologists are not predisposed to consider the archaeological implications of what is now known about the sea.

The continuing lack of integration between wet and dry is underlined by an apparent paradoxical disinclination to consider the archaeology of inland waters, in the Wessex region and elsewhere. Water has been essential to human activity throughout history, not only for drinking but for transport, power, sanitation, agriculture and fisheries. Waterways, natural and artificial, are central to virtually every settlement in Wessex, but I am struck by the apparent reluctance of archaeologists to investigate if it means they might get their feet wet. Even key waterside monuments go unrecorded from water level downwards.

Anticipating the next 5, 10 or 50 years I look forward to seamless interpretation of the whole historic environment of Wessex, both wet and dry, encapsulated for example in (pre-)histories of the region's major river and estuary catchments. By the time that CBA Wessex celebrates it centenary I would expect the writers to be much more confident of the contribution being made by archaeology in the marine zone to their key periods and themes. But I would also expect the impulse to collect these contributions within a single marine chapter to be regarded as anachronistic. Having had a short history, perhaps 'Marine Archaeology' in Wessex should be allowed only a short future!

The experimental earthworks

Peter Fowler

Two new, 'ancient' archaeological sites have appeared in the Wessex landscape during the second half of the 20th century. Each is in a National Nature Reserve (NNR). Each has already been excavated several times under archaeological direction, and numerous finds have been made; but the next excavations will not take place until 2024 and 2027 respectively, with a gap of 64 years to final excavations in, respectively, 2088 and 2091. What on earth is going on here?

The two earthworks are an outcome of the Charles Darwin centenary meeting of the British Association for the Advancement of Science (BAAS) in 1958. As archaeological excavators and receivers of material from the excavations of others, Richard Atkinson, Ian Cornwall, Geoffrey Dimbleby, Peter Jewell and Bruce Proudfoot were only too well aware of the ignorance about the processes going on within archaeological sites – for example about rates of ditch sedimentation. So a research committee was formed 'to investigate by experiment the denudation and burial of archaeological structures'. On that first committee, in addition to the five men named above, were Paul Ashbee, Peter Fowler, Edward Pyddoke and Peggy Wilson. It was decided that the first (and, as it turned out, the only) project would be to build simple earthworks, a bank and a ditch, on different subsoils and monitor the superficial and internal changes to them through time. Long-term site tenure and security were immediate concerns, and hence the choice of sites in NNRs.

One bank and ditch was built on Upper Chalk on Overton Down, near Avebury, Wiltshire, in 1960; another on Tertiary Sands and Clays on Morden Bog, near Wareham, Dorset, in 1963. The two main earthworks do not simulate any particular type of archaeological site, though they obviously echo aspects of long and round barrows, linear ditches, hillforts and indeed any other type of site

Fig 6.8 General view from the west of Overton Down experimental earthwork, 21 March 1964, showing, towards the end of the fourth winter, ditch sedimentation and turf collapse from the berm (© Peter Fowler and the Council for British Archaeology)

Fig 6.9 General view from the north-west of the Overton Down experimental earthwork, 25 July 2009, 49 years after construction, showing overall vegetation, three hawthorn bushes and recent stock damage at the north-east end, where the 2024 section is due to be cut (© Peter Fowler)

enclosed by a bank and ditch. Results from them, therefore, could be relevant to a wide range of archaeological circumstance. The study of morphological change was helped by placing markers in known positions with a view to finding them during excavation and seeing how far, if at all, each had travelled.

Another facet of the experiment concerned materials such as flints, wood, bone, textiles and leathers, buried in the bank to be studied more for their changes *in situ* than for their movement. Since archaeological science has developed as a sub-discipline in its own right since the earthworks were built, these buried materials and their micro-environments can now be observed and analysed in ways not envisaged in 1960.

The methodology common to both earthworks is that each is sectioned at intervals of 2, 4, 8, 16, 32, 64 and 128 years: at Overton Down, in 1962, 1964, 1968, 1976, 1992, 2024 and 2088; at Morden Bog, 1964 (additional early section because of rapid geomorphological changes), 1965, 1967 (actually 1968), 1972 (1973), 1979 (1980) and 1995 (1996), 2027 and 2091. That the latter was not sectioned on time on four occasions represents the difficulties encountered by Committee members in meeting their self-imposed regime through a generation and more. Nevertheless, both earthworks have been monitored closely over and above the periodic sections, and a large archive of data and materials now exists. This has itself brought its own challenges of order and accessibility, and the archive is currently seeking a permanent home.

What have these earthworks contributed to science and archaeology; and – something that was not in the forefront of the originators' minds – to conservation? Answers include:

1. Suggestions about general archaeological issues, for example does 'The apparent speed of pottery destruction at Wareham ... go some way towards explaining the paucity of poorly fired prehistoric pottery on acid and upland soils' and make 'the identification of aceramic cultures in the west and north of Britain more open to debate'?

2. On methodology, 'The experiment has helped to make experimental methodology an accepted part of archaeological practice' and 'the development of a team approach to the application of science in archaeology'.

3. On interdisciplinarity, the project's 'approach is relevant to a range of disciplines concerned with change over time'.

4. The experiment addresses 'issues of medium-term change'.

5. As the experiment was set up so carefully, the sites can be used 'for a range of studies which were not originally foreseen'.

6. On conservation, the vegetational changes on the Overton earthwork in just 24 years document a newly created habitat with 'a floristic composition in some ways comparable with that of old grassland ... This is at variance with the view that species-rich grassland takes centuries to form' and 'shows that disturbance ... can help to maintain diversity in chalk grassland'.

The Committee has so far published four main reports (Jewell 1963; Jewell and Dimbleby 1966; Evans and Limbrey 1974; Bell, Fowler and Hillson 1996), the most recent of which discusses all the matters mentioned here, and provides all the quotations.

An environmental archaeology and geoarchaeological revolution?

Michael J Allen

What are environmental archaeology and geoarchaeology? Why are they relevant? What have they done for archaeology in Wessex? Environmental archaeology is for me, in part, the science of reconstructing the long-term relationship between ancient peoples and the environments they lived in. It is, therefore, central to any understanding of ancient societies. It seeks to interpret the development of the human environment, the interaction of natural environmental change and human activities, and the role of humans in shaping and using the landscape we see around us today. Environmental archaeology has seen a surge of interest in recent years, as it is one of the few disciplines that is able to provide empirical evidence to show how humans have responded to rapid climate change in the past. Various sub-disciplines are involved to document and interpret this relationship, including palaeoethnobotany, geomorphology, palynology, geoarchaeology, landscape archaeology, human biology, and human ecology. The aspects of environmental archaeology I concentrate upon here are mainly those relating to environment, landscape, and land-use, as opposed to those relating to economy and diet.

Environmental archaeology has emerged as an identifiable discipline only in the last 30 years. It has rapidly grown in significance and is now seen as a component of most excavation projects; many universities teach the subject as a standard course component. Environmental archaeology in my mind is strictly related, directly or indirectly, to our understanding of people and communities, and their interaction with their surroundings. It is not just the study of environmental remains *per se*, although detailed study and development of methods is obviously key to the success of the interpretive ability we hold, but it is the application of the resultant data to a wider environmental archaeological enquiry. It is incumbent on the environmental archaeologist to be acutely aware of the key questions being addressed within archaeology, and to engage with these whole-heartedly. Environmental archaeology, that is, a structured environmental approach within archaeology, is ideally suited to analysing the landscape and land-use, especially now that it has progressed beyond being merely a technique for compiling floral, faunal, and climatic sequences and has proved itself as a means to interpret human activity (Evans 1975). Any study of the human environment, however, needs to be thoroughly integrated into the archaeological field of investigation. It is only when questioning of the evidence is designed within an archaeological framework that the use of the natural and environmental sciences as a method of enquiry can be archaeologically relevant.

Environmental archaeology and geoarchaeology in Wessex

Environmental archaeology and geoarchaeology may be relatively new disciplines, but they have now reached maturity and are no longer subservient to 'mainstream' archaeology, providing archaeological interpretation in their own right. This paper will plot that journey and illustrate some of the palaeo-environmental interpretations suggested for regions, study areas, and sites. We have now reached the dawn of a new era where we can question 30-year-old texts and concepts and start to replace them with a new framework.

Following a brief review of how we got to where we are today, I offer several vignettes of how environmental archaeology in Wessex has matured as a discipline and how engagement with environmental archaeological analyses has provided *archaeological* interpretation relevant to our understanding of past communities and their actions. Well before the 50-year period we are discussing here, when archaeology was developing into its own discipline in the early part of the 20th century, the subject as a whole was largely driven by monuments and objects, and environmental archaeology *per se* was unrecognised. Archaeologists working in Wessex, however, occasionally stumbled across some of the macroscopic items that were normally missed and had them identified by biological scientists. These include charcoal from Cunnington's excavations at Woodhenge in the 1920s and the keen observation of the larger snails at Stonehenge from Hawley's *c* 1926 excavations (Allen in Cleal *et al* 1995, 436–7). These provide useful anecdotal information but, importantly, indicate the possibilites that such material might hold.

A start

Admittedly, 50 years ago, there were skilled analysts such as Ian Cornwall (*Soils for the Archaeologist*, 1953; *Bones for the Archaeologist*, 1956) and Frederick Zeuner (*The Pleistocene Period*, 1959) studying bones and soils on archaeological sites, but these were individual studies, largely driven by individual scholars. Descriptions of soils, for instance, at Fussell's Lodge, Robin Hood's Ball, Chick's Hill, Black Down, and Wallis Down, identified the type of soil that had previously existed, and basic analyses undertaken aided in their characterisation (see Macphail 1987 for a fuller list). By the 1950/60s, at the inception of CBA Wessex, there was only a handful of practitioners to engage with excavation and fieldwork. At this time their main aims were to record, characterise, and compile a basic framework of data and chronologies. For instance, precious few Neolithic monuments had been excavated (save perhaps in the Avebury area and Stonehenge itself), and the comprehension of the environment and land-use which accompanied them was essentially non-existent.

The birth of a new discipline in Wessex

In the late 1960s and 1970s a number of energetic, influential biological scientists and the first 'environmental archaeologists' used sites and monument in the region to further their development of palaeo-environmental enquiry. In the 1970s, environmental archaeological studies were strongly influenced by the Department of Human Environment of the Institute of Archaeology, London. This 'team', taught directly by Zeuner and Cornwall, included the pre-eminent practitioners, Geoff Dimbleby (*Plants in Archaeology*, 1967; *The Palynology of Archaeological*

Sites, 1985) and John Evans (*Land Snails in Archaeology*, 1972; *Introduction to Environmental Archaeology*, 1975; *The Environment of Early Man in the British Isles*, 1979). In this decade they set down the foundations for the first full generation of environmental archaeologists – of which Martin Bell, Charly French and I, for instance, are products. The archaeology of Wessex provided the arena for key archeological studies (eg, Colin Renfrew's 'Monuments, mobilization and social organization in Neolithic Wessex', 1973, and Andrew Fleming's 'Territorial patterns in Bronze Age Wessex', 1971), and narratives such as these provided the foundation for the development of environmental enquiry at the landscape and regional scale at which societies operated.

Setting the framework

Detailed site investigations in the late 1970s and 1980s produced nationally significant palaeo-environmental sequences from Neolithic henges at Durrington Walls, Mount Pleasant and Stonehenge, and long barrows such as Maiden Castle, Milbarrow, and Easton Down. This information in turn enabled regional syntheses and hypotheses (Evans 1971) such as the table published by John Evans in 1979 (Evans and Jones 1979; table 26, republished by Roy Entwistle and Mark Bowden in 1991). The chalklands that were previously largely devoid of palaeo-environmental history were shown to have been clothed in post-glacial woodland which was progressively removed and cleared by populations building monuments and establishing farming (Table 6.1; see Allen and Scaife 2007, and Allen 2009 for a summary of this history).

In recent years archaeologists in Wessex have been more pro-active in raising the research profile of environmental archaeology than in other regions. For instance, 'environmental archaeology' was included as a separate topic alongside the conventional period reviews in the Hampshire Research Agenda (Allen in Hinton and Hughes 1996) and the Avebury World Heritage Site research agenda (Allen in Chadburn and Pomeroy 2001). More relevantly it was also given its own short section in the CBA Wessex research agenda *Wessex before Words* (Allen in Woodward and Gardiner 1998).

Complacency, data gathering and lack of direction?

However, with the onset of developer-funded studies in the 1990s and beyond, environmental archaeology in part lost its way. This is still evident today, as developer-funded contract archaeology has been led down the path of data gathering ('stamp collecting'). Interpretation and analysis of data tend to be restricted to the individual site, to the detriment of more holistic and regional interpretation. There has thus been a failure to engage with past societies in the round, instead of focusing on fragments of evidence from their landscapes.

Climatic zone	Godwin Pollen zone	Interglacial chronozone	Archaeological period	Climate and vegetation	Approximate date calibrated BC/(BP)
Sub-atlantic	VIII	Flandrian III	Roman period Iron Age Late Bronze Age	*Deterioration* Cold and wet, general deterioration. High rainfall. Decline of lime. Increase of ash, birch and beech	1250 cal BC (2900 BP)
Sub-boreal	VIIb		Middle Bronze Age Early Bronze Age Final Neolithic	*Stable* Warm and dry, low rainfall, wind-blown deposits. Woodland regeneration in southern England	3200 cal BC (4500 BP)
			Late Neolithic Middle Neolithic Early Neolithic	Declining warmth. Landnam and first agriculture. Elm decline 3800 cal BP (5050BP)	3800 cal BC (5050BP) 4000 cal BC (5200 BP)
Atlantic	VIIa	Flandrian II	Later Mesolithic	*Optimum* Climatic optimum, warm and wet. Increase of 2oC, poly-climax forest. Increase of alder, some clearances	6300 cal BC (7500 BP)
Boreal	VI V	Flandrian I	Mesolithic	*Ameliorating* Continental climate, warm and dry. Asynchronous expansions of mixed oak forest with hazel and successional from pine	8900 cal BC (9500 BP)
Pre-boreal	IV		Early Mesolithic	*Rapid Amelioration* Sharp increase in warmth at 10,000 BP. Birch; juniper and pine woodland	10,000 cal BC (10,000 BP)

Table 6.1. Outline of climatic zonation (after Sir Harry Godwin and Richard West), interglacial chronozone, archaeological periods and basic vegetational change for southern England. This allows pollen zones quoted in many specialist pollen and quaternary geography reports to be equated to the archaeological chronology and activity

A new framework?

Two decades of commercial archaeology have amassed a vast amount of good but disparate evidence. We now find ourselves at a crossroads – one at which we can either become swamped in data, or choose to move on in leaps and bounds if the data are used and interpreted boldly, enabling rigorous challenging of former and new interpretations. The following vignettes illustrate how environmental archaeological studies can engage with archaeological enquiry from prehistoric to medieval periods and from chalkland to aquatic landscapes.

Our understanding of Neolithic henges was vastly advanced by the work of Geoff Wainwright at Durrington Walls, Mount Pleasant, and Marden, but the sites then became fossilised by Scheduled Ancient Monument status that prevented their re-investigation. This has, however, allowed a period of reflection, re-examination, and digestion of the Neolithic as a whole. As a result, these monuments can now be re-investigated with an entirely new set of questions, in a new framework of Neolithic enquiry and with a new set of tools (eg Parker Pearson *et al* 2004). In a similar vein, environmental archaeology, particularly of the chalklands, is now seeing the same process of re-evaluation of original models and the development of new ideas of landscape and land-use histories. This is being led by myself, Charly French and Rob Scaife among others (French *et al* 2003; 2007; Allen 2002). New interpretations are beginning to emerge as illustrated below.

Examples of environmental archaeology and geoarchaeology in Wessex

1: Dorset Heath (1986–91)

A series of sixteen excavations across much of the fragile, protected Dorset Heathland was conducted in advance of infrastructure development relating to the Wytch Farm Oilfield. The excavations revealed evidence of Mesolithic to post-medieval activity (Cox and Hearne 1991, table 3). One of the key studies was that of the pollen (Rob Scaife) which provided an overall interpretation of the vegetation history but, more importantly, of the history of inadvertent change to the landscape by human activity, and the 'manufacture' of the landscape we see today, to the detriment and destruction of the former 'natural' landscape (Allen and Scaife 1991).

The heathland and bog landscape that exists today is undoubtedly beautiful, with significant, rare, and fragile floral and faunal communities and colonies that deserve the protection and management they are afforded (SSSI and AONB). But these complex and rare ecologies that we strive to preserve (Fig 6.10) are not 'natural' in the sense that, without human intervention in the past, they would not be present today. The earlier prehistoric environment was one of 'climax' woodland supported by thick humic woodland soils – brown earths, or even brown forest soils (argillic brown earths). Initial clearance in early prehistory and, certainly, more extensive clearance in the Bronze Age led to depletion of soil nutrients, progressive acidification, soil erosion, and the invasion of heathland

Fig 6.10 Modern view of a part of Wytch Farm heath showing plagioclimax vegetation probably typical of the Iron Age (after Cox and Hearne 1991, pl 33; © Wessex Archaeology)

Fig 6.11 Strenuous augering in Langstone Harbour (© E Wakefield and the Council for British Archaeology)

plants and ultimately podzolisation; ie the creation of heath and heathland soils. The development of podzols and typical ericaceous vegetation is a direct result of prehistoric actions and mismanagement of a former woodland landscape, with the loss of thicker, more fertile, soils. The heathland of today is very fragile, and the now sandy soils are highly susceptible to erosion, but the vegetation needs to be 'culled' to maintain the heathland status by burning or extensive grazing to retard woodland succession. Left to its own devices woodland would start to take hold, podzolisation would eventually be arrested, and brown earth soils would develop. Prehistoric communities had unwittingly, via clearance and cultivation, *created* a completely new Dorset landscape by the end of the Bronze Age.

2: *Langstone Harbour (1993–2000)*

The examination of artefacts and deposits below high water was not a new concept in Wessex. Peat deposits exposed during development in Portsmouth and Southampton docks (1940s and 1950s) enabled the observation of sedimentary and peat sequences, the recovery of artefacts, and the study of pollen sequences which were used to characterise the British vegetation history (eg Godwin 1975). They also demonstrated that the prehistoric landscape clearly extended beyond the current coastline and that sea level was considerably lower than at present. Since then, relatively little archaeological work had been conducted in these intertidal areas and virtually no palaeo-environmental work undertaken. The three harbours, Chichester, Portsmouth, and Langstone, were considered to be infilled deeply incised ancient valleys containing well-buried prehistoric land surfaces – as indeed was evident at both Portsmouth and Southampton. Nevertheless, fieldwork by a young Barry Cunliffe and later more systematic recording by Richard Bradley and Barri Hooper (Bradley and Hooper 1973) recovered extensive distributions of prehistoric artefacts strewn across the poorly accessible intertidal zone. This was reinforced by the similar work of Caroline Cartwright in Chichester harbour in 1982; these studies clearly demonstrated the archaeological potential of these harbours and, by inference, the intertidal zones along the Wessex coastline generally.

The realisation of the potential and fragility of the archaeological resource was recognised by the then County Archaeologist, Mike Hughes, who with great foresight funded, via Hampshire County Council, an archaeological and geoarchaeological survey of Langstone Harbour. Colleagues from a number of different commercial and academic organisations collaborated in a concentrated period of fieldwork that was reliant on a strong geoarchaeological framework involving strenuous augering (Fig 6.11) and extensive fieldwork (Allen and Gardiner 2000). Mapping of the sedimentary architecture provided the basis of our understanding of the present distributions of archaeological artefacts. This, combined with low-tide survey, palynological analysis (Rob Scaife), and the study of waterlogged plant remains and submerged forests (Alan Clapham), enabled a new prehistory of Langstone and our southern coast to be presented. Environmental and geoarchaeological enquiry were pursued with rigour, despite

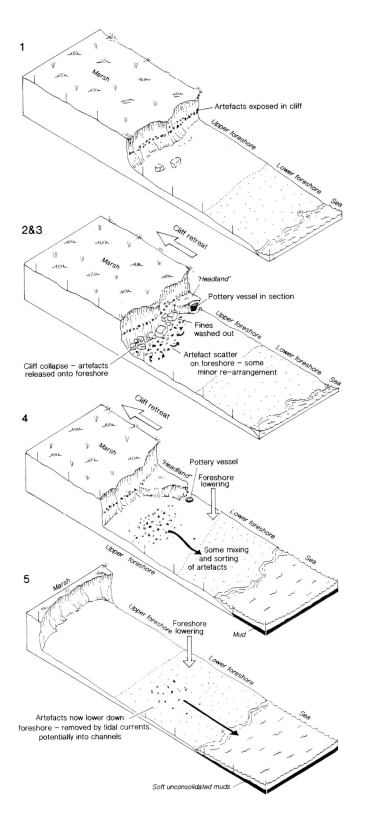

Fig 6.12 Model of the stages of 'cliff' retreat, releasing and eroding artefacts which are then redistributed across the intertidal zone and ultimately lost to the sea (from Allen & Gardiner 2000, fig 59; © Wessex Archaeology)

NEW ANTIQUARIANS

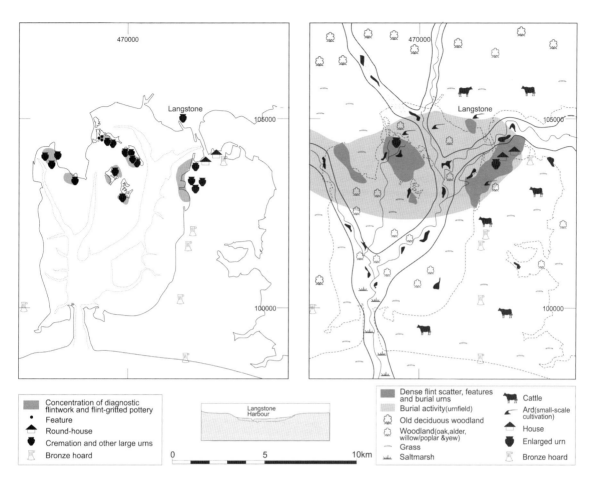

Fig 6.13 Distribution of the later Bronze Age activity in Langstone harbour, and (right) reconstruction of the later Bronze Age landscape and activities (from Allen & Gardiner 2000, fig 64; © Wessex Archaeology)

the difficult and challenging conditions, and demonstrated that Langstone Harbour, far from being a drowned landscape, was a shallowly buried, eroded, and eroding one. Artefacts on the current foreshore had fallen from low cliffs and become exposed, then mixed, before eventually being washed away. (Fig 6.12) What the geoarchaeology indicated was extensive and intensive prehistoric occupation of an area of dry land that is now intertidal and largely inaccessible. The palaeo-environmental evidence suggested a wooded dry environment which was inundated by rising tides and ground water levels. Limited settlement occurred on the slightly higher ground (Fig 6.13) while a large part of the northern harbour was previously a large open flat cemetery in the Bronze Age – hardly the marginal landscape we perceive today.

3: *The* **Mary Rose** *(1982–2005)*

The *Mary Rose*, raised in 1982, was a spectacular international event for Wessex. The archaeology was well documented – but it was also thanks to members of CBA Wessex that the first real structured investigation of the environmental archaeology from a maritime site was instigated. Led by Jennie Coy and Frank Green, a strong

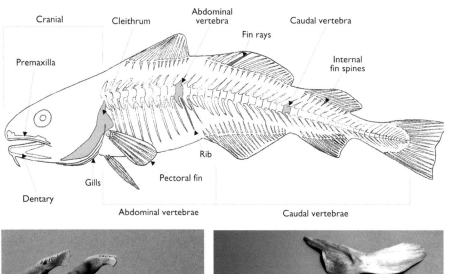

Cranial

Premaxilla

Cleithrum

Abdominal vertebra

Fin rays

Caudal vertebra

Internal fin spines

Dentary

Gills

Pectoral fin

Rib

Abdominal vertebrae

Caudal vertebrae

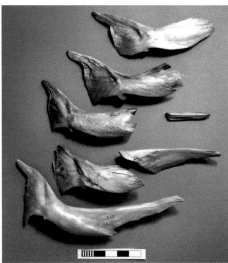

Fig 6.14 Skeleton of cod with typical elements recovered from the *Mary Rose* highlighted (top); two obliquely chopped vertebrae (left), and (right) a selection of butchered cod cleithra showing cuts to remove the head (with modern example at bottom) (All images by permission of S Hamilton-Dyer and The *Mary Rose* Trust; © Sheila Hamilton-Dyer)

environmental programme was incorporated in the later stage of the marine excavation, and in the early stages of what we would now call assessment and post-excavation analysis. The wreck itself provided a wide and largely unprecedented range of artefacts preserved by waterlogging that are normally lost on dryland sites (see Hamer, this volume). Many of these were 'normal' everyday objects not exclusive to the maritime context and provide important information about Tudor life (Gardiner with Allen 2005). The same is true of the range of preserved environmental remains. The understanding, however, of survival and distribution of both was largely achieved by the study of the geoarchaeology and taphonomy of the site. The environmental remains themselves provide one of the best Tudor assemblages in the country and a significant research archive for the study of Tudor farming, economy, and markets – as well as for the provisioning and victualling of the ship. For instance, baskets of plums (bullaces) and apples were recovered, representing a number of different varieties of each. Such information is not normally accessible from more usual charred remains, and possibly suggests supply from a range of orchards. Bones of salted beef and pork had been specifically prepared for provisioning the ship, displaying consistent butchery practices indicating the 'industrial' scale of production necessary to supply not only the *Mary Rose* but the whole Tudor fleet. Similarly butchered and prepared salted cod was stored in casks, each beheaded and gutted so consistently it was almost mechanical. These instances alone allude to the scale of the Tudor economy and market needed to prepare the fleet (Fig 6.14).

4: Stonehenge and the prehistoric chalklands (1997–2007)

I have argued that the landscape contemporary with Stonehenge was open and farmed, and the farming economy was big enough to support the large communities necessary to build Stonehenge (Fig 6.15). The emergence of farmers (as opposed to farming) enabled such a central monument to be constructed, and the risks inherent in a wholesale farming economy (primarily single-point failures) provided the *raison d'être* for these large-scale community-bonding projects (Allen 1997a). At a smaller scale, even the history of use of a Bronze Age barrow can be significantly enhanced by understanding of its wider land-use history. Buckskin barrow in Hampshire was a typical ditched barrow with stake rings, but it contained no primary burial (Allen *et al* 1995). Detailed analysis of land snail evidence was able to show that, contrary to a popular belief that chalkland barrow mounds existed as gleaming white 'beacons' visible from afar, the mound became an overgrown and tangled mass of brambles and grass within years of its construction. This was only cleared centuries later when the mound was re-used and burials were inserted for the first time.

On a larger and more significant scale, others studies of the chalkland landscapes at Stonehenge (Allen 1995; 1997a), Dorchester (Allen 1997b), and Cranborne Chase (French *et al* 2003; 2007; French 2009; Allen 2002) have started to redefine the whole vegetational history and development of the chalklands, which will have a profound effect on our understanding of the archaeological history (Allen and Scaife 2007; Allen 2009; French 2009). No longer is it likely that the whole chalklands from Dover to Dorset were swathed in a uniform post-glacial woodland blanket (see Table 6.1), nor that deep brown forest soils (argillic brown earths) uniformly mantled the chalk. Instead, it seems that the chalklands supported a series of fine- and coarse-grained mosaics of vegetation, broadly comprising woodland. But within that woodland were large areas, perhaps as large as parishes, where woodland development was retarded by natural processes and by animal browsing and grazing. It seems likely that these areas then became the foci of early prehistoric (Mesolithic) activity, having fewer trees, better visibility and a greater diversity of nuts and berries to attract browsing animals. Thus meat and vegetable resources were immediately on hand for Mesolithic and Neolithic hunters. Recent research has not only identified the presence of these landscapes (in strong contrast with, for instance, the South Downs of Sussex) but now shows a very strong correlation between them and the centres of rich, and 'ritual',

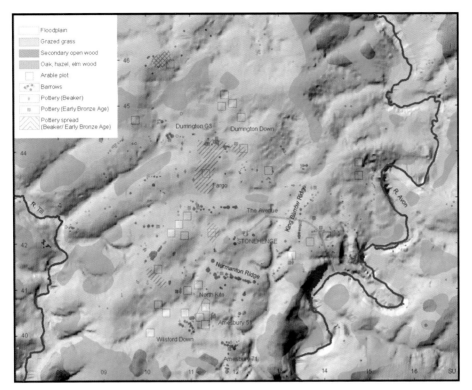

Fig 6.15 Vegetation and land-use in the Stonehenge landscape in the early to middle Neolithic c 4000–3000 cal BC (a) and the Chalcolithic to early Bronze Age c 2550–2600 cal BC (b) (after Allen 1997b; © M J Allen)

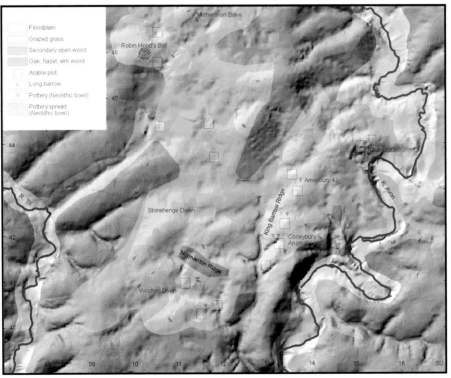

NEW ANTIQUARIANS

landscapes. Hypotheses of 'more open landscapes' have thus been proffered for the Dorchester area, Cranborne Chase and Stonehenge – all major centres of ceremonial monuments in Wessex. Perhaps, therefore, we can start to suggest that settlement locations were driven by natural rather than anthropogenic phenomena – an issue I explore in more depth elsewhere (Allen 2009).

5: Geoarchaeology of rivers and valleys

The late John Evans started to examine chalkland river valleys and demonstrated their archaeological and palaeo-environmental significance. His work in the Kennet (eg Evans *et al* 1988; 1993) and subsequently the Test valleys (currently being brought to conclusion by Paul Davies) demonstrated the archaeological significance of these locations of communication, settlement, and farming. Alluviation had provided a thin sedimentary veneer that masked the archaeology from easy observation and encouraged a misconceived picture of damp, inhospitable conditions and a low use of the resources of valleys and floodplains. These alluvial sediments provided stratified environmental histories that incorporated archaeological event horizons and in turn allowed holistic re-interpretation of land and human activity. Indeed this work inspired that which was later conducted in the Wylye Valley (Allen and Gardiner 2004; Gardiner and Allen 2009).

In contrast to river valleys, chalk dry valleys do not contain permanent water courses or alluvium. Deeply stratified hillwash or colluvium has long been demonstrated to have accumulated in these valleys and these too provide the opportunity to examine long environmental and land-use histories on the chalk downs, dated through the careful recovery and plotting of small eroded artefacts (see Bell 1983). Although long histories have been obtained, most of the original soils and information seem to have been flushed out (Allen 1992). However, two decades of studying such settlements in south-east England have not only provided information on a regional scale but clearly demonstrated, through the recovery of numerous previously unknown Beaker 'settlement' sites (see Allen 2005), the potential for colluvium to mask archaeological information and thus bias the archaeological record obtained through normal archaeological reconnaissance (Allen 1988; 1991). Geoarchaeological and palaeo-environmental enquiry in these locations has opened a whole new landscape for *archaeological* enquiry.

Some concluding thoughts

Commercial archaeology has been good at data collection and site-based interpretation but poor at developing more general narratives and at making wider regional connections. Research has largely been based around projects or small-scale landscapes and has rarely looked at regions or periods.

In 50 years we have seen the development, blossoming and maturing of environmental archaeology within the portfolio of archaeology in Wessex. But where now? There are two main questions to address here: i) what shall we do now; and ii) how can this be accomplished by archaeological practitioners in Wessex? The former is addressed in part in the numerous new research agenda being drafted, of which the Solent–Thames is most relevant to us in Wessex (www.buckscc.gov.uk/bcc/content/index). Some of these themes also emerge from the text above. How do we ensure that archaeological practitioners continue to engage in environmental archaeology and geoarchaeology, and address new and larger themes? The onus is clearly on environmental archaeologists to ensure that their texts and interpretations address *archaeological* questions and are archaeologically relevant. Among archaeological practitioners I see three main players: commercial archaeology conducted by archaeological units; research archaeology conducted (largely though not wholly) via university departments; and thirdly the unpaid amateur research carried out by local and regional societies. It is easy to see how the first two of these can engage with environmental studies, but because environmental archaeology is a specialist scientific discipline, the volunteer sector will find it increasingly difficult to engage in it without either considerable funding and training or the generous (and unpaid) support of individual professional experts in the field. This is clearly an area that requires addressing at both a regional and national level.

Ironically, despite this rich regional history of environmental archaeology the local universities (Bournemouth, Bristol, Reading, Southampton and Winchester) have not, until very recently, made any really significant contribution to the environmental or geoarchaeological study of Wessex landscapes. It is perhaps continued and expanded teaching at this level that will aid the field practitioners and increase the number of specialists that we can entice into Wessex. For the time being it remains a disturbing fact that although a very high proportion of archaeological students successfully complete higher education courses and progress into professional careers, the majority of them do not know what a soil is. Nor do they know the difference between a soil and a sediment – in spite of the fact that these are the very materials they will be intimately involved with for most of their careers!

Acknowledgements

Thanks are due as always, to Julie Gardiner, my personal editor, for improvement in the sense and clarity of the text, and for sorting out the digital images. I am grateful to Sheila Hamilton-Dyer for permission to reproduce her illustrations (Figure 6.14). Thanks are also due to both Wessex Archaeology and the Mary Rose Trust for permission to reproduce figures I have published previously elsewhere.

7

Archaeology and the Public

'Public and private': the role of Wessex Archaeology 1979–2008 and beyond

Sue Davies

The opportunity to celebrate 50 years of the Wessex group of the Council for British Archaeology and to look at the role and development of the major archaeological practice in the region is most welcome. My own career in archaeology – which was entirely unexpected (I was offered a job after finals by David Peacock and Mike Fulford on the UNESCO 'Save Carthage' Project) – spans (I regret to reflect) more than 30 years, most of which have been spent in Wessex, after a brief sojourn in the warmer climes of North Africa.

Local societies and individual members form part of the bedrock of CBA Wessex and in this time I have been lucky enough to work with many of the local societies – in the early days with the Lower Test Valley Archaeological Society and the Andover Archaeological Society at Old Down Farm, but subsequently with many others including the Avon Valley, Christchurch, Dorset and New Forest groups and societies. One of those who cut their teeth in archaeology at Old Down Farm working at the weekends was the schoolboy Mike Heyworth, now Director of the CBA.

It is appropriate to record here the enormous debt that Wessex Archaeology owes to Bill Putnam, who died on 14 October 2008 shortly before the conference was held. Alongside his teaching at Weymouth College and then Bournemouth University and many other commitments, Bill was proud to be Wessex Archaeology's first Chairman of the Board. He led the organisation from 1977 to 1999, guiding it through times of great change. He was a huge influence and saw the potential of a diverse economy – allowing us to invest in and diversify into marine archaeology and other areas. Bill was famous for wearing brown cardigans, especially when visiting site, and while I am not entirely sure how many cardigans he got through when he was Chairman, he was a lovely man, very thoughtful and caring, and with a deep knowledge of his subject and people (Fig 7.1).

Those two decades and the following years saw substantial changes in the ways in which archaeology is practised and funded in the UK. The 1970s saw a growth in organisations funded by local authorities and government which were organised primarily on a territorial basis. By the late 1980s, however, this structure was changing, with a shift from public to private funding and new emphasis on competitive tendering.

Fig 7.1 Bill Putnam, Chairman of Wessex Archaeology from 1977 to 1999, with Lord Montagu, the Chairman of English Heritage, at the opening of the Trust's new Portway House headquarters in 1988 (© Wessex Archaeology)

By the 1990s the principle of offsetting damage, sometimes known as 'polluter pays', was well established and in some ways the implementation of *Planning Policy Guidance 16: Planning and Archaeology* (PPG 16) in 1990 signified not only the formalisation of this but also the withdrawal of government funding for field archaeology apart from strategic projects. On the one hand this brought about a significant period of growth for archaeological companies: many more practices were established, and shortly before the 2008–10 recession started there were more than 3000 archaeologists working in professional practice, with the turnover of the UK sector being estimated at more than £100 million. On the other hand, the changing way in which the work was organised, and in particular the short timescales both for the work and, perhaps more importantly, the lead-in time for excavations (which is typically a matter of weeks), has restricted the opportunities for community involvement.

Wessex Archaeology: a historical sketch

Wessex Archaeology was founded in 1979 and sprang from the Wessex Archaeological Committee. In 1983 it became a registered charity and a company (limited by guarantee), with its charitable object being 'to advance the education of the public in the subject of archaeology'. The object was changed in 2004 to one that – in my view – better reflects archaeology as a process of understanding about people and their landscapes: 'to advance the education of the public in the subjects of arts, culture, heritage and science through the pursuit of archaeology'.

Initially Wessex Archaeology was entirely funded by the Department of the Environment and only worked within the five counties of Berkshire, Dorset, Hampshire, the Isle of Wight, and Wiltshire. From about 1987, however, and almost coincidental with the introduction of competitive tendering, work began to extend across southern England and Wales. With this came a shift in funding. Throughout the 1980s the contribution of developers increased steadily so that by the mid-1990s almost all of the company's income was from this source. In recent years, strategic projects commissioned by the public sector and other sources, such as the Aggregates Levy Sustainability Fund and the Heritage Lottery Fund, have adjusted the balance but the private sector remains the major funding stream.

At the same time as this change in funding streams, Wessex Archaeology began to work more widely, and other companies began to work in Wessex. Most of the older-established companies, such as Oxford Archaeology, are, like Wessex, charities or charitable trusts. A few local government organisations remain but those companies that have been founded more recently have typically been established on a commercial basis. In some cases for-profit companies expanded their geographical base to take advantage of markets – for example during the short life of the Celtic Tiger economy in Eire. There are also companies or consultancies that specialise in certain methods, for example geophysics. In addition there are many sole traders, usually expert in particular disciplines.

With this rapid diversification in the supply of archaeological services has come a feeling of fragmentation. The short lead-in times for fieldwork not only restrict community participation but also make it difficult to work effectively with museums, schools, and other organisations that provide access and learning opportunities. It is also now quite possible for archaeologists to be unaware of important projects taking place quite close by. Even so, there is still a strong charitable flavour in the sector. Until very recently the six largest archaeological organisations in the UK were all charitable companies.

Activities, past and present

In the early 1980s Wessex Archaeology carried out what would now be regarded as a 'traditional' range of land-based excavation and reporting works, surveys, and the writing-up of backlog excavations. Now we have probably the most diverse set of skills and services of any organisation in the UK, covering work on land and in the marine environment. There are more than 50 types of project, from evaluation to geophysics, to building recording, conservation statements and plans, sensitivity analyses, condition surveys, landscape characterisation, marine surveys and Environmental Impact Assessments.

As the range of work has increased so has the size of the practice. To give you some idea of the changes in scale, Wessex Archaeology started with three people

– Ann Woodward as Director, John Iles (the Administration Officer), and me, shortly rising to about fifteen staff, among whom were luminaries such as Peter Cox, Peter Fasham, Chris Gingell, John Hawkes, Sue Lobb, Julian Richards, and Rob Read. And, of course, one Phil Harding, who is still with the company. Through the 1980s our staff level, including fixed-term contracts, averaged about 40, with peaks generated by the Manpower Services Schemes. Through the 1990s we employed an average of 70–80 staff, but by 2000 we had more than 100. By 2003 there were 165 and in 2008, before the start of the 2008–10 recession, at one stage we had more than 200 staff.

The number of projects undertaken has risen from fewer than 100 a year in the 1980s to more than 800 in 2008. These projects span the UK, and some are international. Turnover has also risen, from less than £1 million in the early 1980s to several millions in 2008. This should be seen in perspective. In 2007–08 the archaeological excavations undertaken in the south-east of England in the context of PPG 16 by Wessex Archaeology alone covered some 150 hectares – or 200 football pitches!

While the scale of land-based work has increased – and this includes analytical field survey and also building recording – so too has that in the coastal and marine sector. We now have more than 20 full-time staff with marine expertise, from geophysicists to divers, and projects in this sector account for 18–20 per cent of Wessex Archaeology's annual turnover. Today Wessex Archaeology is the largest provider of coastal and marine archaeology services in the UK.

Change and innovation

Changes have not just been restricted to the range of projects and their size. There have also been major changes in technology and communications. The use of digital survey gear, GPS and lidar is now standard and laser scanning can be deployed (Fig 7.2). The web is crucial in communicating with the public and within the organisation an intranet fulfils a similar role. Multimedia, such as the use of video and podcast, is also playing an ever-increasing role in interpretation and communication.

While we have dedicated staff working in access and learning, working with schools, and supporting training excavations, the demand for opportunities to participate in such excavations far exceeds our current supply capacity (Fig 7.3). On the one hand we need to create new ways of funding and providing these opportunities. On the other hand the increasing use of the web as a method of dissemination also means that a wider range of staff can contribute to our charitable objectives. We are steadily increasing the number of reports available not just through the Archaeology Data Service (ADS) website but also on our own site.

A more unusual result of our outreach activities is that both a school and a pub were named after one of our most important discoveries, the Amesbury Archer! This serves to highlight how popular archaeology has become, largely because of the media. Special mention should be made of *Time Team* in this

Fig 7.2 Modelling
the intervisibility of
monuments in the
Stonehenge Basin: just
one of the many new
techniques pioneered
by Wessex Archaeology
(© Wessex Archaeology)

Fig 7.3 Children spending
a day learning about life
in the Bronze Age at a
real archaeological site
(© Wessex Archaeology)

Fig 7.4 Phil Harding being filmed during a *Time Team* excavation at Salisbury Cathedral (© Wessex Archaeology)

regard, not just for generating so much interest among the general public but also for its role in explaining what archaeologists do and acting as advocates for the sector (Fig 7.4). While Phil Harding may be best known as a *Time Team* star, he does actually work for Wessex Archaeology, and we provide the behind-the-camera archaeological support for each programme, prepare the reports on the excavations, and host those reports on our website.

Interest in our projects can reach far beyond Wessex or the UK. By its nature marine archaeology is international in its scope and this is well shown by the story of the SS *Mendi* (see *British Archaeology* **99**, April–May 2008). She was a troop ship carrying the South African Native Labour Corps to the Western Front in 1917 (Fig 7.5). In thick fog off the Isle of Wight she was accidentally rammed and sunk by a British boat with the loss of 600 lives. The tragedy was not recognised

Fig 7.5 The SS *Mendi* troop ship, sunk off the Isle of Wight in 1917. A recent multibeam scan of the ship by Wessex Archaeology is shown in Figure 6.5 (reproduced by courtesy of the South African Navy)

by the South African government and the story of the *Mendi* became an iconic one in that country's struggle against apartheid, yet was barely known in the UK until recently. The web statistics and a steady flow of media interest show that the story is becoming known around the world.

More of the same? Or something different?

Turning to the future, it is important to recognise that what archaeologists do – studying people and environments – is essentially the study of change. Our involvement in the planning process means that we are involved in managing change and are an integral part of the contemporary sustainability agenda. This challenge – conserving without fossilising the environment we live in, which is the result of activity over millennia – is a difficult one. Changes are in store for the planning framework and its regulatory system in the Planning Policy Statement that will supersede PPGs 15 and 16, but we also all need to change our habits and work better together if we are to have a sustainable future. Archaeologists will have to adapt, as will others. But in order to work better and achieve our objectives in a changing world, we have to understand what matters in it. This demands a thorough understanding of all aspects of significance in the historic environment. And archaeology – as well as archaeologists of all shapes and forms – has the potential to play an important role in understanding what is regarded as significant and why.

While – as long as there are not too many changes to the planning system – we will continue to provide services to a range of people, this work will also entail an ambassadorial or advocacy role, and a political one too. We need to influence policy and decision-makers by explaining why archaeology matters. Cultural heritage is still not well enough considered by government, of whatever political persuasion, and within government there is a lack of joined-up thinking that must change. As we have seen, there is a huge public interest, which should be taken into account, but the sector is varied and fragmented and for it to influence government it needs focus – something that the CBA is beginning to provide.

Archaeology also has a huge role to play in interpreting social values and providing public benefit. It can do this through making an understanding of the past increasingly accessible and relevant, by building social inclusion through enhancing community identity and sense of place, and by helping to sustain a living and dynamic historic environment. It could also make a bigger contribution to key contemporary issues such as the climate-change debate.

But the profession also needs to make sure that it listens to its audiences, which include the voluntary sector, and that it makes the information it creates available. The archaeological sector as a whole can be a shade inward-looking and introspective. This is not a newly developed characteristic but it is one to guard against because the sector is accountable. Ultimately all continuing funding, whether from the public or the private sector, rests on continuing public support and being seen to be relevant. That challenge is before us.

Panel discussion: archaeology and the public

Mike Heyworth

It was fitting that a conference programme looking back on 50 years of archaeology in Wessex should end with a debate on archaeology and the public. The panel members were Sue Davies (Chief Executive of Wessex Archaeology), Marjolein Mussellwhite (Chair of the Basingstoke Archaeological & Historical Society), Julian Richards (a freelance archaeologist with considerable media experience as a presenter and writer), and Katy Whitaker (from the English Heritage National Monuments Record and a local branch leader of the Young Archaeologists' Club), with contributions to the discussions also encouraged from the audience.

Archaeology and the media

The first topic for consideration related to the way in which archaeology was represented on television (through programmes like *Bonekickers*) and through films such as the Indiana Jones series. This subject has been much aired in discussions during the year, particularly in relation to the *Bonekickers* series, which had been heavily criticised by many sections of the archaeological community.

It was generally acknowledged by the panel and the audience that many aspects of the representation of archaeology in the media was helpful in portraying the subject as exciting and involving the thrill of discovery – though there was wariness of the view of archaeology as 'treasure hunting'. The public can discriminate between 'fantasy', such as Indiana Jones, and more documentary-style programmes such as *Meet The Ancestors* or *Time Team*, though one of the concerns about *Bonekickers* was where it was perceived to sit in this spectrum. If it is seen to be a representation of 'real' archaeology then this might be more of a concern, but was that really the intention of the programme makers? It can be argued that their job was to make good television – though from the reaction of most critics they seemed to have singularly failed in this desire!

In general, most people thought that we could wholeheartedly welcome the widespread depiction of archaeology in the media, which was seen as positive and helping to draw people into archaeology in a more active way. The long-running recent storyline on Radio 4's *The Archers* that related to a community archaeology project in Ambridge was quoted as an example of an educative and responsible approach to archaeology and the public. Of far greater concern than Indiana Jones and his like was thought to be the pseudo-documentary programmes that muddle fact and fiction in ways which are potentially very misleading about key aspects of the past. These often pick up on key historical events or myths (such as the Arthurian legends, or the Holy Grail stories, or even alleged alien visits to Earth in the past) and portray them in ways that make it very hard for the audience to distinguish between the facts and the interpretations.

Encouraging participation in archaeology

The discussions on the representation of archaeology in the media led naturally on to the topic of how we could draw more people in to archaeology and persuade them to become active participants. This is a key topic for all local archaeological societies, especially linked with the issue of how to attract a younger audience to engage with traditional routes into the subject.

The panel members brought considerable experience to bear on this topic and had a variety of constructive suggestions to put forward. Inevitably the starting point was the suggestion that we should ask more non-society members why they are not members, and find out their thoughts on what they would actually like to do if they did become involved. How many of our existing societies have pro-active programmes of outreach to go out and engage with non-members?

The Basingstoke Archaeological & Historical Society (www.bahsoc.org.uk) is clearly a good example of a society that does have a very lively programme of activities, inevitably run by a number of energetic people who form the nucleus of the group via their committee. The vigorous promotion of their programme of lectures, site visits, field activities (including excavations), and historical projects are the key to their thriving membership. They work closely with professional archaeologists and historians and provide a range of opportunities for their members to get involved – recognising that this means different things to different people, not all of whom relish the opportunity to take part in excavations or field projects.

Working together, across the different elements of the archaeological sector, is important to maximise the limited resources that a relatively small subject like archaeology can bring to bear. Commercial archaeological contractors, such as Wessex Archaeology (www.wessexarch.co.uk), have a significant role to play in communicating knowledge about the archaeological stories they have uncovered, and the techniques and methodologies that they have used. Many such companies are registered charities and have a particular obligation to deliver public benefit; they can best do this in partnership with voluntary bodies, such as local societies.

For various reasons, including a more risk-averse attitude in society leading to increased attention to matters of health and safety and insurance, it is sometimes more difficult to involve the public in field archaeological projects being run within the strictures of the planning system. However, there are rarely good reasons why it is not possible to allow the public to view the work in progress and access the results of the work through subsequent publications and websites.

Whilst for many members of the public, partly due to TV programmes like *Time Team*, archaeology is all about digging and finding 'stuff', part of the role of anyone delivering public education is to show just how painstaking and forensic modern excavations have to be to recover the full range of evidence available. High standards of work are essential, especially in a study that inevitably destroys much of the evidence it uncovers in a one-off unrepeatable experiment, but there is no reason why this has to exclude non-professionals (in the sense of people not being paid through employment to undertake their activities). Other valuable contributions can also be made through field conservation activities and the FOAM (Friends of Ancient Monuments) group within CBA Wessex are kept busy over the winter months conserving and making accessible archaeological sites across the region.

Interestingly, until it was pointed out from the audience, no-one had mentioned the role of museums in stimulating public participation in archaeology. Museums are already a treasure trove of valuable material, much in need of further work and research to ensure that it is fully catalogued, researched and published.

Two other examples of successful projects to enthuse the public were put forward from the audience. The first was the valuable work of the Sussex Archaeological Society (www.sussexpast.co.uk) involving members in environmental and archaeological science research programmes. Voluntary groups often need particular support with post-excavation programmes where specialist help is required and funds are needed to pay for the specific expertise or the application of scientific techniques, eg radiocarbon dating. More funding is needed to allow societies to have the confidence to undertake fieldwork with the reasonable expectation that they will be able to receive support, particularly in exceptional, unexpected circumstances.

Another example of good practice in working with young people is the Higher Education Field Academy (www.arch.cam.ac.uk/aca/fa) run by Carenza Lewis. In a programme that has much potential to be extended across the UK, but which is currently focused on the East Anglia region, over 450 teenagers have been introduced to practical archaeology through programmes of test-pitting in village gardens. Often initially reluctant to get involved, as soon as the digging starts and the first finds are made the students are usually hooked and it is often hard to stop them! One of the key tricks is to find the right 'champions' among the staff of the individual schools, which is surely a message that has wider application across archaeology. Whether it is in our local archaeological societies, the branches of the Young Archaeologists' Club (www.yac-uk.org) or the growing community archaeology sector, the involvement of keen enthusiasts who are prepared to lead ensures that others will be able and willing to follow.

The last word, perhaps appropriately before the limited time allocated to the debate was used up, came from a senior professional archaeologist who reminded us all that we should never underestimate the capacity and skills of the amateur archaeologist – not only to excavate and undertake other forms of fieldwork, but to go much further with the research and dissemination of their results.

From the rich and varied contributions to the conference debate it is clear that the public appreciation of, and enthusiasm for, archaeology appear to be as high as ever. And over the next 50 years there will be many opportunities to broaden the active participation of the public in archaeology across the Wessex region.

Looking to the future

Barry Cunliffe

Like all good conferences we came away from this weekend having learned a huge amount, with our perspectives sharpened and with our enthusiasms renewed. Each of us will have our own memories of how the various contributions and discussions we have enjoyed have refocused our understanding. What follows is, of necessity, a personal view.

First and foremost we have been reminded of the huge wealth of material evidence and opportunity we have here in Wessex. This may, understandably, make us complacent, encouraging us to see our region as providing the narrative for the rest of the country. Yet, in reality, Wessex is only one region with its own distinctive character, to be considered alongside other equally distinctive regions. Rather than trying to make British prehistory fit the Wessex model we should compare and contrast it with other areas in an attempt to understand something of the kaleidoscope of regional cultures that make up – and have always made up – the British Isles.

Nor is Wessex by any means an homogeneous region. We are all aware of its contrasting geomorphologies, each supporting local economies and probably differing social systems. The time has come for us to try to define and understand these sub-regions and to explore how they articulated with each other and how that interconnectedness changed over time. This requires us not only to look more closely at regional differences but also to break down the narrow, old-fashioned, period-focused approaches which have bedevilled British archaeology for so long, particularly around the prehistory/Roman divide. Continuity may be more significant than change. To give just one example: a study of Iron Age material culture suggests that there was a broad uniformity throughout Wessex until the 4th century BC when distinctive regional patterns begin to emerge which intensify in later centuries and are still visible throughout the Roman interlude, reflected in the vernacular architecture of the period. The long perspective encourages us to ask: is this the result of geomorphology or of deep-rooted territorial differences persisting over the centuries?

Differences in regional cultures inevitably raise questions of boundaries – a subject that has been sadly neglected. Physical boundaries like Bokerley Dyke and the Quarley linear remained significant markers over many hundreds of years and separated culturally distinct regions. Is there any significance in the fact that both are quite closely followed over some distance by county boundaries which would have been formalised in the 8th or 9th century AD?

Another theme to emerge from the conference is the importance of 'place' and 'memory' – issues that are difficult to make tangible with real evidence. The prime example is, of course, Stonehenge, which means all things to all men – and many choose to indulge their fantasies! Speculation aside however, as a 'place' it has existed for more than six millennia in one form or another and its very presence has demanded some form of acknowledgement by successive generations. It would be interesting to try to identify other 'places of significance' in the landscape which remained in people's cognisance over the *longue durée*. Structuring our understanding of place, boundary and regionality through time has much to offer in our attempts to understand the character of Wessex.

We have also, quite properly, reminded ourselves that archaeology has become something of a spectator sport and as a discipline we have a responsibility to satisfy the public appetite for what we do. That appetite is voracious. That this last summer a three-week excavation which I carried out at Brading Roman Villa attracted more than 8000 visitors and kept a team of guides busy from 9 am until 6 pm seven days a week is a measure of the very real interest that the general public has in our work. It was one of our great ancestor figures, Mortimer Wheeler, who, as long ago as the 1920s, reminded us that if we wanted our subject to flourish, engagement with the public would be essential. It is even more so today.

At various points throughout the weekend we looked to the future with occasional nostalgic references to the past. Peter Fowler and I met at the second CBA Wessex conference held in Salisbury in 1959 and we inevitably reminisced about the occasion! How innocent archaeology then was. In no way could we then have anticipated how the discipline was to develop over the next 50 years and to try to crystal gaze now is a rather fruitless exercise. But there are some things that can be said. Archaeology is now well embedded in the infrastructure of local and national government and we are awaiting a new Heritage Protection Bill that will give the heritage even greater security than it now has. As we are all too well aware, the present recession will pose problems but, hopefully, only in the short term. The downturn in building will inevitably mean that commercial archaeological units will come under pressure. Painful though this will be, some good may come of it. It will encourage a greater scrutiny of standards and a louder call for value for money. The pressure to rethink and refocus what commercial archaeology is all about is an opportunity that can be turned to very good purpose.

There is also another, related, issue. Excavation is becoming very expensive partly because of the increased level of post-excavation analysis that is required and partly because of the on-costs which administrators are, understandably, charging for university-based and commercial projects. These factors, exacerbated by the short-termism imposed by the Research Assessment Exercise, are very likely to mean that large, university-led projects will decline in number over the next few decades. But this is by no means a cry of despair – quite the opposite. It will require us to rethink our strategies. I firmly believe that the future for research excavation and fieldwork lies in partnerships between universities, commercial units, and the large body of amateurs who have been the backbone of archaeology in the past and have so much to offer today. Whereas over the last 50 years we have seen these threads separate, over the next 50 years we will, I believe, see them come more closely together to make practical archaeology stronger, more balanced and far more inclusive. In Wessex, where archaeology has always been innovative and where we have an excellent tradition of amateur involvement, we can continue to lead the way.

Bibliography

Addyman, P V & Hill, D H, 1968 Saxon Southampton: a review of the evidence Part I: history, location, date and character of the town, *Proc Hampshire Fld Club Archaeol Soc*, **25**, 61–93

Addyman, P V & Hill, D H, 1969 Saxon Southampton: a review of the evidence Part II: industry, trade and everyday life, *Proc Hampshire Fld Club Archaeol Soc*, **26**

Addyman, P V & Leigh, D, 1973 The Anglo-Saxon village at Chalton, Hampshire: second interim report, *Medieval Archaeol*, **17**, 1–25

Addyman, P V, Leigh, D & Hughes, M, 1972 Anglo-Saxon houses at Chalton, Hampshire, *Medieval Archaeol*, **16**, 13–32

Akerman, J Y, 1853 An account of excavations in an Anglo-Saxon burial ground at Harnham Hill, near Salisbury, *Archaeologia*, **35**, 259–78 and 475–8

Alcock, L, 1972 The Irish sea zone in the pre-Roman Iron Age, in C Thomas (ed), *The Iron Age in the Irish Sea Province*, CBA Res Rep **9**, 99–112. London: CBA

Allen, D F, 1971 The Sark hoard, *Archaeologia*, **103**, 1–31

Allen, J R L & Fulford, M G, 1996 The distribution of south-east Dorset black burnished category 1 pottery in south-west Britain, *Britannia*, **27**, 223–81

Allen, J R L & Fulford, M G, 2004 Early Roman mosaic materials in southern Britain, with particular reference to Silchester (*Calleva Atrebatum*): a regional geological perspective, *Britannia*, **35**, 9–38

Allen, J R L & Fulford, M G, 2007 Burnt Kimmeridgian shale at early Roman Silchester, south-east England, and the Roman Poole-Purbeck complex-agglomerated geomaterials industry, *Oxford J Archaeol*, **26** (2), 167–91

Allen, L G & Gibbard, P L, 1993 Pleistocene evolution of the Solent River of southern England, *Quat Sci Rev*, **12**, 503–528

Allen, M J, 1988 Archaeological and environmental aspects of colluviation in South-East England, in W Groenmann-van Waateringe & M Robinson (eds), *Man-Made Soils* BAR Int Series **410**, 69–92. Oxford: BAR

Allen, M J, 1991 Analysing the landscape: a geographical approach to archaeological problems, in A J Schofield (ed), *Interpreting Artefact Scatters; contributions to ploughzone archaeology* Oxbow Monogr **4**, 39–57. Oxford: Oxbow

Allen, M J, 1992 Products of erosion and the prehistoric land-use of the Wessex chalk, in M G Bell & J Boardman (eds), *Past and Present Soil Erosion: archaeological and geographical perspectives* 37–52. Oxford: Oxbow

Allen, M J, 1997a Environment and land-use; the economic development of the communities who built Stonehenge; an economy to support the stones, in Cunliffe & Renfrew (eds), Science and Stonehenge, *Proc British Academy* **92**, 115–44

Allen, M J, 1997b Landscape, land-use and farming, in R J C Smith, F Healy, M J Allen, E L Morris, I Barnes & P J Woodward (eds), *Excavations along the route of the Dorchester by-pass, Dorset, 1986–88* Wessex Archaeol Rep **11**, 277–83 Salisbury: Trust for Wessex Archaeology

Allen, M J, 2002 The Chalkland Landscape of Cranborne Chase: a prehistoric human ecology, *Landscapes*, **3**, 55–69

Allen, M J, 2005 Beaker settlement and environment on the chalk downs of southern England *Proc Prehist Soc*, **71**, 219–46

Allen, M J, 2009 If you go down to the woods today you're in for a big surprise, in Allen *et al*, *Land and People*, 3–11

Allen, M J & Bayliss, A, 1995 Appendix 2: the radiocarbon dating programme, in Cleal *et al*, *Stonehenge in its Landscape*, 511–35

Allen, M J & Gardiner, J P, 2000 *Our Changing Coast; a survey of the intertidal archaeology of Langstone Harbour, Hampshire*, CBA Res Rep **124**. York: CBA

Allen, M J & Gardiner J, 2004 Neolithic of the Wylye Valley 1: millennium re-investigation of the Corton Long Barrow, ST 9030 4034, *Wiltshire Archaeol Natur Hist Mag*, **97**, 63–77

Allen, M J & Green, M, 1998 The Fir Tree Field shaft: the archaeological potential of solution features in chalk *Proc Dorset Natur Hist Archaeol Soc*, **120**, 25–38

Allen, M J, Morris, M & Clark, R H, 1995 Food for the living: re-assessment of a Bronze Barrow at Buckskin, Basingstoke, Hampshire, *Proc Prehist Soc*, **61**, 157–89

Allen, M J, O'Connor, T & Sharples, N (eds) 2009 *Land and People; papers in honour of John G Evans*, Prehist Soc Res Pap **2**. Oxford: Oxbow Books and the Prehistoric Soc

Allen, M J & Scaife, R G, 1991 The exploitation of the flora and fauna and its impact on the natural and derived landscape, in P W Cox and C M Hearne (eds), *Redeemed from the Heath the archaeology of the Wytch Farm Oilfield* Dorset Natur Hist Archaeol Soc Monogr **9**, 216–20. Dorchester: Dorset Natur Hist Archaeol Soc

Allen, M J & Scaife, R, 2007 A new downland prehistory: long-term environmental change on the southern English chalklands, in A Fleming & R Hingley (eds), *Prehistoric and Roman Landscapes; landscape history after Hoskin*, 16–32. Macclesfield: Windgather Press

Allen, R, 1999 The pageant of history: a re-interpretation of the 13th-century building at King John's House, Romsey, Hampshire, *Medieval Archaeol*, **43**, 74–114

Anderson, A S, Wacher, J S & Fitzpatrick, A P, 2001 *The Romano-British Small Town at Wanborough, Wiltshire*, Britannia Monogr **19**. London: Society for the Promotion of Roman Studies

Annable, F K, Excavation and Fieldwork in Wiltshire: 1957 *Wiltshire Archaeol Natur Hist Mag* **57**, 2–17

Anon, c 1996 *Industrial Berkshire*. Reading: Babtie Group and Berkshire County Council

Arnold, C J & Wardle, P, 1981 Early medieval settlement patterns in England, *Medieval Archaeol*, **25**, 145–9

Ashbee, P, 1960 *The Bronze Age Round Barrow in Britain*. Letchworth: Aldine Press

Ashbee, P, 1978 Amesbury barrow 51: excavation 1960, *Wiltshire Archaeol Natur Hist Mag*, **70/71**, 1–60

Ashbee, P, 1981 Amesbury barrow 39: excavations 1960, *Wiltshire Archaeol Natur Hist Mag*, **74/75**, 3–34

Ashbee, P, 1984 The excavation of Amesbury barrows 58, 61a, 61, 72, *Wiltshire Archaeol Natur Hist Mag*, **79**, 39–91

Ashbee, P, Bell, M & Proudfoot, E, 1989 *Wilsford Shaft: excavations 1960–62*. London: English Heritage

Ashbee, P, Smith, I F & Evans, J G, 1979 Excavation of three long barrows near Avebury, Wiltshire, *Proc Prehist Soc*, **45**, 207–300

Ashton, N, 2008 Transport, curation and resharpening of lithics in the Lower Palaeolithic. *Lithics*, **29**, 6–17

Ashton, N & Lewis, S, 2002 Deserted Britain: Declining Populations in the British Late Middle Pleistocene, *Antiquity*, **76**, 388–96

Ashton, N & McNabb, J, 1994 Bifaces in Perspective, in N Ashton & N David (eds) *Stories in Stone*, Lithic Studies Soc Occ Pap **4**, 182–191. London: Lithic Studies Society

Astill, G G, 1978 *Historic towns in Berkshire: an archaeological appraisal*. Reading: Berkshire Archaeol Comm

Astill, G G & Lobb, S J, 1989 Excavation of prehistoric, Roman and Saxon deposits at Wraysbury, Berkshire, *Archaeol J*, **146**, 68–134

Aston, M & Lewis, C (eds) 1994 *The medieval landscape of Wessex*, Oxbow Monogr **46**. Oxford: Oxbow

Atkinson, R J C, 1956 *Stonehenge*. London: H Hamilton

Barrett, J C, 1980 The pottery of the Later Bronze Age in lowland England, *Proc Prehist Soc*, **46**, 297–320

Barrett, J, Bradley, R & Green, M, 1991 *Landscape, Monuments and Society The Prehistory of Cranborne Chase*. Cambridge: CUP

Barrett J, Bradley, R & Hall, M 1991a *Papers on the Prehistoric Archaeology of Cranborne Chase*, Oxbow Monogr **11**. Oxford: Oxbow

Barton, R N E (ed), 1992 *Hengistbury Head, Dorset: Volume 2 – The Late Upper Palaeolithic and Early Mesolithic Sites*, Oxford Uni Comm Archaeol Monogr **34**. Oxford: Oxford Uni Comm Archaeol

Barton, R N E, 1997 *Stone Age Britain*. London: Batsford and English Heritage

Basford, V, 1980 *The Vectis report: a survey of Isle of Wight archaeology*. Newport: Isle of Wight Archaeol Comm

Bates, R, Bates, M & Dix, J, 2009 Contiguous Palaeo-landscape Reconstruction: transition zone mapping for marine-terrestrial archaeological continuity. Unpublished report for English Heritage: ALSF Project Number 4632

Bates, M R, Wenban-Smith, F F, Briant, R & Marshall, G, 2004 *Palaeolithic Archaeology of the Sussex/Hampshire Coastal Corridor*, English Heritage Archive Report (Project No **3279**). London: English Heritage

Baudrillard, J, 1994 *Simulacra and Simulation. The Body in Theory: Histories of Cultural Materialism*. Ann Arbor: Uni Michigan Press

Bayliss, A & Whittle, A (eds), 2007 Histories of the dead: building chronologies for five southern British long barrows, *Cambridge Archaeol J*, **17**(1) Supplement

Bayliss, A, McAvoy, F & Whittle, A, 2007 The world re-created: redating Silbury Hill in its monumental landscape, *Antiquity*, **81**, 26–53

Bell, M G, 1983 Valley sediments as evidence of prehistoric land-use on the South Downs, *Proc Prehist Soc*, **49**, 119–50

Bell, M, Fowler, P J & Hillson, S W (eds), 1996 *The Experimental Earthwork Project 1960 – 1992*, CBA Res Rep **100**. York: CBA

Bersu, G, 1940 Excavations at Little Woodbury, Wilts, *Proc Prehist Soc*, **6**, 30–111

Besly, E & Bland, R 1983 *The Cunetio Treasure: Roman Coinage of the Third Century AD*. London: British Museum Press

Bevan, B (ed), 1999 *Northern Exposure: interpretative devolution and the Iron Ages in Britain*, Leicester Archaeol Monogr **4**. Leicester: Uni Leicester Archaeol Res Centre

BGS, Cefas, Marine Ecological Surveys, Sussex Sea Fisheries District Committee and Wessex Archaeology, 2010 *South Coast Regional Environmental Characterisation*, BGS Open Report 09/51; MEPF 08/02

Biddle, M, 1967 Two Flavian burials from Grange Road, Winchester, *Antiq J*, **47**, 224–50

Biddle, M, 1972 Excavations at Winchester 1970, ninth interim report, *Antiq J*, **52**, 93–131

Biddle, M, 1983 The study of Winchester: archaeology and history in a British town, *Proc British Academy*, **69**, 93–135

Biddle, M & Kjølbye-Biddle, B, 2007 Winchester: from *Venta* to *Wintanceaster*, in L Gilmour (ed), *Pagans and Christians*, BAR Int Ser **1610**, 189–214. Oxford: Archaeopress

Bingeman, J M, 1985 Interim report on artefacts recovered from *Invincible* (1758) between 1979 and 1984, *Int J Naut Archaeol*, **14**, 19–210

Blackmore, H P, 1864 Discovery of flint implements in the higher level gravel at Milford Hill, Salisbury, *Archaeo J*, **21**, 243–5

Blackmore, H P, 1865 On the discovery of flint implements in the drift at Milford Hill, Salisbury, *Quat J Geol Soc*, **21**, 250–2

Blair, J, 2006 *The Church in Anglo-Saxon England*. Oxford: Oxford University Press

Bond, J, 1994 Forests, chases, warrens and parks in medieval Wessex, in Aston, M & Lewis, C (eds), *The medieval landscape of Wessex*, Oxbow Monogr **4**, 115–586. Oxford: Oxbow

Bonney, D, 1966 Pagan Saxon boundaries and burials in Wiltshire, *Wiltshire Archaeol Natur Hist Mag*, **61**, 25–30

Bonney, D, 1973 The pagan Saxon period, in Crittall, E (ed) *Victoria History of the Counties of England: Wiltshire* Vol **2**(1), 468–84. Oxford: OUP for the Institute of Historical Research

Bonney, D, 1976 Early boundaries and estates in southern England, in P H Sawyer (ed) *Medieval Settlement*. London: Edward Arnold

Boon, G C, 1957 *Roman Silchester*. London: M Parrish

Boon, G C, 1959 The latest objects from Silchester, Hampshire, *Medieval Archaeol*, **3**, 79–88

Boon, G C, 1969 Belgic and Roman Silchester: The excavations of 1954–58, with an excursus on the early history of Calleva, *Archaeologia*, **102**, 1–82

Boon, G C, 1974 *Silchester: The Roman Town of Calleva*. Newton Abbott: David and Charles

Borthwick, A & Chandler, J, 1984 *Our chequered past. The archaeology of Salisbury*. Trowbridge: Wiltshire Library and Museum Service

Bowden, M & McOmish, D, 1987 The required barrier, *Scott Archaeol Rev*, **4**, 76–84

Bowden, M & McOmish, D, 1989 Little boxes: more about hillforts, *Scott Archaeol Rev*, **6**, 12–16

Bowen, H C, 1990 *The Archaeology of Bokerley Dyke*, London: HMSO

Bradley, R, 1976 Maumbury Rings, Dorchester: The Excavations of 1908–13, *Archaeologia*, **105**, 1–97

Bradley, R, 1978 *The Prehistoric Settlement of Britain*. London: Routledge

Bradley, R, 2006 Bridging the two cultures – commercial archaeology and the study of prehistoric Britain, *Antiq J*, **86**, 1–13

Bradley, R & Ellison, A, 1975 *Rams Hill: a Bronze Age defended enclosure and its landscape*, BAR Brit Ser **19**. Oxford: Archaeopress

Bradley, R, Entwistle, R & Raymond, F, 1994 *Prehistoric land divisions on Salisbury Plain: the work of the Wessex linear ditches project*. London: English Heritage

Bradley, R J & Hooper, B, 1973 Recent discoveries from Portsmouth and Langstone harbours: Mesolithic to Iron Age, *Proc Hampshire Fld Club Archaeol Soc*, **30**, 17–27

Brailsford, J W, 1948 Excavations at Little Woodbury, part II, *Proc Prehist Soc*, **14**, 1–23

Brailsford, J W, 1949 Excavations at Little Woodbury, parts IV and V, *Proc Prehist Soc*, **15**, 156–68

Briant, R M, Bates, M R, Schwenninger, J-L & Wenban-Smith, F, 2006 An optically stimulated luminescence dated Middle to Late Pleistocene fluvial sequence from the western Solent Basin, southern England, *J Quat Sci*, **21**, 507–23

Briant, R M & Schwenninger, J-L, 2009 Solent river gravels at Badminston Farm, Hampshire (SU 463 019) in R M Briant *et al*, *The Quaternary of the Solent Basin*, 189–97

Briant, R M, Bates, M R, Hosfield, R T & Wenban-Smith F F (eds), 2009a *The Quaternary of the Solent Basin and West Sussex Raised Beaches: Field Guide*, 42–59, London: Quat Res Ass

Briant, R M, Bates, M R, Boreham, S, Cameron, N G, Coope, G R, Field, M H, Keen, D H, Simons, R M J, Schwenninger, J-L, Wenban-Smith, F F & Whittaker, J E, 2009b Gravels and interglacial sediments at Stone Point Site of Special Scientific Interest, Lepe Country Park, Hampshire, in R M Briant *et al*, *The Quaternary of the Solent Basin*, 171–88

Briant, R M, Wenban-Smith, F F & Schwenninger, J-L 2009c Solent river gravels at Barton on Sea, Hampshire (SZ 230 930), in R M Briant *et al*, *The Quaternary of the Solent Basin*, 161–70

Bridgland, D R, 1994 *Quaternary of the Thames*, Geological Conservation Rev Ser No. **7**. London: Chapman and Hall

Bridgland, D R, 1996 Quaternary river terrace deposits as a framework for the Lower Palaeolithic record, in C S Gamble & A J Lawson (eds), *The English Palaeolithic Reviewed*, 23–39. Salisbury: Wessex Archaeology Ltd

Bridgland, D R, 2001 The Pleistocene evolution and Palaeolithic occupation of the Solent River, in F F Wenban-Smith & R T Hosfield (eds) *Palaeolithic Archaeology of the Solent River* 15–25. Lithic Studies Soc Occ Pap **7**. London: Lithic Studies Society

Bridgland, D R & Harding, P, 1987 Palaeolithic sites in tributary valleys of the Solent River, in K E Barber (ed), *Wessex and the Isle of Wight: Field Guide* 45–57. Cambridge: Quaternary Research Association

Bristow, C R, Freshney, E C, & Penn, I E, 1991 *The Geology of the Country around Bournemouth*, Memoirs of the Geological Survey. London: HMSO

Brown, D, 1997 Pots from houses *Medieval Ceramics*, **21**, 83–94

Brown, G, Field, D & McOmish, D, 1994 East Chisenbury midden complex, Wiltshire, in A P
    Fitzpatrick & E L Morris (eds), *The Iron Age in Wessex: recent research*, 46–49 Salisbury:
    Wessex Archaeology & AFEAF

Brown, G, Field, D & McOmish, D, 2005 *The Avebury Landscape: aspects of the field archaeology of
    the Marlborough Downs*. Oxford: Oxbow

Brown, M & Osgood, R, 2009 *Unearthing Plugstreet: the Archaeology of a Great War Battlefield*.
    Yeovil: Haynes

Budd, P, Montgomery, J, Evans, A & Bareiro, B, 2000 Human tooth enamel as a record of
    the comparative lead exposure of prehistoric and modern people, *The Science of the Total
    Environment*, **263**, 1–10

Burdett, D & Insole, A, 1995 *Discovering an Island: The Roadside Heritage of the Isle of Wight*. Isle
    of Wight: Isle of Wight Society

Burkitt, M C, Paterson, T T & Mogridge, C J, 1939 The Lower Palaeolithic industries near
    Warsash, Hampshire, *Proc Prehist Soc*, **1**, 39–50

Burnett, A M, 1990, Celtic coinage: Britain III, the Waltham St Lawrence treasure trove, *Brit
    Numis J*, **60**, 13–28

Burns, B, Cunliffe, B & Sebire, H, 1996 *Guernsey An island community of the Atlantic Iron Age*,
    Oxford Uni Comm Archaeol Monogr **43**/Guernsey Museum Monogr **6**. Oxford: Oxford Uni
    Comm Archaeol

Bury, H, 1923 Some aspects of the Hampshire Plateau Gravels, *Proc Prehist Soc East Anglia*, **4**(1),
    15–41

Bury, H, 1933 The plateau gravels of the Bournemouth area, *Proc Geol Ass*, **44**, 314–35

Butterfield, C A & Lobb, S J, 1992 *Excavations in the Burghfield area, Berkshire. Developments in
    the Bronze Age and Saxon landscapes*, Trust for Wessex Archaeol Rep **1**. Salisbury: Trust for
    Wessex Archaeology

Calkin, J B & Green, J F N, 1949 Palaeoliths and terraces near Bournemouth, *Proc Prehist Soc*, **15**,
    21–37

Callow, P & Cornford, J M (eds), 1986 *La Cotte de St. Brelade 1961–1978: Excavations by C B M
    McBurney*. Norwich: Geo Books

Campbell, E, 2007 *Continental and Mediterranean imports to Atlantic Britain and Ireland, AD
    400–800*, CBA Res Rep **157**.York: CBA

Carruthers, W, 2005 Mineralised plant remains, in Birbeck, V (ed), *The Origins of Mid-Saxon
    Southampton. Excavations at the Friends Provident St Mary's Stadium 1998–2000*, 157–63.
    Salisbury: Wessex Archaeology,

Cartwright, C R, 1982 Field survey of Chichester harbour, 1982, *Sussex Archaeol Coll*, **122**, 23–7

Catherall, P D, Barnett, M & McClean, H 1984 *The Southern Feeder. The Archaeology of a Gas
    Pipeline*. London: British Gas Corp

Cavanagh, W G, Lee, C B & James, P A, 2005 *The Laconia Rural Sites Project*. London: British
    School at Athens

Cave-Penney, H, 2005 Extensive urban survey, *Wiltshire Archaeol and Natur Hist Soc Mag*, **98**,
    165–212

Centre for Maritime Archaeology, 2009 Maritime and Marine Historic Environment Research
    Framework: Stage One, *Developing a Resource Assessment and Research Agenda for England's
    Maritime Heritage*. Project Design for English Heritage. Southampton: University of
    Southampton

Chadburn, A & Pomeroy-Kellinger M (eds), 2001 *Archaeological Research Agenda for the Avebury
    World Heritage Site*. London: English Heritage and Avebury Archaeol Hist Res Group

Chadwick Hawkes, S, 1994 Longbridge Deverill Cow Down, Wiltshire, House 3: a major round
    house of the Early Iron Age, *Oxford J Archaeol*, **13**, 49–69

Champion, T, 2001 The beginnings of Iron Age archaeology in Wessex, in J R Collis (ed), *Society
    and Settlement in Iron Age Europe*, 9–22

Champion, T C & Collis, J R (eds), 1996 *The Iron Age in Britain and Ireland: recent trends*.
    Sheffield: J R Collis Publications

Chandler, J, 1996 Review of Aston and Lewis (eds) 1994, *Wiltshire Archaeol Natur Hist Soc Mag*, **89**, 154–5

Chisham, C, 2004 Early Mesolithic human activity and environmental change: a case study of the Kennet Valley, Reading: Unpublished PhD Thesis, University of Reading

Churchill, D M, 1962 The stratigraphy of the Mesolithic sites III and V at Thatcham, Berkshire, England, *Proc Prehist Soc*, **28**, 362–70

Clark, J G D, 1966 The invasion hypothesis in British archaeology, *Antiquity*, **40**, 172–89

Clarke, G, 1979 *Pre-Roman and Roman Winchester Part II: the Roman Cemetery at Lankhills*, Winchester Studies Vol **3**. Oxford: Oxford University

Cleal, R M J, Walker, K E & Montague, R, 1995 *Stonehenge in its landscape: Twentieth-century Excavations*, English Heritage Archaeol Rep **10**. London: English Heritage

Collard, M, Darvill, T & Watts, M, 2006 Ironworking in the Bronze Age? Evidence from a 10th-century BC settlement at Hartshill Copse, Upper Bucklebury, West Berkshire, *Proc Prehist Soc*, **72**, 367–422

Collis, J R, 1968, Excavations at Owslebury, Hants, *Antiq J*, **48**, 18–31

Collis, J R, 1970, Excavations at Owslebury, Hants: a second interim report, *Antiq J*, **50**, 246–61

Collis, J R (ed), 1977a *The Iron Age in Britain: a review*. Sheffield: Department of Prehistory and Archaeology, University of Sheffield

Collis, J R, 1977b An approach to the Iron Age, in J R Collis (ed), *The Iron Age in Britain: a review*, 1–7. Sheffield: Department of Prehistory and Archaeology, University of Sheffield

Collis, J R, 1994, The Iron Age, in B Vyner (ed), *Building on the Past: a celebration of 150 years of the Royal Archaeological Institute*, 123–48. London: Royal Archaeological Institute

Collis, J R, 2001a Récentes controverses sur l âge du Fer en Wessex , in J R Collis (ed), *Society and Settlement in Iron Age Europe*, 23–36

Collis, J R (ed), 2001b *Society and Settlement in Iron Age Europe Actes du XVIIIe colloque de l'Association Française pour l'Étude de l'Age du Fer, Winchester, (April 1994)*, Sheffield Archaeol Monogr **11**. Sheffield: J R Collis Publications

Collis, J R, 2003 *The Celts Origins, myths inventions*. Stroud: Tempus

Conneller, C & Ellis, C, 2007 A Late Upper Palaeolithic site at La Sagesse Convent, Romsey, Hampshire, *Proc Prehist Soc*, **73** 191–228

Copley, G J, 1954 *The Conquest of Wessex in the 6th century*. London: Phoenix House

Corfield, M C (ed), 1978 *A Guide to the Industrial Archaeology of Wiltshire*. Trowbridge: Wiltshire County Council

Corney, M, 1989 Multiple ditch systems and Late Iron Age settlement in central Wessex, in M Bowden, D Mackay & P Topping (eds), *From Cornwall to Caithness: some aspects of British field archaeology*, BAR Brit Ser **209**, 111–28. Oxford: Archaeopress

Corney, M, 2001 The Romano-British nucleated settlements of Wiltshire, in Ellis (ed), *Roman Wiltshire and After*, 5–38

Cornwall, I, 1953 *Soils for the Archaeologist*. London: Pheonix House

Cornwall, I, 1956 *Bones for the Archaeologist*. London: Pheonix House

Cosh, S R & Neal, D S, 2005 *Roman Mosaics of Britain*, Vol II, *South-West Britain*. London: Illuminata for the Society of Antiquaries of London

Cossons, N (ed), 2000 *Perspectives in Industrial Archaeology*. London: Science Museum

Cotton, M A, 1947 Excavations at Silchester, *Archaeologia*, **92**, 121–68

Cox, P W & Hearne, C M, 1991 *Redeemed from the Heath the archaeology of the Wytch Farm Oilfield*, Dorset Natur Hist Archaeol Soc Monogr **9**

Cramp, R, 2006 *Corpus of Anglo-Saxon sculpture Volume VII: South-West England*. Oxford: Oxford University Press

Crawford, O G S, 1922 *The Andover District: An Account of Sheet 283 of the One-inch Ordnance Map*. Oxford: Oxford University Press

Crawford, O G S, 1924 *Air Survey and Archaeology*, Ordnance Survey Professional Pap New Ser No **7**. London: HMSO

Crawford, O G S & Keiller, A, 1928 *Wessex from the Air*. Oxford: Clarendon Press

Crawford, O G S, Ellaway, J R and Willis, G W, 1922 The antiquity of man in Hampshire, *Pap and Proc Hampshire Fld Club Archaeol Soc*, **9** (2), 173–88

Crittall, E (ed), 1973 *A History of Wiltshire*, Vol **I**(2). Oxford: Oxford University Press for the Institute of Historical Research

Crossley, D, 1987 Sir William Clavell's glasshouse at Kimmeridge, Dorset: the excavations of 1980–81, *Archaeol J*, **144**, 340–82

Cunliffe, B 1976 *Excavations at Portchester Castle. Volume 2: Saxon*, Rep Res Comm Soc Antiq London, **33**. London: Society of Antiquaries of London

Cunliffe, B, 1972 Saxon and medieval settlement pattern in the region of Chalton, Hampshire *Medieval Archaeol*, **16**, 1–12

Cunliffe, B, 1974 *Iron Age Communities in Britain* (1st edn). London: Routledge and Kegan Paul

Cunliffe, B, 1975 *Excavations at Portchester Castle, Vol I, Roman*, Rep Res Comm Soc Antiq London, **32**. London: Society of Antiquaries of London

Cunliffe, B, 1984 *Danebury An Iron Age hillfort in Hampshire Vol 1: the Excavations 1969–1978: the Site; Vol 2: the Excavations 1969–1978: the Finds*, CBA Res Rep **52**. London: CBA

Cunliffe, B, 1987 *Hengistbury Head, Dorset, Vol 1: The Prehistoric and Roman Settlement, 3500 BC – AD 500*, Oxford Univ Comm Archaeol Monogr **13**. Oxford: Oxford Uni Comm Archaeol

Cunliffe, B, 1992 Pits, preconceptions and propitiation in the British Iron Age, *Oxford J Archaeol*, **11**, 69–84

Cunliffe, B, 1993 *Wessex to AD 1000*. London: Longman

Cunliffe, B, 1995 *Danebury An Iron Age hillfort in Hampshire Vol 6: A hillfort Community in Perspective*, CBA Res Rep **102**. York: CBA

Cunliffe, B, 2000 *The Danebury Environs Programme The prehistory of a Wessex landscape*, Vol 1 Introduction, Oxford Uni Comm Archaeol Monogr **48**. Oxford: Oxford Uni Comm Archaeol

Cunliffe, B, 2005 *Iron Age Communities in Britain* (4th edn). London: Routledge and Kegan Paul

Cunliffe, B, 2008 *The Danebury Environs Roman Programme A Wessex landscape during the Roman era*, Vol 1 Overview, Oxford Uni Comm Archaeol Monogr **70**. Oxford: Oxford Uni Comm Archaeol

Cunliffe, B & de Jersey, P, 1997 *Armorica and Britain: cross-Channel relationships in the late first millennium BC*, Oxford Uni Comm Archaeol Monogr, **45**. Oxford: Oxford Uni Comm Archaeol

Cunliffe, B & Fulford, M G, 1982 *Corpus Signorum Imperii Romani, Great Britain, Vol 1(2) Bath and the Rest of Wessex*. Oxford: Oxford University Press for the British Academy

Cunliffe, B & Poole C, 1991 *Danebury An Iron Age hillfort in Hampshire Vol 4: the Excavations 1979–88: the Site; Vol 5: the Excavations 1979–88: the Finds*, CBA Res Rep **73**. London: CBA

Cunliffe, B & Poole, C 2008 *The Danebury Environs Roman Programme A Wessex Landscape during the Roman Era*, Vol 2 (pts 1–7), Oxford Univ School of Archaeol Monogr **71**. Oxford: Oxford University School of Archaeology

Cunliffe, B & Renfrew, C (eds), 1997 Science and Stonehenge, *Proc British Academy* **92**. Oxford: OUP

Cunnington, M E, 1923 *The Early Iron Age Inhabited Site at All Cannings Cross, Wiltshire*. Devizes: George Simpson

Cunnington, M E & Cunnington, B H, 1913 Casterley Castle excavations, *Wiltshire Archaeol Natural Hist Mag*, **38**, 53–105

Cunnington, M E & Cunnington, B H, 1917 Lidbury Camp, *Wiltshire Archaeol Natural Hist Mag*, **40**, 12–36

Dacre, M & Ellison, A, 1981 A Bronze Age urn cemetery at Kimpton, Hampshire, *Proc Prehist Soc*, **47**, 147–203

Dale, W, 1896 The Palaeolithic implements of the Southampton gravels, *Pap and Proc Hampshire Fld Club Archaeol Soc*, **3**, 261–4

Dale, W, 1912 On the -mplement-bearing gravel beds of the lower valley of the Test, *Proc Soc of Antiq*, **24**, 108–16

Darvill, T C, 2005 *Stonehenge World Heritage Site: an archaeological research framework*. London and Bournemouth: English Heritage and Bournemouth University

Darwin-Fox, W, 1862 When and how was the Isle of Wight severed from the mainland? *The Geologist*, **5**, 452–4

Davis, O, Sharples, N & Waddington K (eds), 2008 *Changing Perspectives on the First Millennium BC*. Oxford: Cardiff Studies in Archaeology

DCMS, 2008 *Historic Environment Records (HERs): draft guidance for local authorities in England*. London: DCMS

Dicks, J, 2009 The Rowland's Castle Romano-British pottery industry, *J Roman Pottery Studies*, **14**, 51–66

Dimbleby, G W, 1967 *Plants in Archaeology*. London: John Baker

Dimbleby, G W, 1985 *The Palynology of Archaeological Sites*. London: Academic Press

Downey, R, King, A, & Soffe, G, 1980 The Hayling Island temple and religious connections across the Channel, in W Rodwell (ed), *Temples, Churches and Religion: Recent Research in Roman Britain*, BAR **77**(1), 289–304. Oxford: Archaeopress

Draper, S, 2004 Roman estates to English parishes? The legacy of Desmond Bonney reconsidered, in R Collins and J Gerrard (eds), *Debating Late Antiquity in Britain AD 300–700*, Oxford: BAR Brit Ser **365**, 55–64. Oxford: Archaeopress

Driver, J T, 2000 A 'perilous, covetous man'; the career of Thomas Tropenell, Esq *c* 1405–88, *Wiltshire Archaeol Natur Hist Soc Mag*, **93**, 82–9

Dyer, C, 2003 The archaeology of small towns, *Medieval Archaeol*, **47**, 85–114

Dyer, K R, 1975 The buried channels of the 'Solent River', southern England, *Proc Geol Ass*, **86**(2), 239–45

Eagles, B, 2001 Anglo-Saxon presence and culture in Wiltshire *c* AD 450 – *c* 675, in Ellis (ed), *Roman Wiltshire and After*, 199–233

Eckardt, H, Chenery, C, Booth, P, Evans, J A, Lamb, A & Müldner, G, 2009 Oxygen and strontium isotope evidence for mobility in Roman Winchester, *J Archaeol Sci*, **36**, 2816–25

Ehrenreich, R M, 1985 *Trade, Technology, and the Ironworking Community in the Iron Age of Southern Britain*, BAR Brit Ser **144**. Oxford: Archaeopress

Ellis, C J & Rawlings, M, 2001 Excavations at Balksbury Camp, Andover 1995–97, *Proc Hampshire Fld Club Archaeol Soc*, **56**, 21–94

Ellis, M, 1975 *Hampshire Industrial Archaeology: A Guide*. Southampton: Southampton University Industrial Archaeology Group

Ellis, P (ed), 2000 *Ludgershall Castle Excavations by Peter Addyman 1964–1972*, Wiltshire Archaeol Natur Hist Soc Monogr **2**. Devizes: Wiltshire Archaeol Natur Hist Soc

Ellis, P (ed), 2001 *Roman Wiltshire and After. Papers in honour of Ken Annable*. Devizes: Wiltshire Archaeol Natur Hist Soc

Ellison, A, 1980 Settlements and regional exchange: a case study in J Barrett & R Bradley (eds), *Settlement and Society in the British Later Bronze Age*, BAR Brit Ser **83**, 127–40. Oxford: Archaeopress

Ellison, A B, 1981 *A policy for archaeological investigation in Wessex: 1981–1985*. Salisbury: Trust for Wessex Archaeology

Emery, A, 2006 *Greater medieval Houses of England and Wales 1300–1500 Volume III: southern England*. Cambridge: Cambridge University Press

English Heritage, 1996 *England's Coastal Heritage: a statement on the management of coastal archaeology*. London: English Heritage and RCHM(E)

English Heritage, 1998 *Identifying and protecting Palaeolithic remains*. London: English Heritage

English Heritage, 2000 *Managing Lithic Scatters*. London: English Heritage

Entwistle, R & Bowden, M, 1991 Cranborne Chase: the molluscan evdience, in J Barrett, R Bradley & M Hall (eds), *Papers on the Prehistoric Archaeology of Cranborne Chase*, Oxbow Monogr **11**, 20–48. Oxford: Oxbow

Erskine, J, 2007 The West Wansdyke: an appraisal of the dating, dimensions and construction techniques in the light of excavated evidence, *Archaeol J*, **164**, 80–108

Evans, C, 1989 Archaeology and modern times: Bersu's Woodbury 1938 and 1939, *Antiquity*, **63**, 436–50 (Reprinted in G Carr and S Stoddart (eds), *Celts from Antiquity*, Cambridge: Antiquity Papers **2**, 145–60)

Evans, J, 1897 The *Ancient Stone Implements, Weapons and Ornaments of Great Britain* (2nd edn). London: Longmans, Green and Co

Evans, J A, Chenery, C A & Fitzpatrick A P, 2006 Bronze Age childhood migration of individuals near Stonehenge, revealed by strontium and oxygen isotope tooth enamel analysis, *Archaeometry*, **48** (2), 309–22

Evans, J, Pitts, M and Williams, D, 1985 An excavation at Avebury, Wiltshire, 1982, *Proc Prehist Soc*, **51**, 305–10

Evans, J, Stoodley, N & Chenery, C, 2006 A strontium and oxygen isotope assessment of a possible fourth century immigrant population in a Hampshire cemetery, southern England, *J Archaeol Sci* , **33**, 265–72

Evans, J G, 1971 Habitat changes on the calcareous soils of Britain; the impact of Neolithic man, in D D A Simpson (ed), *Economy and Settlement in Neolithic and Early Bronze Age Britain and Europe*, 27–73. Leicester: Leicester University Press

Evans, J G, 1972 *Land Snails in Archaeology* London: Seminar Press

Evans, J G, 1975 *Introdcution to Environmental Archaeology* London: Paul Elek

Evans, J G, 1979 *The Environment of Early Man in the British Isle* London: Paul Elek

Evans, J G, 1984 Stonehenge – the environment in the Late Neolithic and Early Bronze Age and a Beaker burial, *Wiltshire Archaeol Natur Hist Mag*, **78**, 7–30

Evans, J G & Jones, H, 1979 Mount Pleasant and Woodhenge: the land Mollusca, in G J Wainwright, *Mount Pleasant, Dorset: Excavations 1970–1971*, Res Rep Soc Antiq, **37**, 190–213. London: Society of Antiquaries of London

Evans, J G & Limbrey, S, 1974 The experimental earthwork on Morden Bog, Wareham, Dorset, England: 1963–1972, *Proc Prehist Soc*, **40**, 170–202

Evans, J G, Limbrey, S, Maté, I & Mount, R, 1988 Environmental change and land-use history in a Wiltshire river valley in the last 14,000 years, in J C Barrett & I A Kinnes (eds), *The Archaeology of context in the Neolithic and Bronze Age; recent trends*, 97–103. Sheffield: J R Collis

Evans, J G, Limbrey, S, Maté, I & Mount, R, 1993 An environmental history of the Upper Kennet valley, Wiltshire, for the last 10,000 years, *Proc Prehist Soc*, **59**, 139–95

Evans, J G & Smith, I F, 1983 Excavations at Cherhill, North Wiltshire, *Proc Prehist Soc*, **49**, 43–117

Evison, V I, 1988 *An Anglo-Saxon cemetery at Alton, Hampshire*, Hampshire Fld Club Archaeol Soc Monogr **4**. Winchester: Hampshire Fld Club Archaeol Soc

Fagan, B M, 1958 A Palaeolith from Chard Junction, *Proc Dorset Natur Hist Archaeol Soc*, **80**, 94–5

Fairbrother, J R, 1990 *Faccombe Netherton: excavation of a Saxon and medieval manorial complex*, 2 vols. London: British Museum

Farwell, D E & Molleson, T I, 1993 *Excavations at Poundbury 1966–80*, Vol II, Dorset Nat Hist Archaeol Soc Monogr **11**. Dorchester: Dorset Nat Hist Archaeol Soc

Fasham, P J, 1979 The excavation of a triple barrow in Micheldever Wood, Hampshire MARC 3 Site R4, *Proc Hampshire Fld Club Archaeol Soc*, **35**, 5–40

Fasham, P J, 1985 *The Prehistoric Settlement at Winnall Down, Winchester*, Hampshire Fld Club Monogr **2**. Winchester: Hampshire Fld Club & Archaeol Soc

Fasham, P J, 1987a The medieval settlement at Popham, excavations 1975 and 1983, *Proc Hampshire Fld Club Archaeol Soc*, **43**, 83–124

Fasham, P J, 1987b A *'Banjo' Enclosure in Micheldever Wood, Hampshire*, Hampshire Fld Club Archaeol Soc Monogr **5**. Winchester: Hampshire Fld Club & Archaeol Soc

Fasham, P J, Farwell, D E & Whinney, R J B, 1989 *The Archaeological Site at Easton Lane, Winchester*, Hampshire Fld Club Archaeol Soc Monogr **6**. Winchester: Hampshire Fld Club & Archaeol Soc

Fasham, P J & Keevill, G (with Coe, D), 1995 *Brighton Hill South (Hatch Warren): an Iron Age farmstead and deserted medieval village in Hampshire*, Trust for Wessex Archaeol Rep **7**. Salisbury: Trust for Wessex Archaeology

Fasham, P J & Whinney, R J B, 1991 *Archaeology and the M3*, Hampshire Fld Club Monogr **7**. Winchester: Hampshire Fld Club & Archaeol Soc

Field, N H, 1992 *Dorset and the Second Legion New Light on a Roman Campaign*. Tiverton: Dorset Books

Firth, A, 2002 *Managing Archaeology Underwater*, BAR Int Ser **1055**. Oxford: Archaeopress

Fitzpatrick, A P, 1994 Outside in: the structure of an early Iron Age house at Dunston Park, Thatcham, Berkshire, in Fitzpatrick & Morris (eds), *The Iron Age in Wessex*, 68–72

Fitzpatrick, A P, 1997 Everyday life in Iron Age Wessex , in Haselgrove & Gwilt (eds), *Reconstructing Iron Age Societies: new approaches to the British Iron Age*, Oxbow Monogr **71**, 87–95. Oxford: Oxbow

Fitzpatrick, A P, 1998 The everyday study of the Iron Age, in A Woodward & J Gardiner (eds), *Wessex before Words Some new research directions for prehistoric Wessex*, 13–14. Salisbury: Wessex Archaeology

Fitzpatrick, A P, 2002 The Amesbury Archer: a well-furnished Early Bronze Age burial in southern England, *Antiquity*, **76**, 629–30

Fitzpatrick, A P, 2009 In his hands and in his head: the Amesbury Archer as a metalworker, in P Clark (ed), *Bronze Age Connections, Cultural connections in Bronze Age Europe, the Second Dover Bronze Age Boat Conference*, 176–88. Oxford: Oxbow

Fitzpatrick, A P, in press *The Amesbury Archer and the Boscombe Bowmen: early Bell Beaker burials at Boscombe Down, Wiltshire, Great Britain Excavations at Boscombe Down, Wiltshire, Vol 1*. Salisbury: Wessex Archaeology

Fitzpatrick, A P, Evans, J & Chenery, C, 2004 Was Stonehenge really built by Welshmen? *British Archaeology*, **78**, 14–15

Fitzpatrick, A P & Morris, E L (eds), 1994 *The Iron Age in Wessex: recent work*. Salisbury: Association Française pour l'Étude de l'Age du Fer

Fleming, A, 1971 Territorial patterns in Bronze Age Wessex, *Proc Prehist Soc*, **37**(1), 138–66

Foster, J, 1980 *The Iron Age Moulds from Gussage All Saints*, Brit Mus Occas Pap **12**. London: British Museum Press

Fowler, P J, 1967 *Wessex*. London: Heinemann Educational Books

Fowler, P J, 1983 *The Farming of Prehistoric Britain*. Cambridge: Cambridge University Press

Fowler, P J, 2000 *Landscape Plotted and Pieced Landscape History and Local Archaeology in Fyfield and Overton, Wiltshire*, Rep Res Comm Soc Antiq London, **64**. London: Society of Antiquaries of London

Fowler, P J, 2004 East of Avebury: ancient fields in a local context, in R Cleal & J Pollard (eds), *Monuments and Material Culture: papers in honour of an Avebury archaeologist: Isobel Smith*, 130–8. Salisbury: Hobnob Press

French, C, 2003 *Geoarchaeology in Action*. London: Routledge

French, C, 2009 A landscape tale of two soil histories in lowland zones of England: the fen-edge of Cambridgeshire and the downland of Cranborne Chase, in Allen *et al*, *Land and People*, 89–104

French, C, Lewis, H, Allen, M J, Scaife, R G & Green, M, 2003 Archaeological and palaeo-environmental investigations of the Upper Allen Valley, Cranborne Chase, Dorset (1998–2000): a new model of earlier Holocene landscape development, *Proc Prehist Soc*, **69**, 201–34

French, C, Lewis, H, Allen, M J, Green, M, Scaife, R G & Gardiner J, 2007 *Prehistoric landscape development and human impact in the upper Allen valley, Cranborne Chase, Dorset*, McDonald Instit Monogr. Cambridge: McDonald Institute for Archaeological Research

Frere, S S (ed), 1960 *Problems of the Iron Age in Southern Britain*, Uni of London Instit Archaeol Occas Pap **11**. London: University of London

Frere, S S, 1976 The Silchester church: the excavation by Sir Ian Richmond in 1961, *Archaeologia*, **105**, 277–302

Friel, I, 1993 Henry V's Grace Dieu and the wreck in the River Hamble near Bursledon, Hampshire, *Int J Naut Archaeol*, **22**(1), 3–19

Froom, R, 2005 *Late Glacial Long Blade Sites in the Kennet Valley*, British Museum Research Publication No. **153**. London: British Museum

Fulford, M G, 1975 *New Forest Roman Pottery*, BAR Brit Ser **17**. Oxford: Archaeopress

Fulford, M, 1984 *Silchester: Excavations on the Defences 1974–80*, Britannia Monogr, **5**. London: Society for Roman Studies

Fulford, M, 1989 *The Silchester Amphitheatre The Excavations of 1979–85*, Britannia Monogr **10**. London: Society for Roman Studies

Fulford, M, 2008 Nero and Britain: the palace of the client king at *Calleva* and imperial policy towards the province after Boudicca, *Britannia*, **39**, 1–13

Fulford, M, Champion, T & Long, A, 1997 *England's Coastal Heritage: a survey for English Heritage and the RCHME*, English Heritage Archaeological Report **15**. London: English Heritage

Fulford, M & Clarke, A, 2002 Victorian excavation methodology: the Society of Antiquaries at Silchester in 1893, *Antiquaries J*, **82**, 285–306

Fulford, M & Clarke, A, 2010 *Silchester: City in Transition The Mid-Roman Occupation of Insula IX, c AD 125–250/300 A report on excavations undertaken since 1997*, Britannia Monogr **25**. London: Society for Roman Studies

Fulford, M, Clarke, A & Eckardt, H, 2006 *Life and Labour in Late Roman Silchester Excavations in insula ix since 1997*, Britannia Monogr, **22**. London: Society for Roman Studies

Fulford, M G, Powell, A B, Entwistle, R & Raymond, F, 2006 *Iron Age and Romano-British Settlements and Landscapes of Salisbury Plain*, Wessex Archaeol Rep **30**. Salisbury: Wessex Archaeology

Fulford, M & Timby, J, 2000 *Late Iron Age and Roman Silchester Excavations on the site of the forum basilica 1977, 1980–86*, Britannia Monogr **15**. London: Society for Roman Studies

Gaffney, C & Gator, J, 2003 *Revealing the Buried Past: Geophysics for archaeologists*. Stroud: Tempus

Gaffney, V & Tingle, M, 1989 *The Maddle Farm Project: An Integrated Survey of Prehistoric and Roman Landscapes on the Berkshire Downs*, BAR Brit Ser **200**. Oxford: Archaeopress

Gale, J, Hewitt, I & Russell, M 2008 Excavations at High Lea Farm, Hinton Martell, Dorset: an interim report on fieldwork undertaken during 2006–7, *Proc Dorset Natur Hist Archaeol Soc*, **129**, 105–14

Gamble, C S & ApSimon, A M, 1986 Red Barns – Portchester in S N Collcutt (ed), *The Palaeolithic of Britain and its Nearest Neighbours: Recent Trends*, 8–12. Sheffield: Dept of Archaeology, University of Sheffield

Gardiner, J & Allen, M J, 2009 Peopling the landscape; prehistory of the Wylye valley, Wiltshire, in Allen *et al*, *Land and People*, in Allen *et al*, *Land and People*, 77–88

Gardiner, J, with Allen, M J (eds), 2005 *Before the mast; life and death aboard the* Mary Rose. *The Archaeology of the* Mary Rose Vol **4**. Portsmouth: Mary Rose Trust Ltd

Gardiner, M, 2000 Vernacular buildings and the development of the later medieval domestic plan, *Medieval Archaeol*, **44**, 159–80

Geake, H, 2002 Persistent problems in the study of Conversion-period burials in England, in S Lucy & A Reynolds (eds), *Burial in early medieval England and Wales*, Soc Medieval Archaeol Monogr **17**, 144–55

Gerrard, C, 2003 *Medieval archaeology. Understanding traditions and contemporary approaches*. London/New York: Routledge

Gibson, A, 1998 *Stonehenge and Timber Circles*. Stroud: Tempus

Gilchrist, R & Sloane, B, 2005 *Requiem, The medieval monastic cemetery in Britain*. London: Museum of London Archaeological Service

Gillings, M, Pollard, J, Wheatley, D & Peterson, R, 2008 *Landscape of the Megaliths: excavation and fieldwork on the Avebury monuments 1997–2003*. Oxford: Oxbow

Gingell, C, 1988 Twelve Wiltshire round barrows Excavations in 1959 and 1961 by F de M and H L Vatcher, *Wiltshire Archaeol Natur Hist Mag*, **82**, 19–76

Gingell, C, 1992 *The Marlborough Downs: a later Bronze Age landscape and its origins*, Wiltshire Archaeol Natur Hist Soc Monogr **1**. Devizes: WANHS/Trust for Wessex Archaeology

Godwin H, 1975 *The History of the British Flora* (2nd edn) Cambridge: CUP

Goldberg, P & Macphail, R I, 2006 *Practical and theoretical geoarchaeology.* London: Blackwell Publishing

Goodier, A, 1984 The formation of boundaries in Anglo-Saxon England; a statistical study, *Medieval Archaeol*, **28**, 1–21

Graham, A H & Davies, S M, 1993 *Excavations in Trowbridge, Wiltshire, 1977 and 1986–1988*, Trust for Wessex Archaeol Rep **2**. Salisbury: Trust for Wessex Archaeology

Graham, A, 2006 *Barton Field, Tarrant Hinton, Dorset Excavations 1968–1984*, Dorset Natur Hist Archaeol Soc Monogr **17**. Dorchester: Dorset Natur Hist Archaeol Soc

Graham, A, Draper, J & Watts, M, 2005 *The Town Mill Lyme Regis: Archaeology and History AD1340–2000.* Lyme Regis: Town Mill Trust

Grant, A, 1984 Animal husbandry, in Cunliffe, *Danebury An Iron Age hillfort in Hampshire*, 496–548

Grant, A, 1991 Animal husbandry in Cunliffe, *Danebury An Iron Age hillfort in Hampshire Vol 3: the Excavations 1979–88: the Site; Vol 42: the Excavations 1979–88: the Finds*, CBA Res Rep **73**, 447–87. London: CBA

Graves, P C, 2000 *The form and fabric of belief: an archaeology of the lay experience in medieval Norfolk and Devon*, BAR Brit Ser **311**. Oxford: BAR

Green, C P, 1988 The Palaeolithic site at Broom, Dorset, 1932–41: from the record of C E Bean Esq, FSA, *Proc Geol Ass*, **99**, 173–80

Green, C & Rollo-Smith, S, 1984 The excavation of eighteen round barrows near Shrewton, Wiltshire, *Proc Prehist Soc* **50**, 255–318

Green, M, 2000 *A Landscape Revealed: 10,000 Years on a Chalkland Farm.* Stroud: Tempus

Green, M, 2007 Wyke Down henge 2 and associated Late Neolithic settlement in French *et al, Prehistoric landscape development and human impact in the upper Allen valley, Cranborne Chase*, 83–94 and 307–335

Green, M, 2009 Secrets of a secret landscape – the Dorset Cursus complex in Barker, K (ed) *The Chase, the Hart and the Park: an Exploration of the Historic Landscapes of the Cranborne Chase and West Wiltshire Downs Area of Outstanding Natural Beauty* Cranborne: Cranborne Chase and West Wiltshire Downs AONB

Green, M & Allen, M J, 1997 An early prehistoric shaft on Cranborne Chase, *Oxford J Archaeol*, **16**, 121–32

Gregory, M, 2003 The restoration of Crux Easton wind engine, *Hampshire IA Soc J*, **11**, 1–13

Griffiths, N, 2001 The Roman army in Wiltshire, in Ellis (ed), *Roman Wiltshire and After*, 39–72

Grimes, W F, 1968 *The excavation of Roman and medieval London.* London: Routledge and Kegan Paul

Grinsell, L V, 1958 *The archaeology of Wessex.* London: Methuen

Gupta, S, Collier, J, Palmer-Felgate, A, Dickinson, J, Bushe, K & Humber, S, 2004 Submerged Palaeo-Arun River: reconstruction of prehistoric landscapes and evaluation of archaeological research potential. Unpublished report for English Heritage: ALSF Project Number 3277/3543

Gurney, D, 1985 Phosphate and magnetic susceptibility survey, in F Pryor & C French, *Archaeology and Environment in the lower Welland valley*, East Anglian Archaeology **27**, 38–41. Cambridge: Cambridgeshire Archaeological Committee

Hambleton, E, 1999 *Animal Husbandry Regimes in Iron Age Britain: a comparative analysis of faunal assemblages from British Iron Age sites*, BAR Brit Ser **282**. Oxford: BAR

Harden, D B (ed), 1956 *Dark-Age Britain Studies presented to E T Leeds.* London: Methuen

Harding, D W, 1972 *The Iron Age in the Upper Thames Basin.* Oxford: Clarendon

Harding, D W, 1974 *The Iron Age in Lowland Britain.* London and Boston: Routledge and Kegan Paul

Harding, D W, 2005 The Atlantic Scottish Iron Age: external relations reviewed, in V E Turner, R A Nicholson, S J Dockrill and J M Bond (eds), *Tall Stories? 2 millennia of brochs*, 32–51. Lerwick: Shetland Amenity Trust

Harding, D W, Blake, I M & Reynolds, P J, 1993 *An Iron Age Settlement in Dorset: excavation and reconstruction*, Uni Edinburgh Dept of Archaeol Monogr **1**. Edinburgh: University of Edinburgh

Harding, P A, 1998 An interim report of an archaeological watching brief on Palaeolithic deposits at Dunbridge, Hants, in N Ashton, F Healy and P Pettitt (eds), *Stone Age Archaeology: Essays in Honour of John Wymer*, Oxbow Monogr **102** and Lithic Studies Soc Occas Pap No. **6**, 72–6. London: Oxbow

Harding, P A & Bridgland, D R, 1998 Pleistocene deposits and Palaeolithic implements at Godolphin School, Milford Hill, Salisbury, *Wilts Archaeol Natur Hist Mag*, **91**, 1–10

Harding, P A, & Newman, R, 1997 The excavation of a turf sided lock at Monkey Marsh, Thatcham, Berks, *Ind Archaeol Rev*, **XIX**, 31–48

Hare, J N, 1988 'Bishop's Waltham Palace, Hampshire: William of Wykeham, Henry Beaufort and the transformation of a medieval episcopal palace', *Archaeol J*, **145**, 222–54

Hare, J, 1993 Netley Abbey: monastery, mansion and ruin, *Proc Hampshire Fld Club Archaeol Soc*, **49**, 207–28

Hare, J, 1994 Agriculture and rural settlement in the chalklands of Wessex: Wiltshire and Hampshire from *c* 1200 to *c* 1500, in Aston and Lewis (eds), *The medieval landscape of Wessex*, 159–71

Hare, J, 2007 Church building and urban prosperity on the eve of the Reformation: Basingstoke and its parish church, *Proc Hampshire Fld Club Archaeol Soc*, **62**, 181–92

Harrison, R J, 1980 *The Beaker Folk*. London: Thames and Hudson

Hase, P, 1994 The Church in the Wessex heartlands, in Aston & Lewis (eds), *The Medieval Landscape of Wessex*, 47–81

Haselgrove, C & Gwilt, A (eds), 1997 *Reconstructing Iron Age Societies: new approaches to the British Iron Age*, Oxbow Monogr **71**. Oxford: Oxbow

Haselgrove, C & Moore, T (eds), *The Later Iron Age in Britain and Beyond: recent work*. Oxford: Oxbow

Haselgrove, C & Pope, R (eds), 2007 *The Earlier Iron Age in Britain and the Near Continent*. Oxford: Oxbow

Haselgrove, C, Armit, I, Champion, T, Creighton, J, Gwilt, A, Hill, J D, Hunter, F & Woodward, A, 2001 *Understanding the British Iron Age: an agenda for action*. Salisbury: Iron Age Res Seminar and Prehist Soc

Haslam, J, 1976 *Wiltshire towns: the archaeological potential*. Devizes: Wiltshire Archaeol & Natur Hist Soc

Hauser, K, 2008 *Bloody old Britain O G S Crawford and the archaeology of modern life*. London: Granta Books

Hawkes, C F C, 1931 Hillforts, *Antiquity*, **5**, 60–97

Hawkes, C F C, 1959 The ABC of the British Iron Age, *Antiquity*, **3**, 170–82 (Reprinted in G Carr and S Stoddart (eds), *Celts from Antiquity*, Antiquity Papers, **2**. Cambridge: Antiquity Publications 131–44)

Hawkes, C F C, Myres, J N L and Stevens, C G, 1930 St Catharine's Hill, Winchester, *Proc Hampshire Fld Club*, **11**, 1–286

Hawkes, J W & Fasham, P J, 1997 *Excavations on Reading Abbey waterfront sites 1979–1981* Wessex Archaeol Rep **5**. Salisbury: Wessex Archaeology

Hawley, E, 1912 *Old Sarum Excavation Fund. Report of the Excavation Committee to the Society of Antiquaries for 1911*. London: The Society of Antiquaries

Healy, F, Heaton, M & Lobb, S J, 1992 Excavations of a Mesolithic Site at Thatcham, Berkshire, *Proc Prehist Soc*, **58**, 41–76

Hearne, C M & Birbeck, V, 1996 The Canford Magna golf course project 1993–94, *Proc Hampshire Fld Club Archaeol Soc*, **118**, 33–50

Hill, J D, 1989 Re-thinking the Iron Age, *Scott Archaeol Rev*, **6**, 16–24

Hill, J D, 1993 Can we recognise a different European past? A contrasting archaeology of later prehistoric settlements in southern England, *J European Archaeol*, **1**, 57–75

Hill, J D, 1995a *Ritual and Rubbish in the Iron Age of Wessex A study on the formation of a particular archaeological record*, BAR Brit Ser **242.** Oxford: BAR

Hill, J D, 1995b How should we study Iron Age hillforts? A contextual study from southern England, in J D Hill and C Cumberpatch (eds), *Different Iron Ages: studies on the Iron Age in temperate Europe*, BAR Int Ser **602**, 45–66. Oxford: BAR

Hill, J D, 1996 Hillforts and the Iron Age of Wessex, in Champion & Collis (eds), *The Iron Age in Britain and Ireland Recent trends*, 95–116

Hinton, D A, 1977 *Alfred's Kingdom Wessex and the South 800–1500.* London: Dent

Hinton, D A, 1990 Excavations at the old church, Otterbourne, *Proc Hampshire Fld Club Archaeol Soc*, **46**, 73–89

Hinton, D A, 1992 Revised dating of the Worgret structure, *Proc Dorset Nat Hist Archaeol Soc*, **114**, 258–9

Hinton, D A, 1994 The archaeology of eighth- to eleventh-century Wessex, in Aston and Lewis (eds), *The Medieval Landscape of Wessex*, 33–46

Hinton, D A, 2005 Debate: south Hampshire, 'East Wessex' and the *Atlas of Rural Settlement in England, Landscape History*, **27**, 71–6

Hinton, D A, 2008 *The Alfred Jewel.* Oxford: Ashmolean Museum

Hinton, D A, 2010 Some finds from deserted medieval villages, in C Dyer & R L C Jones, *Deserted villages revisited.* Hertford: Hertfordshire University Press

Hinton, D A & Oake, M K, 1983 The Anglo-Saxon church at Yateley, *Proc Hampshire Fld Club Archaeol Soc*, **39**, 111–20

Hinton, D & Hughes, M (eds), 1996 *Archaeology in Hampshire: a framework for the future.* Hampshire: Hampshire County Council

Hodder, I, 1974a The distribution of Savernake Ware, *Wiltshire Archaeol Nat Hist Mag*, **69**, 67–84

Hodder, I, 1974b Some marketing models for Romano-British coarse pottery, *Britannia*, **5**, 340–59

Hodson, F R, 1960 Reflections on the 'ABC' of the British Iron Age, *Antiquity*, **34**, 138–40

Hodson, F R, 1962 Some pottery from Eastbourne, the Marnians and the pre-Roman Iron Age in southern England, *Proc Prehist Soc*, **28**, 140–55

Hodson, F R, 1964, Cultural groupings within the British pre-Roman Iron Age, *Proc Prehist Soc*, **30**, 99–110

Horsey, I P, 1992 *Excavations in Poole 1973–1983*, Dorset Natur Hist & Archaeol Soc Monogr **10**

Hosfield, R T, 1999 The Palaeolithic of the Hampshire Basin: a regional model of hominid behaviour during the Middle Pleistocene, BAR Brit Ser **286**. Oxford: Archaeopress

Hosfield, R T & Chambers, J C, 2004 *The Archaeological Potential of Secondary Contexts.* English Heritage Archive Report (Project No **3361**)

Hosfield, R T & Chambers, J C, in press, Genuine diversity? The Broom biface assemblage, *Proc Prehist Soc*, **75**

Hosfield, R T, Straker, V & Gardiner, P, with contributions by Brown, A G, Davies, P, Fyfe, R, Jones, J and Tinsley, H, 2008 Palaeolithic and Mesolithic in C J Webster (ed), *The Archaeology of South West England. South West Archaeological Research Framework: Resource Assessment and Research Agenda*, 23–62. Taunton: Somerset County Council

Hosfield, R T, Wenban-Smith, F F & Grant, M J, 2009 Palaeolithic and Mesolithic archaeology of the Solent Basin and western Sussex region: an overview, in R M Briant *et al*, *The Quaternary of the Solent Basin*, 42–59

Hudson, K, 1963 *Industrial Archaeology: An Introduction.* London: John Baker

Hughes, M, 1976 *The small towns of Hampshire. The archaeological and historical implications of development.* Southampton: Hampshire Archaeological Committee

Hughes, M, 1989 Hampshire castles and the landscape, *Landscape History*, **11**, 27–60

Hughes, M, 1994 Towns and villages in medieval Hampshire, in Aston & Lewis (eds), *The medieval landscape of Wessex*, 195–212

HWTMA (Hampshire and Wight Trust for Maritime Archaeology), Bournemouth University and Southampton University, 2007 England's Historic Seascapes: Solent and Isle of Wight and Adjacent Marine Zone Pilot Area – Technical Report. Unpublished Report for English Heritage: ALSF Project Number 4728

HWTMA, 2008 *A Year in Depth: the annual report of Hampshire and Wight Trust for Maritime Archaeology 2007/8*. Southampton: HWTMA

HWTMA/NAS, 2009 *Forton Archaeology Project: Forton's forgotten fleet*. Hampshire and Wight Trust for Maritime Archaeology/Nautical Archaeology Society

Jacobi, R, 1981 The last hunters in Hampshire, in S Shennan and R T Schadla-Hall (eds) *The Archaeology of Hampshire*, Hampshire Fld Club Archaeol Soc Monogr **1**, 10–25. Hampshire: Hampshire Fld Club Archaeol Soc

James, S, 1999 *The Atlantic Celts: ancient people or modern invention?* London: British Museum

James, T B & Robinson, A M, 1988 *Clarendon Palace: the history and archaeology of a medieval palace and hunting lodge near Salisbury, Wiltshire*, Rep Res Comm Soc of Antiq of London **45**. London: Society of Antiquaries

Jay, M & Richards, M P, 2007 British Iron Age diet: staple isotopes and other evidence. *Proc Prehist Soc*, **73**, 169–90

Jesson, M & Hill, D (eds), 1971 *The Iron Age and its Hillforts*, Southampton Uni Monogr Ser **1**. Southampton: Southampton University

Jewell, P A (ed), 1963 *The Experimental Earthwork at Overton Down, Wiltshire, 1960*. London: Brit Ass Advancement of Science

Jewell, P A & Dimbleby, G W (eds), 1966 The experimental earthwork on Overton Down, Wiltshire, England: the first four years, *Proc Prehist Soc*, **32**, 313–42

JNAPC, 1989 *Heritage at Sea: proposals for the better protection of archaeological sites underwater*. London: Joint Nautical Archaeology Policy Committee, National Maritime Museum

Johnston, D E J, 1977 The Central Southern Group of Romano-British Mosaics, in J Munby and M Henig (eds), *Roman Life and Art in Britain A Celebration in Honour of the 80th Birthday of Jocelyn Toynbee*, BAR Brit Ser **41**, 195–215. Oxford: BAR

Jones, J D & Stead, I M, 1969 An Early Iron Age warrior-burial found at St Lawrence, Isle of Wight, *Proc Prehist Soc*, **35**, 351–4

Jones, M, 1995 Patterns in agricultural practice: the archaeobotany of Danebury in its wider context, in Cunliffe, *Danebury*, 43–50

Jones, M, 2007, A feast of Beltain; reflections on the rich Danebury harvests, in P de Jersey, C Gosden, H Hamerow & G Lock (eds), *Communities and Connections: essays in honour of Barry Cunliffe*, 142–53. Oxford: Oxford University Press

Juson D, 1999 Genesis of Southampton Football Club: an account of the development of Association Football in Southampton and St Mary's Church of England Young Men's Association Football Club, 1885–1888. Unpublished BA dissertation, Univ of Leicester

Keen, L, 1989 Coastal salt production in Norman England, *Anglo-Norman Studies*, **11**, 133–79

Keen, L & Ellis, P, 2005 *Sherborne Abbey and School Excavations 1972–1976 and 1990*, Dorset Natur Hist & Archaeol Soc Monogr **16**

Kinnes, I, 1998 This is the place where time meets space, in H Sebire (ed), *Guernsey Connections: archaeological and historical papers in honour of Bob Burns*, 26–38. Guernsey: La Société Guernesiaise

Kohn, M & Mithen, S, 1999 Handaxes: products of sexual selection? *Antiquity*, **73**, 518–26

Ladle, L, forthcoming, *Excavations at Bestwall, Wareham, Vol 2*. Dorset Natur Hist Archaeol Soc Monogr. Dorchester: Dorset Nat Hist & Archaeol Soc

Last, J 2006 Barrow Clump, Figheldean, Wiltshire: interim report on excavations 2003–4. English Heritage unpublished research report

Lawson, A J, 2000 *Potterne 1982–85 Animal husbandry in later prehistoric Wiltshire*, Wessex Archaeol Rep **17**. Salisbury: Wessex Archaeology

Lawson, A J, 2007 *Chalkland: an archaeology of Stonehenge and its region*. Salisbury: Hobnob Press

Leeds, E T, 1913 *The archaeology of the Anglo-Saxon settlements*. Oxford: Clarendon Press

Leeds, E T, 1954 The growth of Wessex, *Oxoniensia*, **19**, 45–60

Leeds, E T & Shortt, H de S, 1953 *An Anglo-Saxon cemetery at Petersfinger, near Salisbury, Wiltshire*. Salisbury: South Wiltshire and Blackmore Museum

Leonard, A G K, 1987 *The saving of Tudor House, Southampton*. Southampton: Paul Cave Publications

Lewis, C, 1994 Patterns and processes in the medieval settlement of Wiltshire, in Aston & Lewis (eds), *The medieval landscape of Wessex*, 171–93

Light, A, Schofield, A J & Shennan, S J, 1995 The middle Avon valley survey: a study in settlement history, *Proc Hampshire Fld Club Archaeol Soc*, **50**, 43–102

Lilley, K D, 2002 *Urban life in the Middle Ages 1000–1400*. Basingstoke: Palgrave

Linderholm, J, 2007 Soil chemical surveying: a path to a deeper understanding of prehistoric sites and societies in Sweden, *Geoarchaeology*, **22**, 417–38

Lithic Studies Society, 2004 *Research Frameworks for Holocene Lithics in Britain*. Salisbury: Lithic Studies Society

Lucas, R N, 1993 *The Romano-British villa at Halstock, Dorset Excavations 1967–1985*, Dorset Nat Hist and Archaeol Soc Monogr **13**. Dorchester: Dorset Nat Hist & Archaeol Soc

Lucy, S, 2000 *The Anglo-Saxon way of death*. Stroud: Sutton Publishing

Machin, A J, Hosfield, R T & Mithen, S J, 2007 Why are some handaxes symmetrical? Testing the influence of handaxe morphology on butchery effectiveness, *J Archaeol Sci*, **34**(6), 883–93

Macphail, R I, 1987 A review of soil science in archaeology in England, in H C M Keeley (ed), *Environmental Archaeology: a regional review Vol* **2**, Historic Buildings and Monuments Commission for England Occas Pap No **1**, 322–77

Madgwick, R, 2008 Patterns of modification of animal and human bones in Wessex: revisiting the excarnation debate, in O Davis, N Sharples & K Waddington (eds), *Changing Perspectives on the First Millennium BC*, 99–118. Oxford: Cardiff Studies in Archaeology

Maltby, M, 1985 The animals bones, in Fasham, *The Prehistoric Settlement at Winnall Down*, 97–112 and 137–8

Maltby, M, 1994 The animal bone from a Romano-British well at Oakridge II, Basingstoke, *Proc Hampshire Fld Club and Archaeol Soc*, **49**, 47–76

Marsden, P, 2003 *Sealed by Time: The Loss and Recovery of the Mary Rose*. Portsmouth: The Mary Rose Trust Ltd

Marshall, G D, 2001 The Broom pits: a review of research and a pilot study of two Acheulian biface assemblages, in F F Wenban-Smith and R T Hosfield (eds), *Palaeolithic Archaeology of the Solent River*, Lithic Studies Soc Occas Pap No. **7**, 77–84. London: Lithic Studies Society

McBurney, C B M & Callow, P, 1971 The Cambridge excavations at La Cotte de St. Brelade, Jersey A preliminary report, *Proc Prehist Soc*, **37**, 167–207

McKee, A, 1982 *How We Found the Mary Rose*. London: Souvenir Press

McNabb, J, 2007 *The British Lower Palaeolithic: Stones in Contention*. Abingdon: Routledge

McOmish, D, 1996, East Chisenbury: ritual and rubbish at the British Bronze Age–Iron Age transition, *Antiquity*, **267**, 68–76

McOmish, D, Field, D & Brown, G, 2002 *The Field Archaeology of the Salisbury Plain Training Area*. Swindon: English Heritage

McPherron, S P, 1996 A re-examination of the British biface data, *Lithics*: Newsletter of the Lithic Studies Society, **16**, 47–63

Meaney, A L & Hawkes, S C, 1972 *Two Anglo-Saxon cemeteries at Winnall*, Soc Medieval Archaeol Monogr Ser **4**

Mercer, R & Healy, F, 2008 *Hambledon Hill, Dorset, England: excavation and survey of a Neolithic monument complex and its surrounding landscape*. London: English Heritage

Metcalf, D M, 2005 The first series of sceattas minted in southern Wessex: Series W, *Brit Numis J* **75**, 1–17

Mileson, S A, 2009 *Parks in medieval England*. Oxford: Oxford University Press

Millett, M, 1986 An early Roman cemetery at Alton, Hampshire, *Proc Hampshire Fld Club Archaeol Soc*, **42**, 43–87

Millett, M & Graham, D, 1986 *Excavations on the Romano-British Small Town at Neatham, Hampshire, 1969–79*, Hampshire Fld Club Monogr **3**. Farnham: Hampshire Fld Club Archaeol Soc

Mithen, S J, 1998 Hunter-Gatherers of the Mesolithic, in J Hunter & I Ralston (eds), *The Archaeology of Britain: an introduction from the Upper Palaeolithic to the Industrial Revolution*, 35–57. London: Routledge

Momber, G, 2000 Drowned and deserted: a submerged prehistoric landscape in the Solent, *Int J Naut Archaeol*, **29**(1), 86–99

Momber, G, 2001 Recent investigation of deeply submerged human occupation site on the floor of the Western Solent, in R G McInnes and J Jakeways (eds), *Coastal change, climate and instability: final technical report*, Vol 2 Palaeoenvironmental Study Areas, Study Area P1, 36–41. LIFE Project no. 97 ENV/UK/000510. Ventnor: Isle of Wight Centre for the Coastal Environment

Momber, G & Geen, M, 2000 The application of the submetrix ISIS 100 Swath bathymetry system to the management of underwater sites, *Int J Naut Archaeol*, **29**(1), 154–62

Momber, G, Tomalin D, Scaife, R, Satchell, J and Gillespie J, in press, *Mesolithic occupation at Bouldnor Cliff and the submerged prehistoric landscapes of the Solent*, CBA Res Rep **164**. York: CBA

Monk, M A & Fasham, P J, 1980 Carbonised plant remains from two Iron Age sites in central Hampshire, *Proc Prehist Soc*, **46**, 321–44

Montgomery J, Budd P & Evans J A, 2000 Reconstructing the lifetime movements of Ancient people: a Neolithic case study from southern England, *European Journal of Archaeology*, **3**, 370–85

Moore, P (ed), 1984 *A Guide to the Industrial Archaeology of Hampshire and the Isle of Wight*. Southampton: Southampton University Industrial Archaeology Group

Moore, P, 1992 The Restoration of the Golden Lion Brewhouse, Southwick, *Southampton University I A Group J*, **1**, 1–7

Moorhead, T S N, 1997 A reappraisal of the Roman coins in T W Brooke's excavation of a late Roman well at *Cunetio* (Mildenhall), *Wiltshire Archaeol Natur Hist Soc Mag*, **90**, 42–54

Morris, E L, 1994 Production and distribution of pottery and salt in Iron Age Britain: a review, *Proc Prehist Soc*, **60**, 371–93

Morris, E L, 1996 Iron Age artefact production and exchange, in Champion & Collis (eds), *The Iron Age in Britain and Ireland: recent trends*, 41–65

Morse, M A, 2005 *How the Celts came to Britain: Druids, ancient skulls and the birth of archaeology*. Stroud: Tempus

Morton, A D, 1992 The rediscovery of the evidence, in A D Morton (ed), *Excavations at Hamwic*: Vol 1, CBA Res Rep **84**, 4–15. London: CBA

Munby, J & Renn, D, 1985 Description of the castle buildings, in B Cunliffe and J Munby, *Excavations at Portchester Castle, Volume IV: medieval, the inner bailey*, Rep Res Comm Soc Antiq London **43**, 72–119. London: Society of Antiquaries of London

Munby, J, Barber, R & Brown, R 2007 *Edward III's Round Table at Windsor*. Woodbridge: Boydell

Mussi, M & Villa, P, 2008 Single carcass of *Mammuthus primigenius* with lithic artifacts in the Upper Pleistocene of northern Italy, *J Archaeol Sci*, **35**, 2606–13

Musty, J & Algar, D, 1986 Excavations at the deserted medieval village of Gomeldon, near Salisbury, *Wiltshire Archaeol Natur Hist Soc Mag*, **80**, 127–69

Neal, D S & Cosh, S R, 2009 *Roman Mosaics of Britain*, Vol III, *South-East Britain*. London: Illuminata for the Soc Antiq London

Needham, S, 2008 In the Copper Age, *British Archaeology*, **101**

Needham, S & Ambers, J, 1994 Redating Rams Hill and reconsidering Bronze Age enclosure, *Proc Prehist Soc*, **60**, 225–43

O'Connor, B, 1980 *Cross-channel Relations in the Later Bronze Age*, BAR Int Ser **91**. Oxford: BAR

O'Connor T & Evans J, 2005 *Environmental Archaeology; principles and methods* (2nd edn). Stroud: Sutton

Oliver, M, 1993 The Iron Age and Romano-British settlement at Oakridge, *Proc Hampshire Fld Club and Archaeol Soc*, **48**, 55–94

Ordnance Survey, 1933 *Celtic Earthworks of Salisbury Plain based on air photographs Old Sarum*. Southampton: Ordnance Survey

Ordnance Survey, 1934 *Map of Neolithic Wessex*. Southampton: Ordnance Survey

Oswald, A, 1997, A doorway on the past: practical and mystic concerns in the orientation of roundhouse doorways, in A Gwilt and C Haselgrove (eds), *Reconstructing Iron Age Societies*, Oxbow Monogr, **71**, 87–95. Oxford: Oxbow

Palmer, R 1976 Interrupted ditch enclosures in Britain: the use of aerial photography for comparative studies, *Proc Prehist Soc*, **42**, 161–86

Palmer, R, 1984 *Danebury An Iron Age Hillfort in Hampshire: an aerial photographic interpretation of its environs* (RCHM(E) Suppl Ser **6**/*Danebury* Vol **3**). London: Royal Commission on Historical Monuments (England)

Palmer, S, 1999 *Culverwell Mesolithic habitation site, Isle of Portland, Dorset: excavation report and research studies*, BAR Brit Ser, **257**. Oxford: Archaeopress

Papworth, M, 2008 *Deconstructing the Durotriges: a definition of Iron Age communities within the Dorset environs*, BAR Brit Ser, **462**. Oxford: Archaeopress

Parker Pearson, M, 1996 Food, fertility and front doors in the first millennium BC, in C Champion & Collis (eds), *The Iron Age in Britain and Ireland: recent trends*, 117–32

Parker Pearson, M & Ramilisonina, 1998 Stonehenge for the ancestors: the stones pass on the message, *Antiquity*, **72**, 308–26

Parker Pearson, M & Richards, C, 1994 Architecture and order: spatial representation and archaeology, in M Parker Pearson and C Richards (eds), *Architecture and Order: approaches to social space*, 38–72. London: Routledge

Parker Pearson, M, Chamberlain, A T, Collins, M J, Craig, O E, Marshall, P, Mulville, J, Smith, H, Chenery, C, Collins, M J, Cook, G, Craig, G, Evans, J, Hiller, J, Montgomery, J, Schwenninger, J-L, Taylor, G and Wess, T, 2005 Evidence for mummification in Bronze Age Britain, *Antiquity*, **79**, 529–46

Parker Pearson, M, Cleal, R, Marshall, P, Needham, S, Pollard, J, Richards, C, Ruggles, C, Sheridan, A, Thomas, J Tilley, C, Welham, K, Chamberlain, A, Chenery, C, Evans, J, Knüsel, C, Linford N, Martin, L, Montgomery, J, Payne, A & Richards, M, 2007 The age of Stonehenge, *Antiquity*, **81**, 617–39

Parker Pearson, M, Pollard, J, Richards, C, Thomas, J, Tilley, C, Welham, K & Albarella, U, 2006 Materializing Stonehenge: the Stonehenge Riverside Project and new discoveries *J Material Culture*, **11**, 227–61

Parker Pearson, M, Richards, C, Allen, M, Payne, A, & Welham, K, 2004 The Stonehenge Riverside project research design and initial results, *J Nordic Archaeol Science*, **14**, 45–60

Payne, A, Corney, M & Cunliffe, B, 2006 *The Wessex Hillforts Project Extensive survey of hillfort interiors in central southern England*. London: English Heritage

Peacock, D P S, 1967 The heavy mineral analysis of pottery: a preliminary report, *Archaeometry*, **10**, 97–100

Penn, K J, 1980 *Historic towns in Dorset*, Dorset Natur Hist Archaeol Soc Monogr **1** Dorchester: Dorset Natur Hist Archaeol Soc

Percival, J, 1980 *Living in the Past*. London: BBC

Petersen, F F, 1981 *The Excavation of a Bronze Age Cemetery on Knighton Heath, Dorset*, BAR Brit Ser **98**. Oxford: BAR

Pettitt, P B, 2008 The British Upper Palaeolithic, in J Pollard (ed), *Prehistoric Britain*, 18–57. London: Blackwell Studies in Global Archaeology

Pettitt, P B, Gamble, C & Last, J (eds), 2008 *Research and Conservation Framework for the British Palaeolithic*. London: English HeritagePiggott, S, 1962 *The West Kennet Long Barrow Excavations 1955–56*. London: HSMO

Piggott, S, 1954 *Neolithic Cultures of the British Isles*. Cambridge: Cambridge University Press

Piggott, S, 1966 A scheme for the Scottish Iron Age, in A L F Rivet (ed), *The Iron Age in Northern Britain*, 1–16. Edinburgh: Edinburgh University Press

Pitt-Rivers, A H L F, 1887 *Excavations in Cranborne Chase, Vol 1*. London: privately printed

Pitt-Rivers, A H L F, 1888 *Excavations in Cranborne Chase, Vol 2*. London: privately printed

Pitt-Rivers, Lt-Gen [A] 1890 *King John's House, Tollard Royal, Wiltshire*. Privately printed

Pitt-Rivers, A H L F, 1892 *Excavations in Cranborne Chase, Vol 3*. London: privately printed

Pitt-Rivers, A H L F, 1898 *Excavations in Cranborne Chase, Vol 4*. London: privately printed

Pitts, M, 1982 On the road to Stonehenge: report on investigations beside the A344 in 1968, 1979 and 1980, *Proc Prehist Soc*, **48**, 75–132

Pitts, M, 1996 The stone axe in neolithic Britain, *Proc Prehist Soc*, **61**, 311–71

Pitts, M, 2001 *Hengeworld* (2nd edn). London: Random House

Pitts, M, 2006 Isobel Smith obituary, *The Guardian*, 17 January 2006

Pitts, M & Whittle, A, 1992 The development and date of Avebury, *Proc Prehist Soc*, **58**, 203–12

Platt, C, 1973 *Medieval Southampton. The port and trading community, AD 1000–1600*. London: Routledge and Kegan Paul

Platt, C & Coleman-Smith, R, 1975 *Excavations in medieval Southampton* (2 vols). Leicester: Leicester University Press

Platt, C & Coleman-Smith, R, 1975 *Excavations in Medieval Southampton 1953–1969 Vol 1 The excavation reports; Vol 2 The finds*. Leicester: Leicester University Press

Plets, R M K, Dix, J K & Best, A I, 2008 Mapping of the buried Yarmouth Roads wreck, Isle of Wight, UK, using a Chirp sub-bottom profiler, *Int J Naut Archaeol*, **37**(2), 360–73

Plets, R M K, Dix, J K, Adams, J R, Bull, J M, Henstock, T J, Gutowski, M & Best, A I, 2009 The use of a high-resolution 3D Chirp sub-bottom profiler for the reconstruction of the shallow water archaeological site of the *Grace Dieu* (1439), River Hamble, UK, *J Archaeol Sci*, **36**(2), 408–18

Pollard, J & Reynolds, A, 2002 *Avebury The biography of a landscape*. Stroud: The History Press Ltd

Ponting, K G (ed), 1973 *The Industrial Archaeology of Wiltshire*. Devizes: Wiltshire Archaeol Natur Hist Soc

Powell, A B, 2009 Two thousand years of salt making at Lymington, Hampshire, *Proc Hampshire Fld Club Archaeol Soc*, **64**, 9–40 (Hampshire Studies 2009)

Prehistoric Society, 1999 *Research Frameworks for the Palaeolithic and Mesolithic of Britain and Ireland*. Salisbury: The Prehistoric Society

Pryor, F & French, C, 1985 *Archaeology and Environment in the lower Welland valley*, East Anglian Archaeol, **27**. Cambridge: Cambridgeshire Archaeological Committee

Pugh, R B & Crittall, E (eds), 1957 *A History of Wiltshire*, Vol I(1). Oxford: Oxford University Press

Putnam, B, 2004 An industrial tramway in Puddletown Forest, *CBA Wessex News* 11, September 2004

Putnam, B, 2005 Current news of the industrial tramway in Puddletown Forest, *Dorset Ind Archaeol Soc Bull*, **12**, 1

Putnam, B, 2007 *Roman Dorset*. Stroud: The History Press Ltd

Rahtz, P, 1959 Holworth medieval village excavation, *Proc Dorset Natur Hist Archaeol Soc*, **81**, 127–47

Rahtz, P, 2001 *Living Archaeology*. Stroud: Tempus Publishing

RCHM(E), 1952 *An Inventory of the Historical Monuments in the County of Dorset Vol 1, West Dorset*. London: HMSO

RCHM(E), 1959 Wareham west walls, *Medieval Archaeol*, **3**, 120–38

RCHM(E), 1960 *A Matter of Time: an archaeological survey*. London: HMSO

RCHM(E), 1970a *An Inventory of the Historical Monuments in the County of Dorset Vol 2, South-East* (3 parts). London: HMSO

RCHM(E), 1970b *An Inventory of the Historical Monuments in the County of Dorset Vol 3 Central Dorset* (2 parts). London: HMSO

RCHM(E), 1972 *An Inventory of the Historical Monuments in the County of Dorset Vol 4, North Dorset*. London: HMSO

RCHM(E), 1975 *An Inventory of the Historical Monuments in the County of Dorset Vol 5, East Dorset*. London: HMSO

RCHM(E), 1979a *Long Barrows in Hampshire and the Isle of Wight*. London: HMSO

RCHM(E), 1979b *Stonehenge and its Environs*. Edinburgh: HMSO

RCHM(E), 1980 *Ancient and historical monuments in the City of Salisbury Vol 1*. London: HMSO

Reid, C, 1885 The Flint Implements of Bemerton and Milford Hill, *Wilt Archaeol Natur Hist Mag*, **22**, 117–23

Reid, C, 1903 *The Geology of the County around Salisbury*. Memoir of the Geological Soc

Renfrew, C, 1973 Monuments, mobilisation and social organisation in neolithic Wessex, in C Renfrew (ed), *The Explanation of Culture Change: models in prehistory*, 539–58. London: Duckworth

Reynolds, P J, 1979 *Iron Age Farm: the Butser experiment*. London: Colonnade

Richards, C & Thomas, J, 1984 Ritual activity and structured deposition in later Neolithic Wessex, in R Bradley and J Gardiner (eds), *Neolithic Studies: a review of some current research*, BAR Brit Ser **133**, 189–218. Oxford: BAR

Richards, J, 1978 *The archaeology of the Berkshire Downs: an introductory survey*, Berks Archaeol Comm publ No. **3**. Reading: Berks Archaeol Comm

Richards, J, 1990 *The Stonehenge Environs Project*. English Heritage Archaeol Rep **16**. London: English Heritage

Richards, M P, Hedges, R E M, Molleson, T I & Vogel, J C, 1998 Stable isotope analysis reveals variations in human diet at the Poundbury Camp cemetery site, *J Archaeol Sci*, **25**, 1247–52

Richmond, I A & Brailsford, J W, 1968 *Hod Hill Vol **2** Excavations carried out between 1951 and 1958*. London: British Museum

Riley, R C, 1987 *The Industrial Archaeology of the Portsmouth Region*. Portsmouth: Portsmouth City Council

Rivet, A L F, 1958 *Town and Country in Roman Britain*. London: Hutchinson University Library

Roberts, E, 1986 The Bishop of Winchester's fishponds in Hampshire 1150–1400, *Proc Hampshire Fld Club Archaeol Soc*, **42**, 125–38

Roberts, E, 1998 The rediscovery of two major monastic buildings at Wherwell, *Proc Hampshire Fld Club Archaeol Soc*, **53**, 137–53

Roberts, E, 2003 *Hampshire houses 1250–1700 Their dating and development*. Winchester: Hampshire County Council

Roberts, M R, 1995 Excavations at Park Farm, Binfield, 1990: an Iron Age and Romano-British settlement and two Mesolithic flint scatters, in I Barnes, W A Boismier, R M J Cleal, A P Fitzpatrick & M R Roberts (eds), *Early Settlement in Berkshire: Mesolithic-Roman Occupation in the Thames and Kennet Valleys*. Salisbury: Trust for Wessex Archaeology

Roe, D A, 1968 *A Gazetteer of the British Lower and Middle Palaeolithic Sites*, CBA Res Rep **8**. London: CBA

Roffey, S, 2007 *The medieval chantry chapel: an archaeology*. Woodbridge: Boydell Press

Rowlands, M J, 1976 *The Production and Distribution of Metalwork in the Middle Bronze Age in southern England*, BAR Brit Ser **31**. Oxford: BAR

Rule, M, 1982 The Mary Rose: *The Excavation and Raising of Henry VIII's Flagship*. London: Conway Maritime Press

Rule, M & Monaghan, J, 1993 *A Gallo-Roman Trading Vessel from Guernsey*, Guernsey Museum Monogr **5**

Russel, A, 2002 Anglo-Saxon, in N Stoodley (ed), *The Millennium Publication: A Review of Archaeology in Hampshire 1980–2000*, 20–5. Hampshire: Hampshire Fld Club Archaeol Soc

Salter, C & Ehrenreich, R M, 1984, Iron Age metallurgy in central southern Britain, in B W Cunliffe & D Miles (eds), *Aspects of the Iron Age in Central Southern England*, Oxford Uni Comm for Archaeol Monogr **2**, 146–61. Oxford: Oxford University Press

Sauer, E W, 2005 Inscriptions from Alchester: Vespasian's base of the Second Augustan Legion(?), *Britannia*, **36**, 101–33

Saunders, A, 1989 *Fortress Britain Artillery fortification in the British Isles and Ireland*. Liphook: Beaufort Publishing

Saunders, P, 1986 *Channels to the past: the Salisbury drainage collection*. Salisbury: Salisbury and South Wiltshire Museum

Saunders, P, 1991 Hugh de Saumarez Shortt, 1912–1975, in P and E Saunders (eds), *Salisbury and South Wiltshire Museum medieval catalogue part 1*, 11–13. Salisbury: Salisbury and South Wiltshire Museum

Schofield, J, Beck, C & Drolliner, H, 2003 The archaeology of opposition: Greenham Common and Peace Camp, Nevada, *Conservation Bulletin*, **44**, 47–9

Schreve, D C, 2006 The taphonomy of a Middle Devensian (MIS 3) vertebrate assemblage from Lynford, Norfolk, UK, and its implications for Middle Palaeolithic subsistence strategies, *J Quat Sci*, **21**(5) 543–56

Scobie, G D, Zant, J M & Whinney, R, 1991 *The Brooks, Winchester A preliminary report on the excavations 1987–88*, Winchester Museums Service Archaeology Report **1**. Winchester: Winchester Museums Service

Scott, I R, 1996 *Romsey Abbey Report on the excavations 1973–1991*, Hampshire Fld Club Archaeol Soc Monogr **8**. Hampshire: Hampshire Fld Club Archaeol Soc

Scott, K, 1980 Two hunting episodes of Middle Palaeolithic age at La Cotte de St. Brelade, Jersey, Channel Islands, *World Archaeology*, **12**(2), 137–52

Scott, K, 1986 The bone assemblages of layers 3 and 6, in Callow & Cornford (eds), *La Cotte de St. Brelade*, 159–83

Scott, K, 1989 Mammoth bones modified by humans: Evidence from La Cotte de St. Brelade, Jersey, Channel Islands, in R Bonnichsen and M H Sorg (eds), *Bone Modification*. University of Maine at Orono: Center for the Study of the First Americans

SELRC, 1992 *Annual Report 1991*. Lampeter: Severn Estuary Levels Research Committee

Semple, S & Williams, H, 2001 Excavation on Roundway Down, *Wiltshire Archaeol Natur Hist Soc Mag*, **94**, 236–9

Shakesby, R A & Stephens, N, 1984 The Pleistocene gravels of the Axe Valley, Devon, *Reports Trans Devon Assoc Advancement Science*, **116**, 77–88

Sharples, N M, 1991 *Maiden Castle: excavations and field survey 1985–86*, English Heritage Archaeological Report **19**. London: HMSO

Shaw, A D & White, M J, 2003 Another look at the Cuxton handaxe assemblage, *Proc Prehist Soc*, **69**, 305–13

Shennan, S, 1985 *Experiments in the collections and analysis of archaeological survey data: the East Hampshire Survey*. Sheffield: Dept Archaeol & Prehist

Shore, T W & Elwes, J W, 1889 The New Dock excavation at Southampton, *Proc Hampshire Fld Club Archaeol Soc*, **1**, 43–56

Slocombe, P (ed), 2008 *A Guide to the Industrial Archaeology of Wiltshire*. Telford: Association for Industrial Archaeology

Smith, D J, 1965 Three fourth-century schools of mosaics in Roman Britain, in G Picard and H Stern (eds), *La Mosaique gréco-romaine* II, 269–90. Paris: École Française de Rome

Smith, D J, 1984 Roman mosaics in Britain: a synthesis in R Farioli Campanati (ed), *Il Mosaico Antico* III, Ravenna; Edizioni del Girasole 357–80

Smith, I F, 1965 *Windmill Hill and Avebury: excavations by Alexander Keiller, 1925–1939*. Oxford: Clarendon Press

Smith, K, 1977 The excavation of Winklebury Camp, Basingstoke, Hampshire, *Proc Prehist Soc*, **43**, 31–129

Smith, R A, 1900 Anglo-Saxon remains, in Victoria History of the Counties of England *A History of Hampshire and the Isle of Wight* Vol 1, 373–98. Westminster: Archibald Constable

Smith, R A, 1906 Anglo-Saxon remains, in Victoria History of the Counties of England, *A History of Berkshire*, Volume 1, 229–50. Westminster: Archibald Constable

Smith, R J C, Healy, F, Allen, M J, Morris, E L, Barnes, I & Woodward, P J, 1997 *Excavations along the route of the Dorchester by-pass, Dorset, 1986–88*, Wessex Archaeol Rep No. **11**. Salisbury: Wessex Archaeology

Southampton Gaslight and Coke Co, 1948 *Centenary 1848–1948*. Privately published (copy in Southampton Archives Service)

Sparey-Green, C, 1987 *Excavations at Poundbury. Volume I: the settlements*, Dorset Natur Hist Archaeol Soc Monogr Ser **7**. Dorchester: Dorset Natur Hist Archaeol Soc

St John Hope, W H, 1910 *Old Sarum Excavation Fund Report of the Excavation Committee to the Society of Antiquaries for 1909*. London: The Society of Antiquaries

Stanier, P, 1993 Dorset limekilns: a first survey, *Proc Dorset Archaeol Natur Hist Soc*, **115**, 33–49

Stanier, P, 1996 The quarried face: evidence from Dorset's cliffstone quarries, in P Newman (ed), *The Archaeology of Mining and Metallurgy in South-West Britain, Mining History: Bulletin Peak District Mines Hist Soc*, **13**(2), 1–9

Stanier, P, 2000 *Stone Quarry Landscapes*. Stroud: Tempus Publishing

Stanier, P, 2002 *Dorset in the Age of Steam: A history and archaeology of Dorset industry, 1750–1950*. Tiverton: Dorset Books

Stanier, P, 2006 *Wiltshire in the Age of Steam: A history and archaeology of Wiltshire industry, 1750–1950*. Tiverton: Halsgrove

Stead, I M, 1998 *The Salisbury Hoard*. Stroud: Tempus

Stone, J F S, 1958 *Wessex Before the Celts*. London: Thames and Hudson

Stopford, J, 1985 Danebury: an alternative view, *Scott Archaeol Rev*, **4**, 70–5

Stringer, C, 2006 *Homo Britannicus: The Incredible Story of Human Life in Britain*. London: Penguin

SWARF, 2005 *South-West Archaeological Research Framework: Research Agenda* http://www.somerset.gov.uk/somerset/cultureheritage

Tabor, R, 2008 *Cadbury Castle: the hillfort and landscapes*. Stroud: The History Press Ltd

Tate, P 2005 Ambassador to the past, *British Archaeology* **85**, 66

Tatton-Brown, T, 1991 Building the tower and spire of Salisbury Cathedral, *Antiquity*, **65**, 74–96

Taylor, C, 1970 *Dorset*. London: Hodder and Stoughton

Taylor, C, 1994 The regular village plan: Dorset revisited and revised, in Aston & Lewis (eds), *The medieval landscape of Wessex*, 213–18

Taylor, H M & Taylor, J, 1965 *Anglo-Saxon architecture* (2 vols). Cambridge: CUP

Thomas, N, 2005 *Snail Down, Wiltshire: the Bronze Age barrow cemetery and related earthworks in the parishes of Collingbourne Ducis and Collingbourne Kingston: excavations 1953, 1955 and 1957*, Wiltshire Archaeol Natur Hist Soc Monogr **3**. Trowbridge: Wiltshire Archaeol Natur Hist Soc

Thomsen, M H, 2000 The Studland Bay wreck, Dorset, UK: hull analysis, *Int J of Naut Archaeol*, **29**(1), 69–85

Timby, J, 2001 A reappraisal of Savernake Ware, in Ellis (ed), *Roman Wiltshire and After*, 73–84

Tomalin, D, 1993 Maritime Archaeology as a Coastal Management Issue: a Solent case study from the SCOPAC coast, in *The Regional Coastal Groups – after the House of Commons Report SCOPAC: Seminar Papers and Proceedings*, 93–112. Littlehampton: Standing Conference on Problems Associated with the Coastline

Tomalin, D J, Simpson, P & Bingeman, J M, 2000 Excavation versus sustainability in situ: a conclusion on 25 years of archaeological investigations at Goose Rock, a designated historic wreck-site at the Needles, Isle of Wight, England, *Int J Naut Archaeol* **29**(1), 3–42

Toms, P, Hosfield, R T, Chambers, J C, Green, C P & Marshall, P, 2005 *Optical dating of the Broom Palaeolithic sites*, Devon and Dorset Centre for Archaeology Report **16**/2005. London: English Heritage

Townend, S, 2007 What have reconstructed roundhouses ever done for us? *Proc Prehist Soc*, **73**, 97–112

Tweddle, D, Biddle, M & Kjølbye-Biddle, B, 1995 *Corpus of Anglo-Saxon sculpture Volume IV: South-East England*. Oxford: OUP

Tyers, P A, 1996 *Roman Pottery in Britain*. London: Batsford

Ulmschneider, K, 1999 Archaeology, history and the Isle of Wight in the middle Saxon period, *Medieval Archaeol*, **43**, 19–44

Vander Linden, M, 2006, *Le phénoméne campiforme dans l Europe du 3e millénaire avant notre ère Synthèse et nouvelles perspectives*, BAR Int Ser **1470**. Oxford: Archaeopress

Velegrakis, A F, Dix, J K & Collins, M B, 1999 Late Quaternary evolution of the upper reaches of the Solent River, Southern England, based upon marine geophysical evidence *J Geol Soc London*, **156**, 73–87

Wacher, J 1995 *The Towns of Roman Britain* (2nd edn). London: Routledge

Wainwright, G J, 1968 The excavation of a Durotrigian farmstead near Tollard Royal in Cranborne Chase, southern England, *Proc Prehist Soc*, **34**, 102–47

Wainwright, G J, 1969 The excavation of Balksbury Camp, Andover, Hants, *Proc Hampshire Fld Club*, **26**, 1969 (1970), 21–55

Wainwright, G J, 1971 The excavation of a later Neolithic Enclosure at Marden, Wiltshire, *Antiq J*, **51**, 177–239

Wainwright, G J, 1979a *Mount Pleasant, Dorset Excavations 1970–1971*, Rep Res Comm Soc Antiq London No. **37**. London: Soc Antiq London

Wainwright, G J, 1979b *Gussage All Saints An Iron Age Settlement in Dorset* Dept Environment Archaeol Rep **10** London: HMSO

Wainwright, G J, 1997 Future directions for the study of Stonehenge and its landscape, in Cunliffe & Renfrew (eds), Science and Stonehenge, 335–41

Wainwright, G J & Cunliffe, B W, 1985 Maiden Castle: excavation, education, entertainment? *Antiquity*, **59**, 97–100

Wainwright, G J & Davies, S M, 1995 *Balksbury Camp, Hampshire Excavations 1973 and 1981*, English Heritage Archaeological Rep **4**. London: English Heritage

Wainwright, G J, Lawson, A J & Gardiner J, 1995 Future directions, in Cleal *et al*, *Stonehenge in its Landscape*, 492–3

Wainwright, G J & Longworth, I H 1971 *Durrington Walls: Excavations 1966–68*, Rep Res Comm Soc Antiq London No. **29** London: Soc Antiq London

Wainwright, G J & Spratling, M G, 1973 The Iron Age settlement of Gussage All Saints, *Antiquity*, **47**, 109–20 (Reprinted in G Carr and S Stoddart (eds), *Celts from Antiquity*, Cambridge, Antiquity Papers 2, 187–214)

Wait, G A, 1985 *Ritual and Religion in Iron Age Britain*, BAR Brit Ser **149**. Oxford: BAR

Walker, K E & Farwell, D, 2000 *Twyford Down, Hampshire Archaeological investigations on the M3 motorway from Bar End to Compton, 1990–93*. Hampshire Fld Club Monogr **9**. Winchester: Hampshire Fld Club

Watkins, D R, 1994 *The Foundry. Excavations on Poole waterfront 1986/7*, Dorset Natur Hist Archaeol Soc Monogr **14**. Dorchester: Dorset Natur Hist Archaeol Soc

Watson, K & Gale, A, 1990 Site evaluation for marine sites and monuments records: Yarmouth Roads wreck investigations, *Int J Naut Arch*, **19**(3), 183–92

Webster, C J (ed), 2008 *The Archaeology of South West England: South West Archaeological Research Framework: Resource Assessment and Research Agenda*. Taunton: Somerset County Council

Wenban-Smith, F F, 2001 LSS excursion to Priory Bay, Isle of Wight, *Lithics*, **22**, 53–4

Wenban-Smith, F F & Hosfield, R T (eds), 2001 *Palaeolithic Archaeology of the Solent River*, Lithic Studies Soc Occas Pap No. **7**. London: Lithic Studies Soc

Wenban-Smith, F F, Bates, M R, Marshall, G D & Schwenninger, J-L, 2009 The Pleistocene sequence at Priory Bay, Isle of Wight, in R M Briant *et al*, *The Quaternary of the Solent Basin*, 123–37

Wenban-Smith, F F, Gamble, C S & ApSimon, A, 2000 The Lower Palaeolithic site at Red Barns, Porchester: bifacial technology, raw material quality, and the organisation of archaic behaviour, *Proc Prehist Soc*, **66**, 209–56

Wessex Archaeology, 1993 *The Southern Rivers Palaeolithic Project: Report No 1 1991–1992 The Upper Thames Valley, the Kennet Valley and the Upper Solent Drainage System*. Salisbury: Wessex Archaeology and English Heritage

Wessex Archaeology, 2002a Hampshire Salterns: a cartographic study of the Hampshire salt industry. Unpublished report for Hampshire County Council: WA ref: 49211.01

Wessex Archaeology, 2002b Hampshire Coastline: digital mapping of the historic coastline of Hampshire. Unpublished report for Hampshire County Council: WA ref: 49211.02

Wessex Archaeology, 2004a England's Shipping: Year 2 Report. Unpublished report for English Heritage: ALSF Project Number 3323; WA Ref: 51552.05

Wessex Archaeology, 2004b Artefacts from the Sea: Year Two Report (Revised). Unpublished report for English Heritage: ALSF Project Number 3322; WA Ref. 5141.06

Wessex Archaeology, 2004c Artefacts from the Sea: Catalogue of the Michael White Collection. Unpublished report for English Heritage: ALSF Project Number 3322; WA Ref: 51541.05a

Wessex Archaeology, 2006 On the Importance of Shipwrecks. Final Report: Volume 1. Unpublished report for English Heritage: ALSF Project Number 3767; WA Ref: 58591.02a

Wessex Archaeology, 2007 Wrecks on the Seabed R2: Assessment, Evaluation and Recording. Year 2 Report. Unpublished report for English Heritage: ALSF Project Number 3877; WA Ref: 57454.03(a)

Wessex Archaeology, 2008 Seabed Prehistory: Gauging the Effects of Marine Aggregate Dredging – Final Report. Volume II Arun. Unpublished report for English Heritage: ALSF Project Number 3876; WA Ref: 57422.32

Wessex Archaeology, 2010 Assessing Boats and Ships: 1860–1913. Unpublished report for English Heritage: ALSF Project Number 5693; WA Ref. 70861.01

Westaway, R, Bridgland, D R & White, M J, 2006 The Quaternary uplift history of central southern England: evidence from the terraces of the Solent River system and nearby raised beaches, *Quat Sci Rev*, **25**, 2212–50

Westley, K, Dix, J & Quinn, R, 2004 A Re-assessment of the Archaeological Potential of Continental Shelves. Unpublished report for English Heritage: ALSF Project Number 3362

Wheeler, R E M, 1943 *Maiden Castle, Dorset*, Rep Res Comm Soc Antiq London No. **12**. Oxford: Soc Antiq London

Wheeler, R E M & Richardson, K M, 1957 *Hillforts of Northern France*, Rep Res Comm Soc Antiq, **19**. London: Soc Antiq London

Whimster, R P, 1981 *Burial Practices in Iron Age Britain: a discussion and gazetteer of the evidence c 700 BC – AD 43*, BAR Brit Ser **90**. Oxford: BAR

White D A, 1971 Early man in Cranborne Chase: preliminary results of the survey work of Martin Green and Barry Lewis, *Proc Dorset Natur Hist and Archaeol Soc*, **93**, 176–82

White, D A, 1982 *The Bronze Age Cremation Cemeteries at Simons Ground, Dorset*, Dorset Natur Hist Archaeol Soc Monogr **3**. Dorchester: Dorset Natur Hist Archaeol Soc

White, M J, 1998 On the significance of Acheulean biface variability in southern Britain, *Proc Prehist Soc*, **64**, 15–44

White, M J & Schreve, D C, 2000 Island Britain – peninsula Britain: palaeogeography, colonisation, and the Lower Palaeolithic settlement of the British Isles, *Proc Prehist Soc*, **66**, 1–28

White, M, Scott, R & Ashton, N, 2006 The Early Middle Palaeolithic in Britain: archaeology, settlement history and human behaviour, *J Quat Sci*, **21**(5), 525–41

Whittaker, K, Beasley, M, Bates, M & Wenban-Smith, F F, 2004 The lost valley, *British Archaeology* **74**, 22–7

Whittle, A, 1997 *Sacred Mound, Holy Rings. Silbury Hill and the West Kennet Palisade Enclosures: a later Neolithic complex in north Wiltshire*. Oxford: Oxbow

Wilkinson, T J & Murphy, P L, 1995 *The Archaeology of the Essex Coast, Volume I: the Hullbridge Survey*, East Anglian Archaeology No. **71**. Chelmsford: Essex County Council

Williams, D F, 1977 The Romano-British black-burnished industry: an essay on characterisation by heavy mineral analysis, in D P S Peacock (ed), *Pottery and Early Commerce: characterisation and trade in Roman and later ceramics*, 163–220. London/ New York: Academic Press

Williams, D F, 2002 Purbeck Marble in Roman and Medieval Britain, in D A Hinton (ed), *Purbeck Papers*, 126–31. Oxford: Oxbow

Williams, D L, 1991 *Salvage! Rescued from the Deep*. Shepperton: Ian Allen

Williams-Freeman, J P, 1915 *Field Archaeology as illustrated by Hampshire*. London: Macmillan

Wilson, C A, Cresser, M S & Davidson, D A, 2008 Multi-element soil analysis: an assessment of its potential as an aid to archaeological interpretation, *J Archaeol Sci*, **35**, 412–24

Wilson, C E, 1981 Burials within settlements in southern Britain during the Pre-Roman Iron Age, *Bulletin Inst Archaeol Uni London*, **18**, 127–69

Wilson, D M & Hurst, J G, 1958 Medieval Britain in 1957, *Medieval Archaeol*, **2**, 183–214

Woodward, A, 2002 Beads and beakers: heirlooms and relics in the British early Bronze Age, *Antiquity*, **76**, 1040–47

Woodward, A & Gardiner, J (eds), 1998 *Wessex Before Words: some new research directions for prehistoric Wessex*. Salisbury: CBA Wessex

Woodward, P J, 1987 The excavation of an Iron Age and Romano-British Settlement at Rope Lake Hole, Corfe Castle, Dorset, in N Sunter, and P J Woodward, *Romano-British Industries in Purbeck*, Dorset Archaeol Natur Hist Soc Monogr **6**, 125–84. Dorchester: Dorset Archaeol Soc

Woodward, P J, 1991 *The South Dorset Ridgeway Survey and excavations 1977–84*, Dorset Natur Hist Archaeol Soc Monogr **8**. Dorchester: Dorset Archaeol Soc

Woodward, P J, Davies, S M & Graham, A H, 1993 *Excavations at the Old Methodist Chapel and Greyhound Yard, Dorchester, 1981–1984*, Dorset Natur Hist Archaeol Soc Monogr **12**. Dorchester: Dorset Natur Hist Archaeol Soc

Wymer, J J, 1958 Archaeological notes: Palaeolithic and Mesolithic, *The Berkshire Archaeol J*, **56**, 56–7

Wymer, J J, 1962 Excavations at the Maglemosian sites at Thatcham, Berkshire, England, *Proc Prehist Soc*, **28**, 329–61

Wymer, J J, 1977 *Gazetteer of Mesolithic Sites in England and Wales*, CBA Res Rep No. **20**. London: CBA

Wymer, J J, 1996 The Palaeolithic and Mesolithic in Hampshire, in D A Hinton & M Hughes (eds), *Archaeology in Hampshire: a framework for the future*. Winchester: Hampshire County Council

Wymer, J J, 1999 *The Lower Palaeolithic Occupation of Britain* Vols 1 & 2. Salisbury: Wessex Archaeology and English Heritage

Yates, M, 1999 Change and continuities in rural society from the later Middle Ages to the sixteenth century: the contribution of west Berkshire, *Economic History Review*, **52**, 617–37

Young, C J, 2000 *Excavations at Carisbrooke Castle, Isle of Wight, 1921–1996*, Trust for Wessex Archaeol Rep **18**. Salisbury: Wessex Archaeology

Zuener, F, 1959 *The Pleistocene Period*. London: Hutchinson

Index

Entries in bold refer to the illustrations